709.04
745.2 WES

KU-875-230

NORTHAMPTON COLLEGE
LIBRARY

7
B

NORTHAMPTON COLLEGE
R17436A 0098

modernism

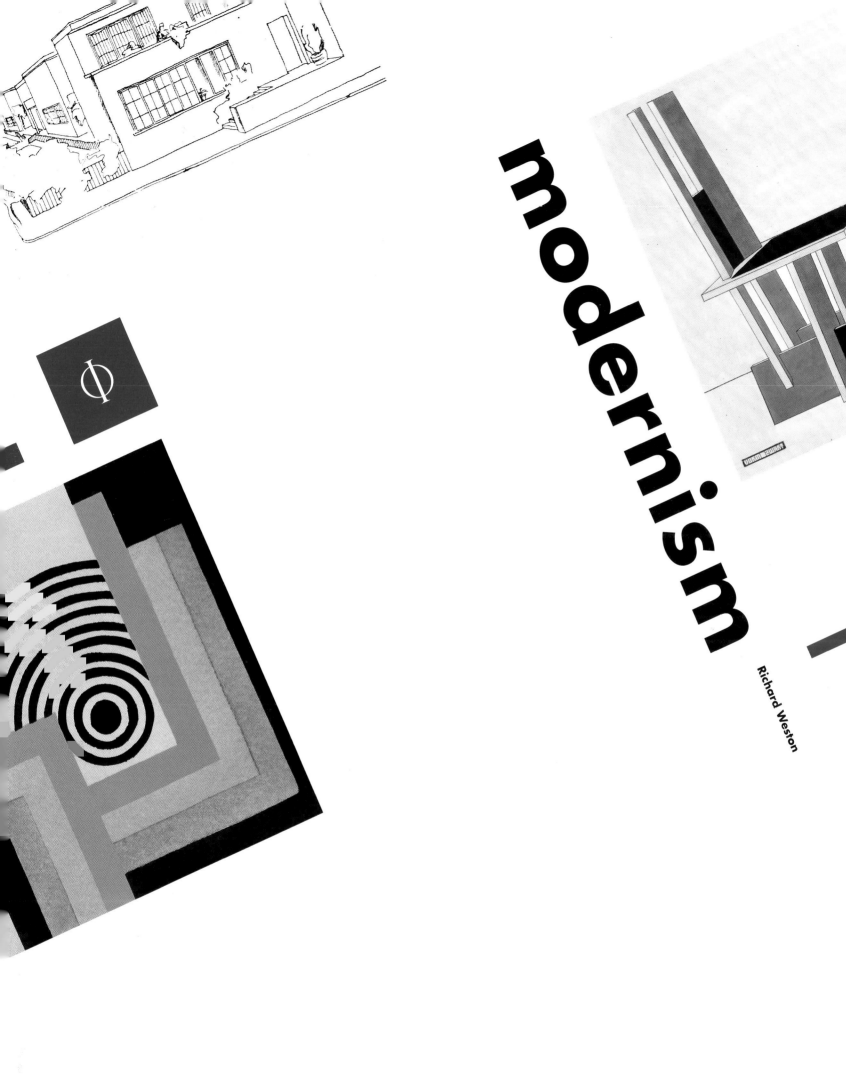

modernism

Richard Weston

In memory of my mother

Phaidon Press Limited
Regent's Wharf
All Saints Street
London N1 9PA

First published 1996
© Phaidon Press
Limited 1996

A CIP catalogue
record for this book is available
from the
British Library

ISBN 0 7148 2879 3

All rights reserved. No part
of this publication may
be reproduced, stored in
a retrieval system or transmitted,
in any form or by any means,
electronic, mechanical, photo-
copying, recording or otherwise,
without the prior permission
of Phaidon Press Limited.

Printed in Hong Kong

Author's Acknowledgements

This book would not have been
possible without the work of
countless scholars, some of whose
names appear in the bibliography
but most of whom must remain
anonymous. My friend and
colleague Dr Paul Harries kindly
provided photographs of the Villa
Savoye taken during the brief
period when it was painted in
something like its original colours,
and Dr Catherine Cooke
provided valuable help with the
chapter on Russia. A book as
wide-ranging as this poses special
challenges for all those involved
in its production and I am
grateful for the tireless efforts of
all involved at Phaidon: Roger
Sears, Commissioning Editor;
Elizabeth Rowe, Project Editor;
Sophie Hartley, Picture
Researcher; and Karl Shanahan
for his careful design in
association with David Pocknell.

Photo Credits

l = left, r = right, t = top,
b = bottom

Alvar Aalto Foundation, Helsinki: 190tr; Aerofilms: 217r; Stiftung Archiv der Akademie der Künste, Berlin: 105; AKG Photo, London: 17, 34, 36, 52t & bl, 129l, 134, 173; AKG/Hilbich: 51t & b; Albertina, Loos-archiv, Vienna: 53; Albright-Knox Art Gallery, Buffalo, New York, Bequest of A. Conger Goodyear, 1964: 81; Albright-Knox Art Gallery, Buffalo, New York, Gift of Seymour H. Knox, 1956: 202, 203; Peter Cook/Archipress: 200, 218; S. Couturier/Archipress: 39, 176; Lucien Hervé/Archipress: 10l; *Architects Journal*/EMAP Construction (Photo: John R. Pantlin): 219r; Architectural Association, London/Andrew Minchin: 175t; Architectural Press/EMAP Construction: 217l; Reproduced courtesy of the *Architectural Review*, London: 186b; Ars Libri Ltd., Boston : 147b; © James Austin: 32; The Baltimore Museum of Art: The Cone Collection, formed by Dr Claribel Cone & Miss Etta Cone of Baltimore, Maryland. BMA1950.228: 65; Bauhaus Archiv, Berlin: 124l & r, 136tl, 137; Bauhaus Archiv, Berlin (photo: Hermann Kiessling, Berlin): 128 & 129r; Bauhaus Archiv, Berlin (photo: Lepkowski, Berlin): 136tr; Bauhaus Archiv, Berlin (photo: Markus Hawlik): 136bl; Bauhaus Archiv, Berlin (photo: Staatliche Bildstelle, Berlin): 123t; Bayer AG, Leverkusen: 224b; Bibliothèque du Musée des Arts Decoratifs, Collection Maciet (photo: Jean Loup Charmet): 37; Bildarchiv Foto Marburg: 75l & r, 76, 127; Braun AG: 210; Bridgeman Art Library, London/Christie's, London: 113tl; Bridgeman Art Library, London/Galleria Pictogramma, Rome: 58; Bridgeman Art Library, London/Collection Haags Gemeentemuseum, The Hague: 78t, c & b; Bridgeman Art Library, London/The Hermitage, St. Petersburg: 63; Bridgeman Art Library, London/Collection Kröller-Müller Museum, Otterlo, The Netherlands: 82-3; Bridgeman Art Library, London/Museum of Fine Arts, Budapest: 106; Bridgeman Art Library, London/Private Collection: 68r, 177t; British Architectural Library, RIBA, London: 43, 49, 73c, 164, 175b, 180, 182t, 188b, 192t, 193; Cassina

S.p.A., Milan: 95b; Martin Charles: 40, 41, 44t, 46, 114t & b, 115, 184rt; Chicago Historical Society (ICHi-01066): 54; Christie's Images, London: 141, 151r, 154t, c & b; Peter Cook: 183; Catherine Cooke: 142, 144t & b, 147t, 148t & b, 149, 150, 151l, 152, 158, 159b, 160, 162, 165b; Gerald Zugman/Coop Himmelblau, Vienna: 229r; Det Danske Kunstindustrimuseum, Copenhagen (photo: Ole Woldbye): 215tl; Eastern Bohemia Museum, Hradec Králové, Czech Republic: 73b; Ezra Stoller © Esto. All Rights Reserved: 206l & r, 207, 225; Courtesy Ex Libris, New York: 131l; Courtesy A + H van Eyck Architecten b.v., Amsterdam: 220br; Fiat, London: 216; Mark Fiennes: 47; Fondation Le Corbusier, Paris: 107, 110r, 111t & b, 112, 177b; Frank Lloyd Wright drawings are copyright © 1996 The Frank Lloyd Wright Foundation: 55, 56; Fundación Colección Thyssen-Bornemisza, Madrid: 71; The Galerie Berinson, Berlin: 153, 163; Galerie Welz, Salzburg: 48t; Dennis Gilbert: 118, 119; © Richard Glover: 228b; Courtesy of Michael Graves, Architect: 226l & r; Courtesy of April Greiman, Greimanski Labs, Los Angeles: 227t; Collection Haags Gemeentemuseum, The Hague: 3r, 94r, 178t, c & b; Copyright: Hackman Iittala OY AB (Photo: Osmo Thiel): 215b; Fritz Hansen A/S, Allerød, Denmark: 209l; Photographed by Steve Wisbauer. Courtesy of *Harper's Bazaar*, New York: 198r; Courtesy of Heal's, London: 214; Dr Paul Harries: 90, 113bb; Hedrich Blessing, Chicago: 211t & b; Honolulu Academy of Arts, Gift of John W. Gregg Allerton, commemorating the 40th Anniversary of the Academy, 1967: 109; Angelo Hornak: 2l; Museum Collection, courtesy Annely Juda Fine Art, London: 159; David King Collection: 146, 156; Courtesy of Knoll Archives, New York: 208tr; The Kobal Collection: 117b, 199l; © Balthazar Korab: 57t & b, 196, 197r, 219l; Collection Kröller-Müller Museum, Otterlo, The Netherlands: 79, 92; Kunstmuseum Bern, Hermann and Margrit Rupf-Stiftung (photo: Peter Lauri): 67l; Kunstsammlungen Weimar (photo: Foto-Atelier Louis Held): 122; Manfred Storck/Helga Lade Fotoagentur, Frankfurt: 138tl & tr; Library of the Landesgewerbeanstalt, Nuremberg (photo: Photostudio Petra Kraus,

Lauf): 172t; *Le Figaro*, Paris: 80; The London Transport Museum: 185t; The London Transport Museum (LRT Registered User No. 96/2438): 185b; Maki and Associates,Tokyo (photo: Toshiharu Kitajima): 231; Mitchell Wolfson Jr. Collection, The Wolfsonian. Miami Beach, Florida and Genoa, Italy: 172b, 198l; Musée National d'Art Moderne, Paris (photo: Philippe Migeat © Centre G. Pompidou): 35; Musée Nationale d'Art Moderne, Paris, Centre Georges Pompidou: 61, 208tl; Musée Picasso, Paris (© photo: R.M.N.): 69; Musei Civici Como: 85, 174; Plakatsammlung Museum für Gestaltung, Zurich: 181; Museum of Applied Arts, Helsinki: 190tl; Museum of Finnish Architecture, Helsinki (photo: E. Stoller): 191; Museum of Finnish Architecture, Helsinki/Gustaf Welin: 188t; Photograph courtesy The Museum of Modern Art, New York: 139, 197l; Photograph © 1996 The Museum of Modern Art, New York: 64; The Museum of Modern Art, New York. Gift of Jay Leyda. Photograph © 1996 The Museum of Modern Art, New York: 155; The Museum of Modern Art, New York. Acquired through the Lillie P. Bliss Bequest. Photograph © 1996 the Museum of Modern Art, New York: 67r; Museum of Photography at George Eastman House, Rochester, NY: 121b; The National Swedish Art Museums, Statens Konstmuseer, Stockholm: 187br; National Technical Museum, Prague: 73t; Netherlands Architecture Institute, Rotterdam: 97t, 98b; Novosti (London): 145, 165t; Courtesy Anthony d'Offay Gallery, London: 87; Öffentliche Kunstsammlung Basel, Kunstmuseum. Donation Dr. h.c. Raoul La Roche 1952 (Photo: Öffentliche Kunstsammlung Basel/Martin Bühler): 68; Österreichisches Museum für Angewandte Kunst, Vienna: 25, 50; Frank den Oudsten: 96, 97b, 99, 100l, 100-1, 102t & b, 104b, 126, 179; Richard Pare: 161; Philadelphia Museum of Art: 86; Philadelphia Museum of Art: George W. Elkins Collection: 62;

Reproduced courtesy of Louis Poulson & Co A/S, Copenhagen (Photo: Bent Ryberg, Planet Foto, Copenhagen): 187tl & cl; Private Collection (Photo: Jan Derwig): 94l; Private Collection (Photo: Julian Comrie): 182; Private Collection, Switzerland (Photo Paul Klee Foundation, Bern/Peter Lauri): 138b; Reinhold-Brown Gallery, New York City: 130; Georg Riha, Vienna: 20, 48b; Royal Commission on Historical Monuments, London: 30; Sears, Roebuck and Co: 199r; © 1996 The Oskar Schlemmer Theatre Estate, 79410 Badenweiler, Germany (Photo Archive C. Raman Schlemmer, Oggebbio, Italy): 121t; © Julius Shulman: 212, 213; Paul M. Smith/University of Leicester, Engineering Department: 220bl; Solomon R. Guggenheim Museum, New York, Gift Estate of Katherine S. Dreier, 1953: 93; South American Pictures: 192b; Tony Morrison/South American Pictures: 220t; Margareta Spiluttini, Vienna: 229l; Staatsgalerie Moderner Kunst, Munich (photo: Artothek): 74; The Stapleton Collection: 2-3b, 21, 23t & b, 27, 28t & b, 29, 42, 77, 88tl & tr, 103t, 123b, 131r, 132, 133, 135, 166, 167, 169 l & r, 170, 186t, 204, 215tr; Stedelijk Museum, Amsterdam: 95t, 98t, 103b, 143; Stedelijk Van Abbemuseum, Eindhoven, The Netherlands: 104t; Tim Street-Porter: 194, 195; *The Face*, London: 227b; Times Newspapers Limited, London: 224t; Universität Stuttgart, Germany: 52br; Courtesy of the Trustees of the Victoria & Albert Museum, London: 136br, 187bl, 190b; Vitra GmbH (photo: Hans Hansen): 208b; Washington University Gallery of Art, St. Louis, University purchase, Kende Sale Fund, 1946: 70; © Matthew Weinreb: 31t & b, 33t & b, 44b, 171b, 184l; Richard Weston: 189t & b, 205t & b, 228t; Photo F.R. Yerbury: 38.

contents

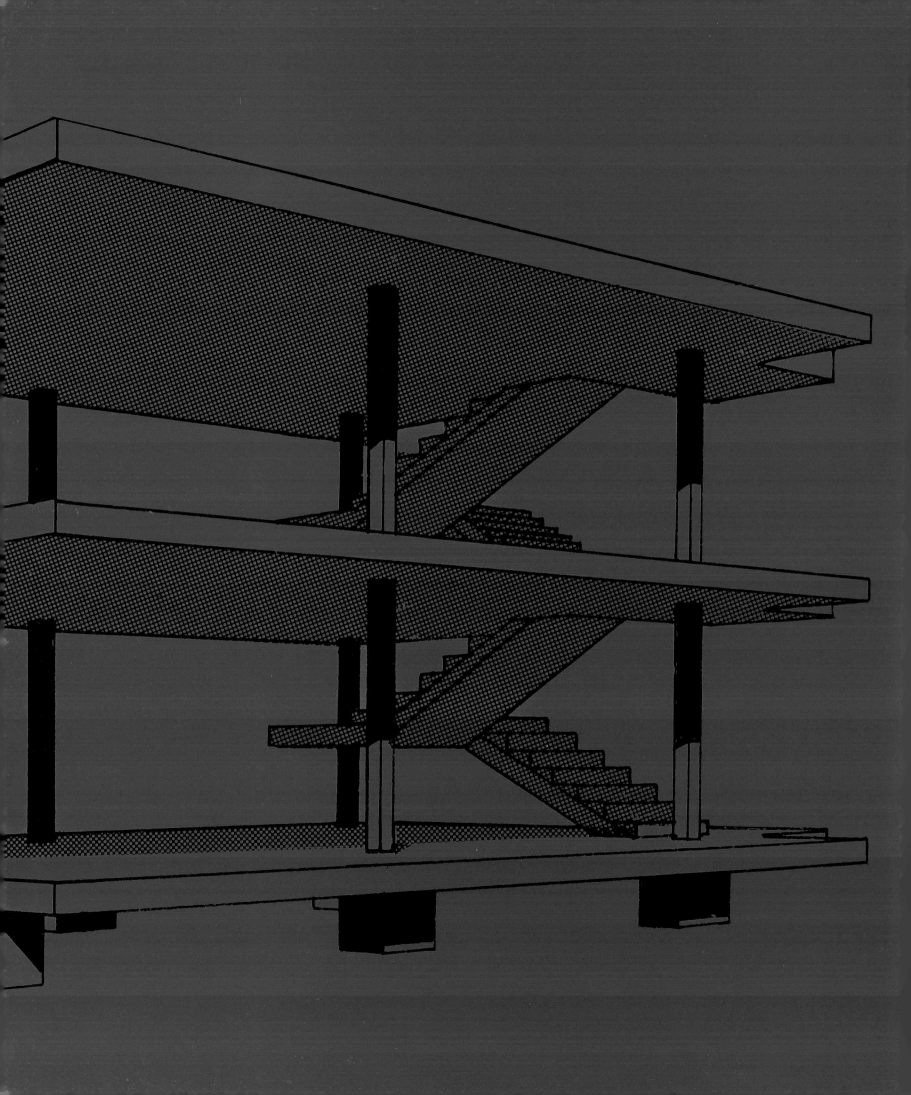

Being modern means being up to date, but being a Modernist is an affirmation of faith in the tradition of the new, which emerged as the creative credo of progressive artists in the early years of the twentieth century. Modernism is the umbrella name for a bewildering array of movements – Cubism, Expressionism, Futurism, Dadaism, Serialism, Surrealism – and ideas – abstraction, functionalism, atonality, free verse – most of which appeared shortly before or after the First World War. It affected all the arts and blossomed in different fields as poets, painters, composers, writers, architects, choreographers, directors and film-makers struggled to come to terms with the 'new times' in which they found themselves. Having uncannily anticipated the collapse of liberal-bourgeois culture which was sealed by the Great War, Modernism came to maturity in the 1920s and flourished above all in the liberal atmosphere of Weimar Germany, where many of the ideas which transformed architecture and design, and in due course the appearance of the everyday world around us, developed.

The Modernist aesthetic reached maturity around 1930, when the capitalist economies were laid low by the Great Depression and the rise of totalitarianism in Germany, Italy and the USSR began to threaten artistic freedom: at the same time as Mussolini was commissioning Modernist architects to design to the glory of Fascism, Hitler was expunging all traces of 'degenerate' Modern Art and Stalin was snuffing out the flames of the great Russian artistic revolution. Most of the leading German Modernists emigrated, many ending up in the United States where they encountered a vigorous consumer economy and the embrace of an establishment eager to assume the mantle of cultural leadership. New York displaced Paris as the creative focus of the art world, and American corporate architecture and domestic design, based on Modernist principles, swept all before them. But it was the Modernist *aesthetic* that was all-conquering: as a revolutionary creative endeavour, Modernism was arguably over – it had become the new academy – but as a force shaping our daily lives its influence was only beginning to be felt.

In writing this book I am conscious that to many people the very word 'Modernism' is anathema. In much of the British press it retains decidedly pejorative overtones, and a recent popular history of architecture begins its account of the Modern period as follows: 'In a century which has witnessed the regimes and genocidal zeal of Stalin, Mao, Hitler and Pol Pot it would perhaps be hyperbolic to refer to the modern movement in architecture as a tragedy or a disaster. Suffice to say that its consequences have been socially

Le Corbusier, Dom-ino house, 1914
Invented as a response to the early devastation of trench warfare in Flanders, the Dom-ino house was a reinforced concrete structural frame with basic services onto which people could build with either the remains of their traditional houses, or factory-made components. After the War, it became a potent emblem of the new spatial freedom of Modernist architecture.

distressing and aesthetically regrettable.' This book is not a defence of Modernism – the works, once some effort has been made to understand them, are their own best defence – but I do write out of sympathy and admiration for what I believe history will judge the most remarkable outpouring of artistic creativity since the early Renaissance. Modernism was closely linked to economic and social modernization, and it can hardly be held wholly accountable for the sins of property speculators and government bureaucracies who employed third-rate architects to cover our cities with cheap, hand-me-down versions of Modernist design.

Before tracing Modernism's nineteenth-century origins, it will be helpful to have an idea of where the story is leading by plunging briefly into the heart of the matter. In 1914 the Swiss-born architect, painter and propagandist Charles-Edouard Jeanneret (who later changed his name to Le Corbusier) designed a housing system he christened 'Dom-ino' after the six dots made by its columns on a plan. Consisting of a prefabricated reinforced-concrete frame and factory-made partitions, windows, doors and other components, it was intended to harness the capacity of modern industry to respond rapidly to a desperate situation – the devastated villages scattered across the battlefields of Flanders. Fifteen years later, lecturing in Buenos Aires, Le Corbusier recounted its origins: it was inspired, he said, by the traditional houses of Flanders, with their almost totally glazed street frontages, and it had taken him over a decade to appreciate its full implications. By comparing the first Dom-ino designs with the Cook House, built in 1926 on the edge of Paris overlooking the Bois de Boulogne, we can see what he meant immediately.

Despite its innovative structural frame, the Dom-ino house could readily have been built using traditional construction methods: the windows are still holes in walls, the room-layout does not exploit the freedom offered by the independent frame and the structure makes no aesthetic contribution to the house as a piece of architecture – neither columns nor slabs are used as elements of the formal composition. In the Cook House, by contrast, the structural system is the basis of an *architectural idea*, embracing the way in which the house is organized and entered, lived-in and lit. Le Corbusier proudly presented it as the first incarnation of 'The Five Points of a New Architecture', which are:

1. The use of columns (which he calls *pilotis*) to raise the house off the ground, freeing the site for the circulation of people and cars, emphasizing the cubic nature of the building by enabling the underside of the first floor slab to be seen and eliminating a basement – which he considered unhealthy in 'tubercular Paris'.
2. Developing the flat roof as a *roof-garden*, recovering the ground 'lost' by building the house and making a private outdoor space for sunbathing, exercise or taking the view.
3. Exploiting the freedom created by the structural frame to position partitions where required – what he called the *free plan*.
4. Glazing, infilling or omitting the non-load-bearing external walls to create privacy, windows or open terraces as desired – the *free facade*.
5. Using a long horizontal window (*la fenêtre en longueur* or ribbon window) to give even and generous lighting (a somewhat dubious claim which was not fully borne out in practice – the reasons were as much aesthetic as practical).

There will be much more to say in Chapter 3 about Le Corbusier's 'New Architecture', and we need pause here only to note how he set about his renewal. Firstly, the New Architecture is *radical*: the 'Five Points' propose a new beginning through a re-formulation of the roots of architecture. In place of the Abbé Laugier's Primitive Hut (the putative origin of the Classical temple in rudimentary timber construction), Le Corbusier offers a machine-age structure and the promise of new freedoms in arranging both plans and facades to create what he considered the eternal qualities of architecture – the 'masterly, correct and magnificent play of volumes brought together in light', experienced as an *architectural promenade* through the building. Secondly, it is an *architectural system* not a prescriptive style and is thus open, in principle, to other interpretations. Thirdly, it aims to exploit *machine-age technology* and *industrial production* in order to solve unprecedented problems – the massive housing need following the ravages of total war – and to enrich daily life with roof-gardens, an abundance of health-giving light and the 'lyricism brought by techniques'. And, finally, it gives compelling formal expression to the *New Spirit* of modernity: the Cook house is like no other built

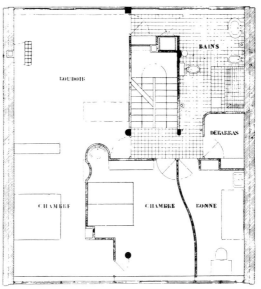

Le Corbusier and Pierre Jeanneret, Cook House, Paris, 1926
The Cook House embodied all 'The Five Points of a New Architecture' Le Corbusier formulated as consequences of the Dom-ino frame. The house is raised on columns, ribbon windows run from edge to edge of the 'free facade', partitions are freely shaped in response to functional or aesthetic requirements, and the pitched roof has been replaced by a garden overlooking the Bois de Boulogne. The plan on the right is of the second floor.

before in the West. You can see over, under and through it, and its forms subtly evoke that most modern of machines, the aeroplane.

All the key concepts can be traced back to the nineteenth century. The architectural promenade was derived from the concept of the picturesque in eighteenth-century English landscape theory and applied to the design of streets and, later, individual buildings. The idea of an architectural system was predicated on the belief that architecture should be grounded in the techniques of construction: initially used almost interchangeably with 'style', by the end of the century it came to mean the antithesis of the academic 'parade of styles'. Finally, the conviction that architecture should express the 'spirit of the age' was ushered in by the Romantic revolution and manifested in repeated calls for a New Style representative of the achievements and character of 'modern life'. This conviction that new technical means and aesthetic forms were needed to express the new life being created by industrialization grew steadily during the nineteenth century, informing the development of all the arts.

The precondition for Modernism was the sense of modernity conceived in the 1780s when Britain, reaping the first rewards of the Industrial Revolution, achieved self-sustaining economic growth, and the French Revolution initiated the long process which would see the ultimate triumph of the bourgeoisie over the *ancien régime*. Its birth, however, was delayed by the Napoleonic Wars, and only when peace finally came in 1815 could the new economic and technical resources be used constructively. The year 1820 saw liberal revolutions in Spain, Portugal and Italy, and in 1824 there was an uprising against Tsar Nicholas – an early manifestation of the social rifts that would lead to the Revolution of 1917. The United States, by contrast, was making rapid strides away from a

struggling former colony and towards a potent nation-state, and the British Empire continued its expansion into the Indian subcontinent. All around the globe the advanced societies were penetrating uncharted territory, subduing, and sometimes annihilating, the native peoples. The foundations of the modern world were effectively laid by 1830.

Accompanying these geopolitical developments was a stream of scientific discoveries and inventions which transformed people's understanding and experience of the world. John Dalton published his atomic theory in 1808; Humphry Davy rose from a poor birth in rural Cornwall to run the Royal Institution and lay the foundations of modern chemistry; his assistant and protégé Michael Faraday emerged from similarly humble origins to do the same for electro-magnetism. In 1830 Charles Lyell published his *Principles of Geology* which established the enormity of geological time and, in conjunction with Charles Darwin's *On the Origin of Species* of 1859, demonstrated how the earth and the organisms it supports evolved – an ultimately irrefutable challenge to the biblical account of creation. The world's first railway, designed to pull coal and passengers from Stockton to Darlington in north-east England, was built by George Stephenson and opened in September 1825, just before the economic crash of 1825–6. The 1820s also saw the invention of the first passenger lift, a host of new machine-tools and the modern type of tin can for preserving food. Altogether more momentous in signalling the arrival of the machine age, however, were the world's first production line and the circular saw for milling timber, both of them the work of Mark Isambard Brunel.

Brunel's biography is the story of a quintessentially modern life. Born and educated in Normandy, he fled the aftermath of the Revolution to seek his fortune in the United States. Finding America did not offer the opportunities he hoped for and hearing of problems satisfying the British Navy's insatiable appetite for handmade rigging blocks (each 74-gun ship needed 922) he hurried to England. In 1801 his ideas for a series of mass-production machines were accepted, and he offered a partnership to the

Farman 'Goliath' aeroplane, illustrated in Le Corbusier's *Vers Une Architecture*, 1923
'Every modern man has the mechanical sense' Le Corbusier declared in his seminal book *Vers Une Architecture*. The Cook house (opposite) reflects his admiration for the planes and cars which illustrated his arguments: note the biplane-like quality of the roof, and the 'cockpit' adjacent to the entrance and car-parking space under the house.

Abbé Laugier, 'The primitive hut', Frontispiece from the second edition of *Essai sur l'architecture*, engraved by Ch. Eisen, 1755
This skeletal timber hut – the putative origin of the Greek temple – haunted French Classical architects. Le Corbusier's drawing of the Dom-ino house structure (page 6) was intended to have a similar iconic power as the origin of a new architecture for the Machine Age.

existing contractor, Fox and Taylor. They declined, however, convinced that machines could not replace skilled craftsmen. The first blocks poured off the line in 1803 and two years later Fox and Taylor lost their contract: they needed 110 tradesmen to Brunel's 10 unskilled hands. The impact of his circular saw was equally emphatic, cutting the cost of milling by 600 per cent; similar machines were soon installed all over Britain. Just as impressive was his boot factory which employed 24 disabled soldiers to produce quality goods at a third or less of the price of handmade boots: they were worn by Wellington's men at Waterloo, and by Napoleon's when he could get them.

Brunel's genius as an inventor was not complemented by a good head for business. The boot factory was hit by the outbreak of peace, leaving him with £5,000 worth of unsold stock and, when his bank collapsed in 1821, he found himself in the debtors' prison. On regaining his liberty (thanks to the intercession of the Duke of Wellington) he put forward, with his son Isambard Kingdom, a proposal for a soft-bed tunnel under the Thames using a machine patented in 1818. Its design was based on a shipworm which tunnels through timber: the principle Brunel observed and adopted is precisely that of a modern boring machine. The creative leap from natural organism to new machine is typical of the great nineteenth-century engineers, and was notably lacking in most architects, whose outlook was dominated by convention – not surprisingly, many of the nineteenth century's most innovative buildings were the work of engineers, not architects. Unfortunately the tunnel was started too near the riverbed and quickly became dangerous; it was temporarily walled up in 1828 and not finished until 1843 and, like the boot factory, proved a financial disaster.

The success of Brunel's production lines was widely acclaimed and emulated; they demonstrated, much to many people's surprise, that machine-tools could in principle replace most, if not all, of the traditional crafts. The social and economic consequences of machine-filled factories are all too familiar: massive migration of people from rural areas to the city and the consequent social and environmental ills of endless acres of crowded, jerry-built housing or, even worse, the depredations of the poorhouse; startling differences in income between capitalists and industrial workers; and the emergence of a middle class of managers, bureaucrats and professionals with sufficient surplus income to sustain the mass-production of *objets d'art*, furniture and other craft products. By the mid-century, as we shall see, the machine-production of art- and craft-objects was the subject of anguished moral-aesthetic arguments across Europe.

NORTHAMPTON COLLEGE LIBRARY

A life like Brunel's would have been impossible before the nineteenth century: travel and communications enabled him to seek his fortune on two continents, and the unprecedented volatility of industrial capitalism made him wealthy one day and a debtor the next. The maelstrom of change in which Brunel and his contemporaries were caught up was given its classic formulation by Karl Marx in *The Communist Manifesto* of 1848:

> Constant revolutionizing of production, uninterrupted disturbance of all social conditions, everlasting uncertainty and agitation distinguish the bourgeois epoch from all earlier ones. All fixed, fast-frozen relations, with their train of ancient and venerable prejudices and opinions are swept away, all new-formed ones become antiquated before they can ossify. All that is solid melts into air, all that is holy is profaned, and man is at last compelled to face with sober senses, his real conditions of life, and his relations with his kind.

The appalling conditions in the industrial cities were amongst the most conspicuous consequences of the 'uninterrupted disturbance of all social conditions'. In Britain, they prompted a range of philanthropic alternatives, from company towns such as Saltaire to the Garden City ideal of Ebenezer Howard, but the damp, airless and rat- and disease-infested slums were less easily tackled. They were the ubiquitous reality against which we must understand the utopian visions of the early twentieth century, such as Charles Garnier's *Cité Industrielle*, Antonio Sant Elia's *Città Nuova*, and Le Corbusier's *Ville Radieuse*. The first city to face modernization head-on was, not surprisingly, Paris – but this was not so much for reasons of public health as to ensure the security of the state. During the first half of the nineteenth century Paris saw its population double while the building of luxury housing and government offices substantially diminished the housing stock. The volatility of the economy in the years after Waterloo produced periodic episodes of mass unemployment which, in the absence of a system of welfare, almost inevitably meant starvation; and epidemics of cholera and typhoid regularly ravaged the crowded old *quartiers*. Against this background it comes as no surprise to learn that between 1827 and 1851 the streets of Paris saw barricades erected on no less than nine occasions: a network of broad, straight streets, affording ample space to deploy the army and good lines of fire, seemed to offer the best defence against potential riots. Following the establishment of the Second Empire in 1852, Napoleon III sketched out suitable street alignments on a

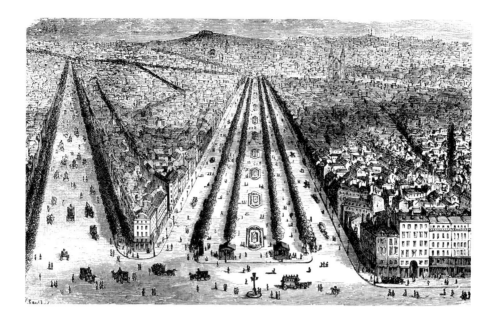

During the 1850s and 1860s, Baron Georges-Eugène Haussmann undertook the vast transformation which established the form of modern Paris. This boulevard covered an old canal, and was one of many intended 'to assure the public peace by [permitting] the circulation not only of air and light but also of troops' so that 'by an ingenious combination the lot of the people will be improved, and they will be rendered less disposed to revolt'.

large map of Paris proudly displayed in his study at Saint-Cloud, and work began soon after. Little progress was made, however, until the following year when – after a further episode of street-fighting – Baron Georges-Eugène Haussmann took charge in his capacity as Préfet de la Seine.

Haussmann relates in his *Mémoires* that his first priority was to 'disencumber the large buildings, palaces and barracks in such a way as to make them more pleasing to the eye, afford easier access on days of celebration, and a simplified defence on days of riot'. Improving the state of the nation's health by 'the systematic destruction of infected alleyways and centres of epidemics' was far from fully achieved, but he had more success in assuring 'the public peace by the creation of large boulevards which will permit the circulation not only of air and light but also of troops' so that 'by an ingenious combination the lot of the people will be improved, and they will be rendered less disposed to revolt'. Haussmann's plans were implemented in three campaigns over seventeen years. He got little help from academically trained architects who found it difficult to adjust to the vast scale of the undertaking, and there were then no trained town-planners. Instead he turned to the chief engineer in charge of bridges and highways, Eugène Belgrand; to Jean Alphand, a landscape gardener with an engineering background; and to his chief surveyor, M. Deschamps, to whom he happily attributed the success of the overall plan. To pay for the massive undertaking Haussmann developed new systems of public finance based on credit raised against the value of the completed improvements, and secured a special fund under his personal control. By 1869, and operating virtually as a benign dictator,

Haussmann had spent two and a half billion francs on the construction of boulevards, squares, gardens, a network of parks, market halls, bridges, sewers and other improvements. In March that year a cost overrun was debated in the Chamber of Deputies, which voted to liquidate the special fund, severely limiting his freedom of action and signalling his impending downfall. The bourgeoisie, who had gained the most from Haussmann's endeavours – expropriation of property being a source of new-found wealth for many – finally turned against him.

Haussmann's contemporaries were understandably disturbed by the scale and pace of change. Slashing great boulevards through dense urban districts inevitably entailed the destruction of established communities and the dislocation of people who, many years before the advent of the car, could not comprehend the need for these massive arteries of the city's new circulatory system. The poor put up little resistance, almost anything being better than the depredations of the old *quartiers*, and most of the bourgeoisie were apparently equally unable to grasp the economic logic of the changes. At their peak, the public works employed a quarter of Paris's labour force, and stimulated a vast expansion of local firms of all kinds – the ground and often mezzanine floors of the typical six-storey tenements were generally occupied by businesses. The speed of the work was just as startling; new boulevards seemed to spring up overnight, complete with thirty-year-old trees in full leaf moved with the help of a specially invented tree-lifting machine.

The street corners were zoned for restaurants and cafés with their delightful – and to modern tourists notoriously expensive – *terrasses*. These soon became the ubiquitous emblem of *la vie parisienne* and were made possible by Haussmann's extravagantly wide pavements, which left plenty of room for trees, benches and slowly moving crowds of pedestrians. Major crossings and terminations of the boulevards were marked by monuments or public buildings: each route visibly led somewhere. Thanks to their many conveniences, the boulevards became the stroller's delight and the home to a new type of urban individual, the *flâneur*, who was a connoisseur of the quintessentially modern life of the boulevards. Alone in the crowds – an unexpected luxury of mass society – the *flâneur* was free to revel in the display of fashion and luxury goods, beautiful women, young lovers and ceaseless traffic.

The first artist to describe the idea of modernity did so amidst the upheavals of Haussmann's Paris. This was the poet Charles Baudelaire in his celebrated essay *The Painter of Modern Life*, published in 1863. 'By "modernity"', he wrote, 'I mean the ephemeral, the contingent, the half of art whose other half is eternal and immutable.' The painter of modern life represents 'the passing moment and all the suggestions of eternity it contains' and directs himself towards the motive forces of modern life. He delights in 'fine carriages and proud horses, ... the sinuous gait of the women, the beauty of the children, happy to be alive and well dressed – in a word, he delights in universal life. If a fashion or the cut of a garment has been slightly modified, if bows and curls have been supplanted by cockades, if bavolets have been enlarged and chignons have dropped a fraction toward the nape of the neck, if waists have been raised and skirts have become fuller, be very sure that his eagle eye will have spotted it.'

This confection may sound more like advertising copy than innovative literature to our ears, but it is typical, as Marshall Berman has argued, of that strand of Modernism 'which sees the whole spiritual adventure of modernity incarnated in the latest fashion, the latest machine, or – and here it gets sinister – the latest model regiment'. Baudelaire's painter takes equal delight in the 'glittering equipment, music, bold, determined glances, heavy solemn moustaches' of a passing regiment, and 'his soul lives with the sound of that regiment, marching like a single animal, a proud image of joy and obedience.' It was in just such a regiment, as Berman points out, that Baudelaire had very probably served in Paris when 25,000 of its citizens were killed in the 1848 Revolution.

No one more clearly anticipated the challenges modern art must face than Baudelaire. The modern painter, he suggested, must 'set up his house in the heart of the multitude, amid the ebb and flow of motion, in the midst of the fugitive and the infinite. . . . His passion and his profession are *to become one flesh with the crowd.*' Plunging into the life of the city he must 'enter into the crowd as though it were an immense reservoir of electrical energy. . . . Or we might compare him to a kaleidoscope gifted with consciousness' able to express 'the attitude and the gesture of living beings, whether solemn or grotesque, and their luminous *explosion* in space.' This plunge into the life of the modern city was not without its risks and in 'Loss of a halo', a prose-poem written in 1865, Baudelaire describes how he 'was crossing the boulevard, in a great hurry, in the midst of a moving chaos, with death galloping at me from every side.' These are powerful images but the visual equivalents of Baudelaire's conscious kaleidoscope, with explosions in space and death galloping from every side, would have to await the fully fledged Modernism which lay forty years into the future.

The salons of the new Paris were the environment which nurtured – albeit unwittingly – the idea of an artistic *avant-garde*, and the

first artist to assert a fully *avant-garde* position, combining a
determination to be new and to shock, was Gustave Courbet. 'My
painting is the only true one,' he said, 'I am the first and only artist
of this century.' Fifty years later, the similarly egotistical American
architect, Frank Lloyd Wright, would make similar claims –
expanding the timescale to five hundred years! Courbet was a
Realist, and his realism influenced the artists whose exhibition in
1874 inspired the first great scandal of modern art: the
Impressionists. Although Impressionism is inextricably linked in the
popular imagination with seemingly carefree landscapes and
leisure, the painters were committed to creating an art of modern
life, and the experience of the urban boulevards and the *places*
figures largely in their work. Take, for example, *La Place du
Théâtre Français* by Camille Pissarro, painted in 1898. Late
Pissarros such as this are famous for their elimination of the
horizon, producing that all-over quality characteristic of much
Modernist painting. Although Pissarro is generally credited with this
innovation, the first horizon-less painting was in fact painted in
1880 by Gustave Caillebotte: entitled *Boulevard Seen from Above*, it
remained in the obscurity of a family collection and was not noticed
again until the Impressionist Centenary Exhibition of 1974. Looking
down on a boulevard was one of the most familiar everyday views
for thousands of Parisians whose apartments lined the new
thoroughfares, but art is based on pictorial conventions and no
artist before Caillebotte had chosen to set his easel before an upper
floor window and *look down*.

Like Degas' pictures of circus performers seen from below, the
view from above was a radical way of reinvigorating the
increasingly jaded pictorial conventions of Realism, and to the

Camille Pisarro, *La Place du
Théâtre Français*, 1898
The view from above became
a favourite of the Impressionists
in the 1890s, the vehicle for
striking new images suggestive
of the anonymity and teeming
life of the modern metropolis
which Baudelaire had identified
as appropriate subject-matter
for the 'painter of modern life'
half a century earlier.

Title page from *Voici des Ailes!* by Maurice Leblanc, 1898

Leblanc's novel celebrated the delights of cycling which, as the lady on the title page clearly suggested, became a metaphor for liberation from social conventions in personal relations, clothing, and marriage – two couples who set out together swapped spouses and returned to new lives.

Modernist artists who revolutionized painting early in the new century it challenged the very convention of the picture as a window-on-the-world. This had dominated both Western art and the Western way of seeing the world since the Renaissance rediscovery of linear perspective, and one of Pissarro's contemporaries wittily suggested that his paintings should properly be exhibited on the floor. Reduced to unrecognizable blobs, people appear to float in the pictorial space, a perfect image of the *experience* as much as of the *appearance*, of urban space, of the anonymity and freedom of the modern city.

Nineteenth-century painters faced another major incentive to renew their art – from photography. Pioneered in France by Nicéphore Niepce and Louis Daguerre and in England by William Henry Fox Talbot, who produced the first negative/positive process in 1841, photography could potentially take over many of painting's 'recording' functions – from portraits, to places, to events. In 1884 George Eastman invented flexible negative film and five years later launched the Kodak No 1 camera and roll film, initiating the era of universal, hand-held snapshots. Photography was but one of many inventions which changed people's whole sense of the world and opened new possibilities of living – amongst the rest were the motor car, airships, aeroplanes, the phonograph, cinema, wireless telegraphy, radio and so forth. New technologies commonly have impacts well beyond anything their inventors envisage, and we gain an amusing but nonetheless revealing insight into this from the novel *Voici des Ailes!* by Maurice Leblanc, published in 1898. The story celebrates the delights of cycling – the modern bicycle, with two equal-sized wheels and pneumatic tyres, was only twelve years old when it was written – and relates the experiences of two married couples touring the French countryside. The new physical freedom of moving through space becomes – as the liberated 'new woman' on the title page clearly announces – an escape from the social conventions of personal relations, clothing, and ultimately marriage itself, since the couples eventually exchange spouses and return to new lives.

The promise of the new technologies was immense. In 1908 the French novelist Valéry Larbaud declared that 'the entire surface of the planet is ours when we want! ... Europe is like one great city' – and this optimism was reflected in much Modernist art, above all in architecture and design whose practitioners were determined to build a new world equal to the expanded possibilities of living. But most early Modernists were also acutely conscious that the world was heading for crisis. Disgusted by the bloated complacency of bourgeois life, disturbed by the burgeoning competition between the major European nations and frequently uprooted from their own national cultures, they projected feelings of alienation and rootlessness, disorientation and detachment. The heroic affirmations of Le Corbusier and the parody and despair of, say, T. S. Eliot's *The Waste Land* (1922) are not so much polar opposites as contrary yet complementary responses to living in a period of unprecedented pluralism, fragmentation and estrangement, in which creation and destruction are inextricably linked. 'A painting', Picasso said, 'is a sum of destructions.'

The roots of Modernism lie deep in the nineteenth century and it is there that we will begin our exploration. The emphasis in the first chapter is on the sources of modern architecture and design, because it is in the applied arts that we find an explicit search for a representative New Style, and the greatest continuity with the twentieth century. The second chapter examines the explosive emergence of Modernism in the arts before the First World War; the War's impact and the consequent 'return to order' during the 1920s are explored in Chapter 3. The October Revolution of 1917 combined with the impact of war to precipitate an astonishing flowering and redefinition of the arts in Russia – the subject of Chapter 4. The consolidation of the Modernist aesthetic and development of the so-called International Style are described in Chapter 5, whilst the final chapter traces the almost universal dissemination of Modernist aesthetics through buildings, magazines, advertising and industrial products as cultural leadership passed to the USA following the Second World War. I conclude with some brief speculations about the Modernist legacy.

This book does not pretend to be a history of Modernism, and I am all too aware of many inevitable omissions. The emphasis throughout is on those developments and ideas which have had the greatest impact on the everyday world, and I have preferred to discuss in detail those movements and individuals whose influence seem to me central, rather than attempt a systematic and necessarily superficial survey: hopefully this approach will do justice to the complexity and richness of the ideas and works discussed. The illustrations and captions are both complementary to the text and designed to tell a parallel story; they are interspersed with quotations from key documents of the period – Modernism produced a blizzard of manifestoes, critical texts and attempts to explain it to a frequently bewildered public. After almost a century, much of that bewilderment remains.

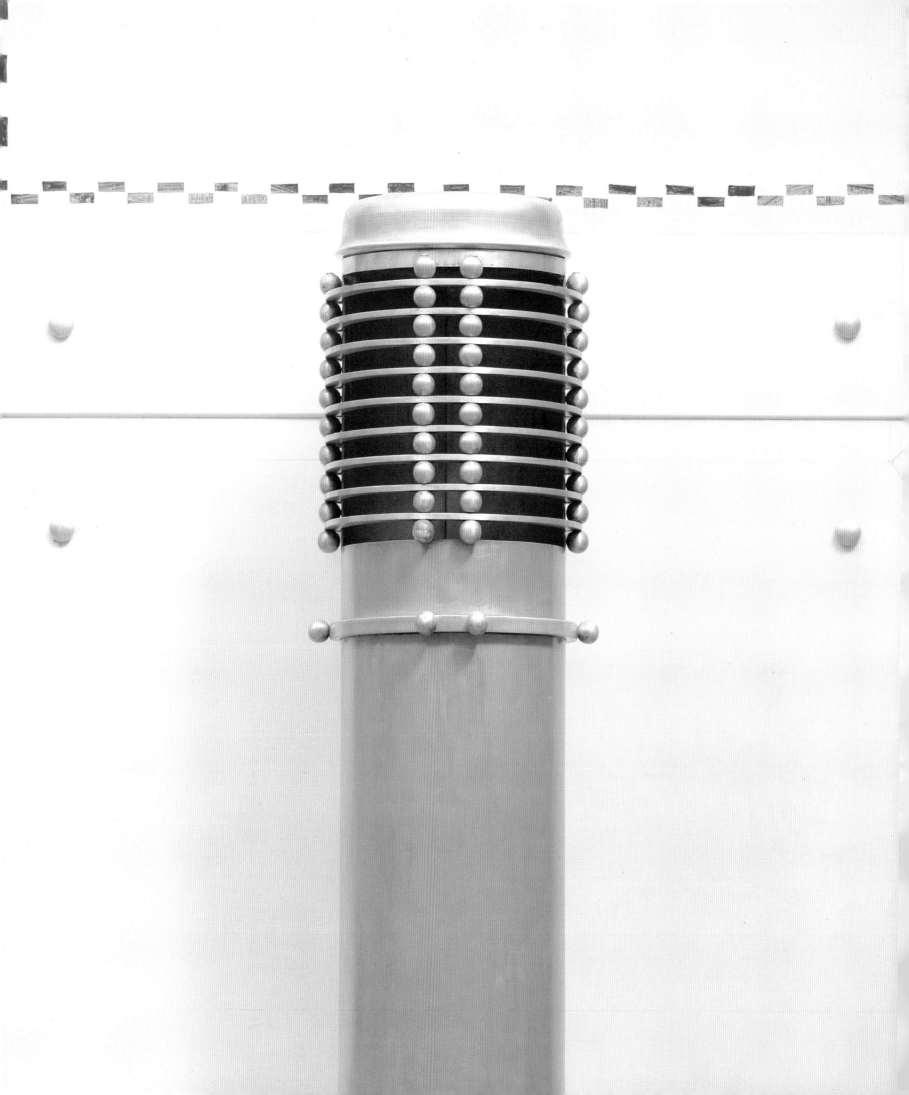

Roots

To recognize the meaning, the form, the purpose of all things of the material modern world with the same truth as the Greeks, among many others, recognized the meaning, form, and purpose of the column. It is not easy nowadays to find the exact meaning and the exact form for the simplest things. Adolf Loos

Opposite: Otto Wagner, Post Office Savings Bank, Vienna, 1903–12
The banking hall in Wagner's masterpiece was one of the finest interiors of the early twentieth century. Its marshalling of all the elements into an integrated whole is epitomized by this elegant cylindrical heat inlet.

Left: Charles Rennie Mackintosh, Textile design, c.1920
Much admired by the Viennese Secessionists, the Scottish architect Mackintosh pioneered a style of decoration which anticipated the geometric purity of Modernism.

The modern arts grew out of the experiences and innovations of the nineteenth century. They were years of bewilderingly rapid change, throughout which most people wanted the arts to reassure by their familiarity, not excite by their novelty – when everything else was changing, surely aesthetic values might remain constant, breakwaters against the tide of time? Most thoughtful artists and architects knew that the answer was no, and their dilemmas were summed up by the simple-sounding question, 'In which style should we build?', asked (as the title of a book published in 1828) by a little-known German architect, Heinrich Hübsch. The question would hardly have been asked before the nineteenth century because it reflected a radically new attitude to the past. Hitherto, history was thought to conform to a pattern into which civilizations were placed according to their stage of 'development'. But in the more liberal climate of the eighteenth century historians examined civilizations on their own merits, valuing features which made them distinctive. The authority of Classical architecture, all but unquestioned since the Renaissance, was challenged, and numerous styles explored: the Gothic came back into favour; archaeological research revealed more fully the miracles of Greece and Egypt; and travellers brought back detailed knowledge of distant China.

Stylistic revivals were not what Hübsch had in mind, however: he wanted to determine the 'right' style for the nineteenth century. In a diary-note, his great contemporary Karl Friedrich Schinkel asked an altogether more daring question: 'Every major period has left behind its own style of architecture. Why should we not try to find a style for ourselves?' Many, such as Théodore Jouffroy, saw eclecticism as the nineteenth century's characteristic mode of thought – the *esprit nouveau*, as he put it in 1825, of the arts and sciences. In architecture, this modern eclecticism would not mean slavishly copying past styles, but synthesizing ideas gleaned from the riches of history. Such syntheses proved beyond the talent of most, and architects specialized in a favourite style, or offered a range, selecting according to their client's preferences, or the appropriateness to the site or brief – such as Gothic for churches and Classical for public buildings.

The dilemmas facing later nineteenth-century architects are neatly summed up by George Gilbert Scott's experience in designing the new Government Offices in Whitehall. He secured the commission in 1868 with a design in his favourite French Gothic, spiced with 'a few hints from Italy'. But the Prime

Minister Lord Palmerston demanded that the buildings be Palladian. Failing to persuade him to accept something 'in the Byzantine of the early Venetian palaces', Scott set to work on a 'beautifully got up' Italian facade. Such stylistic freedom – exercised on a largely unchanging plan – seemed more like licence to those who valued the organic unity of a building: in 'the battle of the styles' architecture was the loser.

The nineteenth century posed new challenges: greenhouses for exotic plants, railway stations, exhibition halls and large open floors for buildings such as knitting mills and department stores. Industry offered materials – iron, steel, and large sheets of glass – not previously available in sufficient quantities for building, and for which past styles offered limited guidance. In a perceptive analysis of architects' stylistic dilemmas, the landscape gardener John Claudius Loudon argued that solving conventional problems required only 'imitative genius', whereas being forced to go beyond historic styles for inspiration would require 'inventive genius'. He suggested new needs, new materials, and 'union' with another art as stimuli, and pointed to three developments – greenhouses, cast-iron construction and suspension bridges – as examples. Perhaps it was there that architects might look for the beginnings of a 'style for ourselves'?

Schinkel's question haunted nineteenth-century architects and writers, and finding 'a style for ourselves' proved difficult. In 1849 the leading French critic César Daly wrote that the public was still waiting for 'a new architecture which will take us out of the sterility of the past and the servility of copying'. And despite his facility, G.G. Scott was concerned that architects were 'content to pluck the flowers of history without cultivating any of their own'. When the great French theorist Eugène-Emmanuel Viollet-le-Duc's lectures, the *Entretiens sur l'architecture*, were published in French (in 1863 and 1872, and in English in 1877 and 1881) they sounded a familiar refrain: lamenting that 'nothing but the confusion of ideas existing in modern times … could have brought about the chaotic state of things', he wondered if the century was 'destined to close without possessing an architecture of its own? Will this age, which is so fertile in discoveries … transmit to posterity only imitations of hybrid works, without character?' It seemed so, because in 1896 Otto Wagner was still lecturing in Vienna about the 'style of our time' in the future tense: 'the new architecture will be dominated by slablike, tabular surfaces and the prominent use of materials in a pure state'.

Eugène-Emmanuel Viollet-le-Duc, Project for a 3,000-seat hall, 1850s
This interior, which illustrated the twelfth of Viollet-le-Duc's *Entretiens sur l'architecture*, was intended to show how a new architecture could arise by combining cast iron and stone. The result, however, is far from convincing.

The Romantic revolution made the search for a representative style intense. The arts, and in particular architecture, were seen as embodiments of the 'Spirit of the Age' – a phrase considered a 'novel expression' by John Stuart Mill in 1831, when he used it as the title of an essay. In German-speaking countries the elusive spirit, known as the *Zeitgeist*, played a key role in the Idealist philosophy founded by Kant. The Idealists saw history as the unfolding of a 'world-plan', in which each age finds its natural expression. This idea had a formative influence on the German-speaking founders of modern art history – Jakob Burckhardt, Heinrich Wölfflin, Alois Riegl and Erwin Panofsky – and through them on two major promoters of Modernist architecture, Nikolaus Pevsner and Sigfried Giedion. In *Space, Time and Architecture* Giedion wrote with pride that it was from Heinrich Wölfflin that he had 'learned to grasp the spirit of an epoch'.

In his doctoral dissertation of 1883, Wölfflin argued that a living style reflected the postures, attitudes, movements and clothing of contemporary life, and that the tendencies of an age were best read in the small-scale decorative arts. The new stylistic freedom did indeed first appear in the decorative arts – Chippendale's pattern-book of 1754 featured Classical, rococo, chinoiserie and Gothic furniture, for example – and could be seen in all its variety at the great international exhibitions: the first, the 'Great Exhibition of the Works of Industry of All Nations', was held in London's Hyde Park in 1851. Its prime movers were Albert, the Prince Consort and President of the Society of Arts, and Henry Cole, a public servant whose accomplishments included originating the Penny Black stamp and inventing the Christmas card. Albert, speaking as a good Victorian *and* a German, said the exhibition would be 'a true test of the point of development at which the whole of mankind has arrived' towards 'that great aim indicated everywhere by history: the union of the human race'. The world flooded London with exhibits, delighting Queen Victoria, who declared it 'the *greatest* day of our history, the *most beautiful* and *imposing* and *touching* spectacle ever seen, and the triumph of my beloved Albert'.

The Exhibition took place in the vast Crystal Palace designed by Joseph Paxton. Most visitors were overwhelmed by its lightness and size, and according to Lothar Bucher (an exile who later became Bismarck's right-hand man), it was 'of such romantic beauty that reproductions of it were soon hanging on the cottage walls of remote German villages'. The exhibits were equally popular: encrusted with 'style', the luxury items exemplified the Victorian delight in accumulation, whether of facts in science, details in a painting, ornament on objects, or money in the bank. This rampant eclecticism might be the true spirit of the age, but it was not what the organizers wished to see, and was especially galling for Cole, who twenty years earlier had sat on a Government Select Committee appointed by the Prime Minister Robert Peel to look into the state of art and design. In 1832 Peel opened the National Gallery in London, with the aim of instilling 'a sense of design in the manufacturers, and of elevating taste in the consumer'. Most consumers visiting the Crystal Palace had clearly not had their taste sufficiently elevated, and Cole and his fellow reformers still had much to do. With machines able to emulate craft skills and simulate precious materials, it was hardly surprising that the new middle classes were eager to surround themselves with affordable signs of wealth and 'taste', nor that educated taste should distance itself by finding aesthetic virtue in the unadorned lines of objects of necessity.

Amidst the profusion of luxuries, the American exhibits were an oasis of calm. The Americans sent practical, cheaply manufactured goods – a reaper, milk pails, boots, guns, axes and other tools. Richard Redgrave, one of Cole's circle, expressed delight in the 'noble simplicity' of these 'objects of absolute utility'. And Gottfried Semper – like Bucher, another German

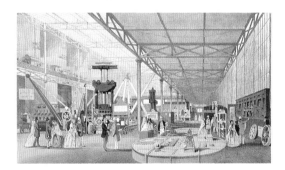

The Crystal Palace at the Great Exhibition of 1851
The raised, cathedral-like crossing (below) was introduced to accommodate a group of mature elm trees. Ornamental fountains and figures had pride of place, forming a striking contrast to the machines (above) shown in the aisles. The most progressive design reformers found art in the machines – and none in the sculptures.

GEBRÜDER THONET.

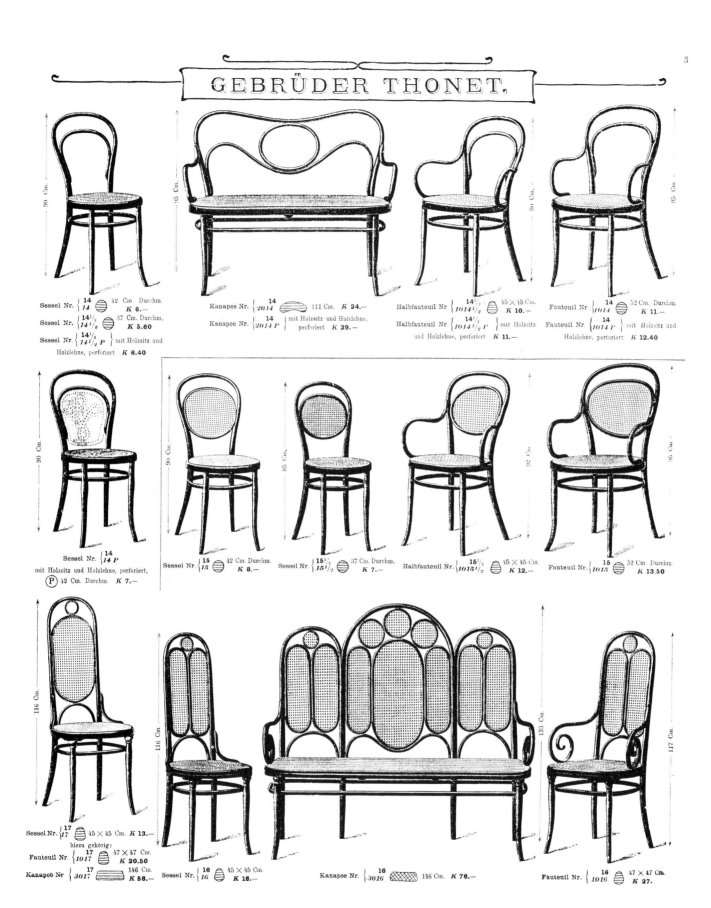

Sessel Nr. {14 / 14} 42 Cm. Durchm. **K 6.—**

Sessel Nr. {14½ / 14½} 37 Cm. Durchm. **K 5.60**

Sessel Nr. {14½ / 14½ P} mit Holzsitz und Holzlehne, perforiert **K 6.40**

Kanapee Nr. {14 / 2014} 111 Cm. **K 24.—**

Kanapee Nr. {14 / 2014 P} mit Holzsitz und Holzlehne, perforiert **K 29.—**

Halbfauteuil Nr. {14½ / 1014½} 45 × 45 Cm. **K 10.—**

Halbfauteuil Nr. {14½ / 1014½ P} mit Holzsitz und Holzlehne, perforiert **K 11.—**

Fauteuil Nr. {14 / 1014} 52 Cm. Durchm. **K 11.—**

Fauteuil Nr. {14 / 1014 P} mit Holzsitz und Holzlehne, perforiert **K 12.40**

Sessel Nr. {14 / 14 P} mit Holzsitz und Holzlehne, perforiert, (P) 42 Cm. Durchm. **K 7.—**

Sessel Nr. {15 / 15} 42 Cm. Durchm. **K 8.—**

Sessel Nr. {15½ / 15½} 37 Cm. Durchm. **K 7.—**

Halbfauteuil Nr. {15½ / 1015½} 45 × 45 Cm. **K 12.—**

Fauteuil Nr. {15 / 1015} 52 Cm. Durchm. **K 13.50**

Sessel Nr. {17 / 17} 45 × 45 Cm. **K 13.—**
hiezu gehörig:
Fauteuil Nr. {17 / 1017} 47 × 47 Cm. **K 20.50**
Kanapee Nr. {17 / 3017} 146 Cm. **K 58.—**

Sessel Nr. {16 / 16} 45 × 45 Cm. **K 18.—**

Kanapee Nr. {16 / 3016} 146 Cm. **K 76.—**

Fauteuil Nr. {16 / 1016} 47 × 47 Cm. **K 27.**

in temporary political exile – praised the exhibits 'in which seriousness of purpose does not permit superfluities, such as carriages, weapons, musical instruments, the perfection and nobility of their forms being strictly prescribed by function'. Perhaps the distinctive new style had been there all along, expressed in industrial products and in the ineffable space conjured by Paxton from small, modular, prefabricated components. It was a machine aesthetic for the first machine age, the philosophical foundations for which had been laid in the mid-eighteenth century, when the first rumblings of the Industrial Revolution were heard in England. 'That Utility is one of the principal sources of beauty has been observed by everybody', noted Adam Smith in 1759, adding that the machine's fitness for purpose rendered 'the very thought and contemplation of it agreeable'. Two years later Henry Home (the future Lord Kames) observed that 'no single property recommends a machine more than its simplicity, not solely for better answering its purpose, but by appearing in itself more beautiful.'

Lovers of the beauty of utility found particular delight in the world of transportation. Thanks to the innovations of engineers such as McAdam and Telford, the industrializing countries were served by rapidly expanding networks of smooth roads, enabling carriages to be made lighter and faster. In England, carriage-driving became fashionable thanks to the Prince Regent and his circle, and the utmost simplicity and lack of any extraneous features were recognized as the mark of elegance and refinement in carriage design. At the century's close Henry van de Velde, the Belgian painter turned architect, ecstatically compared the parade of carriages in Hyde Park to the Elysian mysteries, the procession to the Parthenon, medieval tournaments and legendary feasts of Venetian gondolas, concluding that none compared with 'the harmony and unique rhythm of this festival of modern beauty'.

Horatio Greenough, the American sculptor and pioneer writer on functionalism, similarly believed that if we could 'carry into our civil architecture the responsibilities that weigh upon our ship-building, we should ere long have edifices as superior to the Parthenon for the purposes that we require, as the Constitution or the Pennsylvania is to the galley of the Argonauts. Comparing products of the machine age to the pinnacles of Greek art became a familiar trope of Modernist rhetoric, but in the mid-nineteenth century it was decidedly daring. The Austrian architect Adolf Loos echoed the Greek comparison when, reviewing the

Vienna Jubilee Exhibition of 1898, he exclaimed 'Look at the bicycle! Does the spirit of Pericles' Athens not waft through its forms?' When Loos was writing, calls for furniture, lamps and domestic furniture to be designed like carriages and ships were widely aired, but transferring such thinking to objects with centuries of tradition and less functionally constrained proved difficult, and arguably the only piece of mass-produced furniture to match the elegance of a bicycle or carriage was the bent-wood chair by Michael Thonet.

Born in 1796, Thonet began experimenting with wood-bending in the 1830s. He moved from the Rhineland to Austria at the invitation of Prince Metternich in 1842, and Vienna granted him a patent 'to bend every kind of wood, even the most refractory, by chemico-mechanical means, into any form or curve'. His classic 'No. 14' chair appeared in 1859: inexpensive and elegant, it was an immediate and enduring success. Forty years later, Loos was again reminded of Greece and declared: 'Look at the Thonet chair! Without decoration, embodying the sitting habits of a whole era, is it not out of the same spirit as the Greek chair with its curved feet and its backrest?' In 1925, Le Corbusier chose 'the humble Thonet chair … the most common as well as the least costly of chairs' which nonetheless 'possesses nobility' to furnish the 'Pavilion of the New Spirit' at the Paris exhibition of decorative arts. It looked as fresh then as it did in 1859; it still does, and total sales have now reached well over 50 million.

The challenge of machine production and the stylistic promiscuity following in its wake encouraged a thorough re-evaluation of the fundamentals of architecture, centred around the idea of 'the art of building' as opposed to 'style'. At the century's close, Adolf Loos was in no doubt about where a style of the age should be sought. He said: 'The English and the engineers are our Greeks. From them we get our culture, from them it spreads over the globe. They are the ideal men of the 19th century.'

In 1841 Augustus Welby Northmoor Pugin published his vigorous defence of Gothic, entitled *The True Principles of Pointed or Christian Architecture*. He set out 'the two great rules for design' as follows: first 'that there should be no features about a building which are not necessary for convenience, construction or propriety'; and second, 'that all ornament should consist of enrichment of the essential construction of the building. The neglect of these two rules,' he warned, 'is the cause of all the bad architecture of the present time. Architectural features are continually tacked on

Above: Thonet Brothers, Chair No. 14, 1859
Greatly admired by leading Modernists (Le Corbusier thought they possessed 'nobility'), Thonet chairs had become a ubiquitous part of European café life by the turn of the century.

Opposite: Thonet Brothers catalogue, 1904
Thonet's bent-wood chairs sold in huge numbers throughout Europe and America during the second half of the nineteenth century. The most popular, No. 14, appeared in 1859: still in production, over 50 million copies have now been sold.

buildings with which they have no connection, merely for the sake of what is termed effect.' Pugin's conviction that the 'honest' expression of 'Revealed Construction' was a necessary – although not in itself a sufficient – condition for architecture was widely shared by progressive designers.

In France, Viollet-le-Duc also came to notice in the 1840s as a persuasive advocate of Gothic. But by the time the first volume of the *Entretiens* appeared in 1863, he had extended his analysis to many other architectures, above all to Greek, which he now considered the pre-eminent demonstration of the principles he advocated, and which he summed up as *'la construction faite l'art'* ('construction made art'). The *Entretiens* were among the most widely read books on architecture of the nineteenth century – Frank Lloyd Wright's son, John Lloyd, recalls his father presenting him with a copy with the words: 'In these volumes you will find all the architectural schooling you will ever need.' Viollet's position was made clear in the Introduction. 'All architecture,' he stated, 'proceeds from structure, and the first condition at which it should aim is to make the outward form accord with that structure.' Hence 'if we would invent that architecture of our own times which is so loudly called for, we must certainly seek it no longer by mingling all the styles of the past, but by relying on novel principles of structure.'

Interest in structure as the basis of form was not confined to England and France. In 1846 Karl Bötticher, a German architect and the author of a major study of Greek culture entitled *Die Tectonik der Hellenen* ('The Tectonic of the Greeks'), addressed the Schinkel Festival in Berlin. He argued that Gothic and Greek were incapable of further development, and that for a new style to emerge, a new system of space covering must appear. This, he speculated, would come from the use of iron, and might eventually rival the splendours of Greek and Gothic architecture. Given that Germany did not begin large-scale industrialization until the 1870s, Bötticher showed remarkable prescience in his advocacy of iron. Viollet-le-Duc believed that the combination of iron and masonry would yield genuinely new forms, and included proposals in his *Entretiens* for a kind of 'modern gothic'. But he was a better theorist than designer and the drawings were unconvincing.

Bötticher's book on Greece was only one of several studies to emphasize the importance of construction. This approach culminated in 1899 with the publication of Auguste Choisy's magisterial *Histoire de l'Architecture*, which was acclaimed by Le Corbusier in 1925 as 'the most worthy book there ever was on architecture'. Construction-made-into-art pervades Choisy's approach, and the text was illustrated with isometric projections showing buildings in plan and section to emphasize their three-dimensional spatial and structural organization. The illustrations alone drove home the integral role of construction, and exerted a considerable influence well into the twentieth century. The American architect, Louis Kahn, for example, who rose to prominence in the 1950s, frequently emulated them.

The emphasis on construction culminated at the turn of the century in a growing suspicion about the very words 'architecture' and 'style'. Since Quatremère de Quincy's writings of the 1820s and 30s, the term 'architectural system' had become popular to describe the 'organic' integration of systems of construction, proportion and ornament which 'style' did not adequately convey. The German architect and writer Herman Muthesius crystallized the dilemma in the title – *Stilarchitektur und Baukunst* – of a polemic published in 1902. Whereas 'style architecture' was bad, 'the art of building' was good. He considered the words *moderne* and *Architektur* corrupted, the former through its association with *Mode* (fashion), the latter due to nineteenth-century style-mongering. 'Modern' was first used in association with architecture by Otto Wagner in his *Moderne Architektur* of 1896, but he was so impressed by Muthesius's arguments that he retitled the final edition *Die Baukunst unserer Zeit*. The 'Building-art of our time' was being forged with new materials by engineers, and it was to them, increasingly, that architects looked to see the shape of buildings to come.

'If we want any work of an unusual character and send for an architect,' Prince Albert is reported to have quipped, 'he hesitates, debates, trifles; we send for an engineer and he *does it*.' Taught to revere the past and design from precedent, nineteenth-century architects were ill-prepared for work of 'an unusual character': architecture had become an art of imitation and adaptation rather than invention. Professional engineers, by contrast, relished new technologies and could calculate mathematically the consequences of design decisions. Traditionally, innovations in building were made by trial and error, but gradual evolution was now too slow: the 'spirit of the age' demanded leaps of imagination backed by calculation. The material in which the biggest strides were made was iron, available in bulk thanks to industrial production.

Iron bridges appeared before iron structures in buildings. The first was a 30.5-metre span over the

River Severn, completed in 1779 by Abraham Darby near his Coalbrookdale works. Its form was bulky and modelled on timber, and fifteen years later Thomas Telford designed another bridge over the Severn which spanned nine metres further and used less than half the material. In 1836 Isambard Kingdom Brunel began building one of the first masterpieces of the art, Clifton Suspension Bridge, across a dramatic 210-metre gorge of the river Avon on the edge of Bristol. Massive brick pylons, elegantly tapered and somewhat Egyptianate in style, form a perfect foil to the filigree of iron slung seemingly weightlessly between them: everything here, you are convinced, must be this way and no other. Although the bridge was primarily an exercise in practical intelligence and not 'taste', no calculations told Brunel exactly how to shape the pylons or join cable to masonry. The perfection of line and shape – and it is of the highest order – was the result of a feeling for form as well as skill in calculation. The 'Engineer's Aesthetic' (as Le Corbusier later called it) deserves its own canon, and Clifton is one of its sacred sites: the sheer daring still takes your breath away.

The use of iron in buildings began less conspicuously. In the 1790s large, multi-storey mills with fireproof iron frames were appearing in the British Midlands, and the building system soon found application in dockside warehouses. In 1818 John Nash cut a dash at Brighton Pavilion with cast-iron columns in the Red Drawing Room and kitchen – the latter replete with flamboyant palm-leaf capitals. The slenderness of cast iron was exploited in glasshouses, with Rouhault's in the Paris botanical garden of 1833 setting the pattern for many. The first iron-framed arcade appeared in Paris in 1829 (this was the Galerie d'Orléans in the Palais Royal) and by the mid-century, modular structures comprising cast-iron columns, rolled wrought-iron rails and glazing panels were the standard way of constructing market-halls, exchanges and arcades.

Joseph Paxton mastered the art of prefabrication whilst building glasshouses for the Duke of Devonshire's Chatsworth estate, where he was Head Gardener. He only became involved with the Great Exhibition at the last minute. The sponsors were unhappy with the entries in their architectural competition and Paxton made a suggestion they liked. Working closely with the engineer Charles Fox, he developed a system of prefabricated iron and glass components and it took just six months to erect the 1,848-feet-long structure which covered 800,000 square feet (about four times the area of St Peter's in Rome).

The barrel-vaulted transept – introduced to save some oak trees – used a wooden framework, which meant that structurally the design made no contribution to the search for the 'new system of space covering'. But in every other sense the building was a landmark, and it is debatable whether any individual building since has demonstrated more convincingly the architectural potential of industrial production. Lothar Bucher was in no doubt that 'the Crystal Palace is a revolution in architecture from which a new style will date' and his marvellous description is worth quoting at length:

NORTHAMPTON COLLEGE
LIBRARY

'We see a delicate network of lines without any clue by means of which we might judge their distance from the eye or the real size. The side walls are too far apart to be embraced in a single glance. Instead of moving from the wall at one end to that at the other, the eye sweeps along an unending perspective which fades into the horizon. We cannot tell if this structure towers a hundred or a thousand feet above us, or whether the roof is a flat platform or is built up from a succession of ridges, for there is no play of shadows to enable our optic nerves to gauge the measurements.

If we let our gaze travel downward it encounters the blue-painted lattice girders. At first these occur only at wide intervals; then they range closer and closer together until they are interrupted by a dazzling band of light – the transept – which dissolves into a distant background where all materiality is blended into the atmosphere. . . . It is sober economy of language if I call the spectacle incomparable and fairylike. It is a

Isambard Kingdom Brunel, Suspension bridge over the river Avon at Clifton, 1836
The sheer daring and formal assurance of the great works of nineteenth-century engineering can still take your breath away, and Brunel's suspension bridge across a spectacular gorge is amongst the most inspiring. The Russian emigré architect Berthold Lubetkin said that he chose to live in Clifton to be near it.

Below: Joseph Paxton, Great Conservatory, Chatsworth, 1837–40
Conservatories (or 'stoves') for exotic plants were all the rage amongst wealthy landowners and it was as Head Gardener at the Duke of Devonshire's Chatsworth estate in Derbyshire that Joseph Paxton gained the experience which enabled him to design the Crystal Palace.

Right: John Nash, Royal Pavilion, Brighton, 1818
This plate of the Golden Drawing Room was printed in 1826. The design was notable for its unashamed use of cast-iron columns, the first to be exposed in an interior of such status.

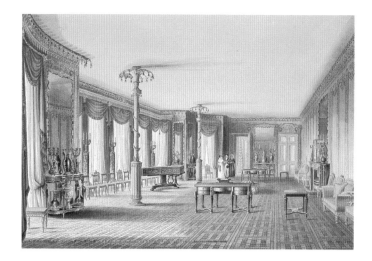

Joseph Paxton, Crystal Palace, London, 1851
The empty interior was photographed in 1852 after the Great Exhibition had ended and shortly before the structure was re-erected (greatly enlarged by Brunel) at Sydenham. It burned down in 1936.

Midsummer Night's Dream seen in the clear light of midday.'

Paxton's triumph did not please everyone. Pugin called it 'Crystal Humbug' and a 'Glass Monster', deeming it a 'bad, vile construction', and John Ruskin was equally dismissive: it confirmed his view that 'higher beauty' would remain 'eternally impossible' in iron, and was, quite simply, 'not architecture'. In a sense he had a point. The space Bucher described so lucidly was unprecedented, as much like an atmospheric landscape as a conventional interior, and almost entirely devoid of the familiar cues from which people were accustomed to make sense of architectural space. It was too vast, too mind-numbingly repetitive and too transparent and diffusely lit to comprehend in traditional terms. As Bucher said, 'contemplating the first great building which was not of solid masonry construction spectators were not slow to realise that here the standards by which architecture had hitherto been judged no longer held good.' A radically new aesthetic of structure, light and space was literally staring them in the face, but few could see it.

In the public's – and most architects' – minds, architecture and engineering were miles apart. We have only to look at London's St Pancras railway station by Barlow and Ordish (1863–5) to see them in uneasy juxtaposition. At 74 metres span, St Pancras boasted the world's largest vault in 1865, completed well before the 'architecture' arrived in 1874 – a red-brick neo-Gothic hotel and administration building by G. G. Scott, which completely obscures, and bears scant relation to, the great vault behind. Brunel and Wyatt's Paddington station (1853–86) fared little better, despite Digby Wyatt's architectural involvement, and Philip Hardwick's hotel and administration building sits almost as awkwardly against Brunel's structure as does Scott's. Wyatt wrote in 1851 apropos the Crystal Palace and other iron structures that 'it has become difficult to decide where civil engineering ends and architecture begins', but the difference – as generally understood – was all too obvious.

Iron was little used in England as an exposed structural material in public buildings – the dome of the British Library's reading room has an iron structure, but it is kept discreetly out of sight, like Victorian children or piano legs with frilly skirts. The worthwhile experiments took place in France, beginning in the 1840s at the Bibliothèque Ste Geneviève in Paris (1843–50) which was designed by Henri Labrouste. Using cast- and wrought-iron members Labrouste created two barrel-vaulted naves forming an independent structure which transmitted no loads to the external walls. The elegant result no doubt inspired Viollet-le-Duc's advocacy of composite iron and masonry construction. In 1854 Labrouste designed the Bibliothèque Nationale in the square courtyard of the Palais Mazarin. The reading room has nine square bays, each with a domical vault supported on slender iron columns and half-round lattice beams. Louis-Auguste Boileau used iron columns and vaulting-ribs in

**Barlow and Ordish,
St Pancras railway station,
London, 1863–5**
On completion, the 74-metre span of the railway shed at St Pancras was the world's largest vault, only to be superseded twenty-four years later by the Machine Hall at the Paris Exhibition of 1889.

the church of St Eugène (1854–55) and five years later
Baltard (the designer of the rambling iron-built central
market known as Les Halles) built St Augustin (1860–1)
with iron piers, arches and a dome.

These buildings are impressive, but the iron still
imitated masonry structure, elaborated with Gothic or
Classical ornament. Just visible through a large glazed
opening in Labrouste's reading room, however, is
something more interesting to modern eyes: the stack
room, which was designed almost without ornament and
made, apart from the timber bookshelves, completely of
iron. Daylight filtered down from wall-to-wall roof lights
through open, gridiron floor plates and stair-treads of
the type found in the engine rooms of ships. Their use
was no doubt strictly functional – to maximize the
passage of light and air – but such is Labrouste's control
that the resulting transparency and layering are akin to
the 'post-Cubist space' of the Modernist aesthetic.
Sigfried Giedion was moved to suggest that 'if there is
a Pazzi Chapel to be found anywhere in contemporary
architecture, it is here'. In the absence of documentary
evidence, however, it is misleading to attribute to
nineteenth-century designers the aesthetic qualities which
modern eyes can see in their work. It is unlikely that
Labrouste saw his stack room as more than an elegantly
efficient, well-lit and ventilated store, and no
photographer before the 1920s would have taken the
views – from a low angle or on a raking diagonal –
with which Giedion illustrated his claim in *Space, Time
and Architecture*. Labrouste was arguably the most original
architect of the mid-century, but he was hardly the
Brunelleschi of modern architecture.

The first department store, Bon Marché, was
established in 1852 and extended by L.A. Boileau and
Gustave Eiffel in 1876, using a cast-iron structure which
permitted large sales areas penetrated by spectacular
light wells, bridges and flamboyant staircases. Boileau
had a highly developed feeling for the possibilities of
glass and iron construction. He noted that 'the spectator
is not aware of the weight of transparent surfaces. These
surfaces are to him air and light, that is to say, an
imponderable fluidity.' And of the kinds of 'luminous
assembly' he created at Bon Marché he observed that
'solid architecture will play the role of a dressed stone
setting; it will have to count just enough to make the
interior daylight vibrate with as much intensity as
possible so that the transverse graded surfaces and the
semi-lit depths which surround it will appear to be as
gay, resonant and well furnished as if they were in the
pure daylight of the outside.' I know of no earlier, and

**Henri Labrouste,
Bibliothèque Ste Geneviève,
Paris, 1843–50**
One of the first architecturally
convincing uses of cast- and
wrought-iron construction,
Labrouste's library comprises
two barrel-vaulted naves
supported independently of the
external walls, anticipating the
separation of enclosure and
structure which became a
principle of Modernist
architecture.

Henri Labrouste, Bibliothèque Nationale, Paris, 1858–68
Sigfried Giedion published pictures of the functional book stacks of Labrouste's library in his seminal book *Space, Time and Architecture* (1941). He saw in the open floor plates – probably first used in the engine rooms of ships – 'the germ of new artistic possibilities'.

few better, descriptions than this of a specifically Modern sense of space and light. Eiffel's structure was, of course, richly ornamented, and as indoor settings for urban theatre the Bon Marché's atria were rivalled only by the stair-hall of Charles Garnier's Opéra.

The two most important exemplars of the Engineer's Aesthetic (together with the Crystal Palace) were created for the 1889 Paris International Exhibition, held to mark the 100th anniversary of the Revolution. They were the Galerie des Machines by Ferdinand Dutert and Victor Contamin, and Gustave Eiffel's tower. The machine hall was the fourth in a line of spectacular structures built for Paris exhibitions. Its 420-metre-long by 115-metre-wide 'nave' had fully glazed ends and was spanned by twenty three-pinned, wrought-iron lattice arches – similar to those at St Pancras, but bigger and with a decisive innovation. The St Pancras arches transmitted a massive bending moment, making foundations heavy and difficult; Contamin introduced a pin-joint, resolving the forces into only vertical and horizontal components. The principle was derived from hinged supports for bridges such as Eiffel's Pont du Garabit of 1884: foundations were simplified and visually the result was stunning. Like ballerinas on points, the 3 metre wide arches touched the earth lightly, appearing to defy gravity and almost hover in space. Contemporaries were awed but disturbed: the proportions were strange, the arches looked too hollow, they lacked a base, seemed out of balance. Expectations based on two and a half millennia of masonry architecture were being turned upside down.

The hall housed a correspondingly impressive display of machines, powered by thirty-two steam engines producing 5,000 horsepower. Machines were the established stars of Paris exhibitions and some 100,000 visitors per day glided through on a kind of travelling crane, participants in a mechanical liturgy of the sublime in Contamin's iron cathedral. The structure was retained after the exhibition but demolished in 1910 – Frantz Jourdain called it an act of 'artistic sadism' – but of course no such fate befell Eiffel's tower. In sheer audacity it outstripped even Contamin's masterpiece – there were precedents for the hall, but none for a 300-metre-high tower (just short of the magic 1,000 feet – but no self-respecting French structure could be measured in English feet).

Eiffel's daring exploits in bridge- and viaduct-construction for the world's ever-expanding railway network had taken him to many countries, and he came to the rescue of the sculptor Bartholdi – and of

Above: Art Nouveau ironwork, 12 Boulevard de Madeleine, Paris
Cast and wrought iron were ideally suited to the sinuous forms typical of Art Nouveau.

Left: Gustave Eiffel, Eiffel Tower, Paris, 1889
Eiffel financed the tower himself and built it against considerable opposition. The open wrought-iron structure offered unprecedented height and views and an interweaving of interior and exterior spaces.

France – by making an armature of iron for the Statue of Liberty. By now he was well on his way to being a folk-hero, or the *magicien de fer* as he became known. A few facts convey the challenge of the tower, which Eiffel completed in two years: 30 draughtsmen worked for 18 months to produce 5,329 drawings of 18,038 separate pieces of metal containing 2.5 million rivet holes. Miraculously only one worker was killed during construction (he was said to be showing off to his girlfriend below). Eiffel used wrought iron because he distrusted the manufacturing methods of the newer steel, and he arranged the finance (just over $1.5 million) for the construction himself. In an interview with the newspaper *Le Temps* he explained the approach to the design as follows:

'I believe that the tower will have its own beauty. The first principle of architectural beauty is that the essential lines of a construction be determined by a

Robert Delaunay, *Eiffel Tower*, 1910
Many of the early Modernists were obsessed with the Eiffel Tower, none more so than Delaunay who tried to represent the way it dominated Paris from every direction by using multiple viewpoints and fragmented planes.

perfect appropriateness to its use. What was the main obstacle I had to overcome in designing the tower? Its resistance to wind. And I submit that the curves of its four piers as produced by our calculations, rising from an enormous base, and narrowing toward the top, will give a great impression of strength and beauty.'

The only major features of the tower for which there was no structural rationale are, in fact, the circular arches between the legs of the piers – but they make for a graceful transition, and Eiffel was concerned that people would be alarmed at the piers' slenderness without them.

The proposal, inevitably, received a mixed reaction. Eiffel might be a folk hero, but he was still an *engineer*, and forty-seven of France's most distinguished academic artists rallied to stop the tower's construction by submitting a *protestation des artistes* to the minister of public works. The tower was declared an insult to the city and to French taste and was reviled as 'the baroque, mercantile imagining of a builder of machines'. Some builder, some imagining.

All protests were brushed aside, however, and the tower's success was overwhelming. The sight of Paris from the air, and the sheer thrill of rising through space to such a height were not to be missed, and by the exhibition's close a continuous stream of almost two million paying visitors had been up, turning the tower's stairs into the spiralling catwalks of a continuous fashion show. At a time when electricity was only just beginning to replace gaslights on the streets of Paris, Eiffel's masterpiece looked magical at night, a tracery of thousands of twinkling lights. There had been nothing like it, and it triumphantly confirmed, as the exhibition's general manager declared, that 'the law of progress is immortal, just as progress itself is infinite'.

The Eiffel Tower retains its hold over Paris, but we struggle to grasp its original impact and meanings. It conquered gravity and wind, challenging and inspiring well into this century and figuring in works by numerous artists – Pissarro, Chagall, Dufy, Henri Rousseau, Picasso, Utrillo and Van Dongen, among others. The tower acquired a radio aerial in 1909, and poets dreamt of 'blue tresses' disappearing into the ether to embrace all nations. And it totally obsessed Robert Delaunay who painted over fifty canvases of the tower between 1909 and 1911. His friend, the poet Blaise Cendrars, described how he attacked it from every angle, but found 'no artistic formula known could resolve plastically the case of the tower'. In the end, to convey its omnipresence in Paris and 'give the impression of vertigo it inspires' he constructed a single image from many points of view. For Delaunay and many Modernists before and after the Great War, Eiffel's tower remained a supreme sign of modernity. In 1925 Le Corbusier wrote that 'it dominates the Art Déco Exposition. Rising above the plaster palaces with their twisted decor, it looks pure as crystal.'

Cast iron, which could only be used in compression, and wrought iron were largely replaced by steel for structural use, and a hidden armature of steel was the key to the other revolutionary building material, reinforced concrete. As with so many innovations, England pioneered modern concrete construction in the late eighteenth century, but the lead soon passed to Heinrich France. François Coignet developed metal mesh reinforcing around 1860, but later sold his patents to Germany. During the last third of the century developments proceeded in parallel in Germany, America, England and France. François Hennebique's 1892 patent included the key innovation of a monolithic joint of interlocked steel bars; his system regained the lead for France and was widely used at the Paris 1900 World's Fair.

Early in the new century several distinguished concrete buildings were built in France, notably by Auguste Perret, in whose office the future Le Corbusier became acquainted with the material. Perret's early buildings, such as the block of flats at 25 bis rue Franklin (1902–3) and the Garage Ponthieu (1905–6), made use of exposed concrete, but only by assimilating it into the familiar rectilinear aesthetic of column-and-beam structures and not really exploiting the new possibilities latent in the material. These were exemplified in the bridges of the Swiss engineer Robert Maillart, the curved slab of the arch and the road-deck working together as active structural elements – in buildings, 'mushroom' columns were used to achieve something similar.

The 1889 Paris exhibition confirmed the engineer's key role in the search for a new architecture. Anatole de Baudot, a pupil of Viollet-le-Duc, told the first International Congress of Architects held alongside the exhibition that 'a long time ago the influence of the architect declined and the engineer, *l'homme moderne par excellence*, is beginning to replace him.' Likewise, after seeing the iron miracles, the novelist Octave Mirbeau suggested that 'it is not in the studios of the painters and sculptors that the revolution so long awaited is

preparing – it is in the factories. . . . From these two colossal embryos – the Galerie des Machines and the Tower – a splendid art, one that our century lacked, will arise: architecture.' Leopold Bauer, writing in 1899, thought 'we moderns must admit that even the Panthéon or Saint Peter's dome must pale before the impression that is called forth by the lower great hall of the Eiffel Tower or by one of its powerful piers.' And finally in 1901 Henry van de Velde declared that the artists 'who have created a new architecture, are the engineers'.

But for all the rhetoric, to most people the art of engineering was not 'art'. The painter Paul Gauguin saw the 1889 exhibition as 'the triumph of iron' but thought architecture still lacked a style of decoration consistent with the material and suggested that 'ornamental bolts' and perhaps 'a sort of gothic lacework of iron' might help. Le Corbusier, in his introduction to Charles Cordat's book on the Tower, said Eiffel 'was pained by not being seen as a creator of beauty' and that he clearly deserved such acclaim because 'his calculations were always inspired by an admirable instinct for proportion, his goal was elegance'.

First to industrialize, Britain was also the first to agonize about the consequences. Worries about machine-production were compounded by the Romantic view of the artist as a creative individual. The Middle Ages came to be seen as the Golden Age before such troubles began, for then the artist was a craftsman, no machines undermined true workmanship and no cult of personality and 'genius' disturbed creative collaboration. Pugin linked architectural to moral values, yet his most influential successor, John Ruskin, always denied any debt to the Catholic fanatic who had worked himself to death at forty in 1851. But Pugin's *True Principles* were the inspiration behind Ruskin's *Seven Lamps of Architecture* which was published in 1849, eight years after Pugin's seminal tract. To Ruskin, religious, social, moral and aesthetic 'truths' were inextricable, and *Seven Lamps* begins with three architectural 'deceits': the suggestion of a structure other than the true one (which damned much Classical architecture); painting surfaces to resemble another material, such as the marbling of wood; and cast or machine-made ornaments. The 'Lamp of Truth' states that 'that building will generally be the noblest, which to an intelligent eye discovers the great secrets of its structure'. In Pugin's terms, this was Revealed Construction.

The finished building and the process of construction were equally inseparable. In the 'Lamp of Life' Ruskin

Robert Delaunay, *Eiffel Tower*, 1926
Delaunay continued to paint the Eiffel Tower in the 1920s, by which time (in common with many others) the fragmentation and dynamism of his early style had given way to a more stable, Classical mode of representation.

says that 'the right question to ask, respecting all ornament, is simply this: Was it done with enjoyment – was the carver happy while he was about it?' because 'to those who love Architecture, the life and accent of the hand are everything.' Ruskin could not abide Classicism: it meant the architect dictating what craftsmen were to do. Whereas in the Gothic, he believed, the medieval craftsmen had enjoyed freedom of expression within an overall framework. In a bravura section of *The Stones of Venice* (1851) entitled 'The Nature of Gothic', Ruskin laid down three rules for the 'Savageness' he loved: '1: Never encourage the manufacture of any article not absolutely necessary in the production of which Invention has no share. 2: Never demand an exact finish for its own sake, but only for some practical or noble end. 3: Never encourage imitation or copying of any kind except for the sake of preserving record of great works.'

Gothic was also characterized by 'Naturalness', achieved through the close observation of natural form (which Ruskin thought a direct revelation of divine truth), and 'Changefulness', which could arise from the response to varied needs, or by extending and adapting buildings in a contemporary style. Ruskin loathed machines and the cheap 'ornament' they churned out, and saw that 'it was possible for men to turn themselves into machines, and to reduce their labour to the machine level'. He thought that in 'the great civilised invention of the division of labour it is not, truly speaking, the labour that is divided; but the man.

Divided into mere segments of men, broken into small fragments and crumbs of life.' The prose-style and moralizing may belong to another world, but the words still challenge, as they did when the high priest of machine-age architecture, Le Corbusier, wrote that Ruskin 'shook our young minds profoundly with his exhortations'.

In the early 1850s Ruskin's exhortations convinced two Oxford University students to give up their ambitions of entering the church and to take up art. Edward Burne-Jones decided on painting, and later joined the Pre-Raphaelite Brotherhood, whilst William Morris entered into an apprenticeship with George Edmund Street, who was perhaps the most original Gothic Revivalist architect and noted for his emphasis on materials. Finding nothing he liked with which to furnish his first studio in 1857, Morris resolved to make what he needed with his friends. The same problem arose in 1861 when, newly wed, he came to occupy the Red House designed for him by Philip Webb. This time he formed a company of 'Fine Art Workmen in Painting, Carving, Furniture and the Metals' with the aim of achieving 'harmony between the various parts' of a building: the Arts and Crafts Movement had begun. In the end Morris did not practise architecture but turned to the decorative arts instead, proving to be a masterly pattern-designer. As he grew older his efforts increasingly focused on changing the world through socialism, declaring: 'It is not this or that tangible steel or brass machine which we want to get rid of, but the

Left: Ferdinand Dutert and Victor Contamin, Galerie des Machines, Paris, 1889
Built for the Centennial Exhibition for the French Republic, the Machine Hall was a tremendous popular success. Great steam-driven machines were a favourite sight at nineteenth-century exhibitions, and here visitors viewed them from a slowly moving gantry.

Opposite: Ferdinand Dutert and Victor Contamin, Galerie des Machines, Paris, 1889
The breathtaking 420-metre-long by 115-metre-wide nave was spanned by twenty three-pinned, wrought-iron lattice arches. The pin-joints at their bases resolved the huge forces into vertical and horizontal components – a decisive innovation which greatly simplified the structural design.

Auguste Perret, Garage Ponthieu, 51 rue Ponthieu, Paris, 1905–6 (destroyed)
The son of a building contractor, Perret designed and built this pioneering example of reinforced concrete construction. The boldly exposed structural frame is exceptional for its date, although its design was clearly rooted in the French Classical tradition.

great intangible machine of commercial tyranny which oppresses the lives of all of us.' His opposition to machines was implacable.

There was also an official design reform movement, in addition to the dogmatic Ruskin-Morris line. In 1847 Henry Cole, Owen Jones, Richard Redgrave and Digby Wyatt formed Summerly's Art Manufactures 'to put the fine arts at the service of manufacturers' – a model for Morris & Company. Two years later they set up the *Journal of Art and Manufactures*, in which they articulated a progressive aesthetic based on Pugin's principles, and in 1851 they opened the South Kensington Museum. The Great Exhibition galvanized Cole and his circle to further efforts: their *Journal* proved influential amongst industrialists, and books such as Ralph Wornum's *Analysis of Ornament* and Owen Jones's widely consulted *Grammar of Ornament*, both published in 1856, were intended to establish principles of good design. The separation of the fine and applied arts accepted by the group – and implemented in government education policy – was anathema to Ruskin, who challenged it directly in *The Two Paths* (1859), where he advocated the study of nature as a common ground for artists and designers.

The influence of Ruskin and Morris was apparent in the later advocacy of craft-work as a tool of 'moral reform', and in a succession of guilds modelled on medieval practice. (Trade guilds had disappeared in England half a century before those in much of continental Europe.) Ruskin led the way with the Guild of St George in 1871; in 1882 A.H. Mackmurdo formed the Century Guild, which published the influential magazine, *The Hobby Horse*, from 1884 to 1891; the still-extant Art Workers Guild was founded in 1884 by four architect-pupils of Richard Norman Shaw led by William Lethaby; and C. R. Ashbee started a Ruskin reading class in 1886, which two years later became the Guild of Handicraft and, in an attempt to recapture the medieval spirit, moved to the unspoilt town of Chipping Campden in the Cotswolds in 1901. Its commitment to communal living, profit sharing and 'joy in labour' was emulated by communities on both sides of the Atlantic.

Disturbed by the squalid housing in which many workers lived, several philanthropic industrialists were moved to found model towns: Saltaire (which, founded in the 1850s, owed much to Robert Owen's earlier New Lanark), Port Sunlight near Liverpool (1889) and Bournville (1898) being amongst the best known. These towns in turn stimulated Ebenezer Howard's 'garden city' ideal, which was originally published in *Tomorrow:*

a Peaceful Path to Real Reform in 1898. The following year the Garden City Association was launched, and work on a new town – Letchworth Garden City, planned by Parker and Unwin – began in 1903. The spirit of Howard's ideas was followed in Garden Suburbs around London, and soon found its way abroad, proving widely influential. For example, Hellerau Garden City (1909), set up near Dresden by Richard Riemerschmid, was the first achievement of the German Garden Cities Association founded in 1902.

In 1894 William Lethaby was appointed Director of the new Central School of Arts and Crafts in London, the first architecture school with workshops for the individual crafts and a precedent for the Bauhaus. He became the spokesman for a group willing to accept machine production: so long as the work was without 'pretence and subterfuge', Lethaby thought it could be 'made beautiful by appropriate handling'. They formed the Design Club in 1909 and the Design and Industries Association in 1915, aiming to work for widespread reform in industry. The catalyst behind both was the Deutscher Werkbund, which held an exhibition in London in 1914.

England's most significant architectural contribution during the late Victorian period was in domestic design, and Webb's Red House was looked to as the pioneer of a new approach. It had sprung from the gritty Gothic Revival vicarages of William Butterfield, with their 'honest' clay tiles and red bricks, which Webb varied according to the local vernacular. The L-shaped plan with a clearly expressed stair-cum-entry hall was widely used, and the stringing of rooms along a corridor, expressed by varied windows, dormers and roofs, yielded a welcome Ruskinian changefulness. The oddity in what appears to be a model of functional planning is that the main rooms face north – as in a Georgian house. Arts and Crafts architecture and the so-called English Free Style both stem from the Red House, and together gave rise to what became known on the Continent as 'The English House'.

In addition to Webb, the early leaders of the 'Free Style' movement were Eden Nesfield and his partner Richard Norman Shaw, whose New Zealand Chambers of 1872–3 put the so-called Queen Anne style on the map. Webb, Nesfield and Shaw drew freely on the work of simple rural buildings, especially in villages built by masons' guilds. They also looked to recognized works of Architecture – the simple, well-proportioned smaller country houses of the late seventeenth and early eighteenth centuries became favourites with Shaw,

having been first tapped by the older Nesfield. 'Queen Anne' was adopted by a new middle class in search of identity. 'Sweetness and light', Matthew Arnold's characterization of the Hellenic virtues, became their watchwords, and they looked to aestheticism and art for art's sake (which had been brought to England from France in the 1860s by the poet Swinburne and art historian Walter Pater) for guidance in furnishing their houses. Queen Anne quickly found its way into many a house via the nursery – in the form of the illustrated books of Walter Crane, Kate Greenaway and Randolph Caldecott.

Of the Arts and Crafts architects, the most important was C.F.A. Voysey. The simplicity of a house such as Perrycroft in the Malvern Hills is still striking and must have astonished when it was built in 1893 – the massive chimneys, battered piers and horizontally ranged windows were markedly original. Voysey interiors rival those of his better-known follower Mackintosh: they are freely planned, light-filled and complemented by artefacts and fabrics of his own design. On seeing his first Voysey fabric, Van de Velde is said to have exclaimed, 'It was as if spring had come all of a sudden.' Voysey summed up his aims in a definition of comfort: 'Repose, Cheerfulness, Simplicity, Breadth, Warmth, Quietness in a storm, Economy of upkeep, Evidence of Protection, Harmony with surroundings, Absence of dark passages, Even-ness of temperature and making the house a frame to its inmates. Rich and Poor alike will appreciate its qualities.' These pragmatic qualities were widely emulated in the garden suburbs of the early twentieth century, but they hardly provided the theoretical foundations for an architectural revolution. English design became known across Europe and America through *The Studio*, an early crafts and interior design magazine started in London in 1893. However, after 1900 leadership of the movement passed to the Continent and the USA.

The English House's most vigorous advocate abroad was Hermann Muthesius, who spent several years attached to the German Embassy in London with a brief to glean the latest ideas in architecture and the applied arts. After returning home he published the three-volume *Das Englische Haus* (1904–5). His aim was to free building from Architecture with a capital 'A' and he concerned himself with plans more than elevations, emphasizing aspect, patterns of circulation and the distinctive shape and character of rooms: in short, the functional logic of buildings. Muthesius believed that 'a truly modern character' could be

Auguste Perret, 25 bis rue Franklin, Paris, 1902–3
The reinforced concrete structural frame is directly expressed on the exterior of these flats, but covered in ceramic tiles and detailed in a way which recalls timber construction.

achieved by keeping out all 'ornamental accessories'. The bathroom exemplified this: he likened it to 'a piece of scientific apparatus' and found in it 'an entirely new art that required no propaganda to win it acceptance, an art based on actual modern conditions and modern achievements that perhaps one day, when all the fashions that parade as modern movements in art have passed away, will be regarded as the most eloquent expression of our age.'

Muthesius's ideals were in total opposition to the style which for many came to typify the turn of the century – Art Nouveau. Like the Arts and Crafts, Art Nouveau was a reaction against stylistic eclecticism and industrialization. It dispelled *fin de siècle* gloom with an outburst of vitality and optimism, blossoming, exotic and precious, in several cities in the 1890s – Paris, Brussels and Munich, Glasgow and Vienna. Yet for all its initial energy it was spent as a creative force in less than a decade and it is tempting to see it as a last desperate effort to greet the new century with a new style. Art Nouveau took its name from the shop Samuel Bing opened in Paris in 1895, which was decorated externally by Frank Brangwyn and had four rooms by Henry van de Velde. Bing hoped it would be a 'meeting ground for all ardent young spirits anxious to manifest the modernness of their tendencies'; youthful ardour was much to the fore as the movement's German name – *Jugendstil* – makes clear. (It was named after the satirical magazine *Jugend*, started in Munich in 1896.) Art Nouveau was patronized by new money, a clientele

Above: C. F. A. Voysey, Perrycroft, Coewall, Worcestershire, 1893–4
Built in the composer Edward Elgar's beloved Malvern Hills, Perrycroft is typical of the restrained style which made Voysey one of the most important Arts and Crafts architects and helped pave the way for early Modernism in England. The tall inclined buttresses became a leitmotif of his houses, whose bright, open interiors were remarkably free of decoration.

Opposite: Philip Webb, Red House, Bexley Heath, Kent, 1859
Designed for William Morris, Red House became the symbolic beginning of the Arts and Crafts Movement. Its dependence upon vernacular traditions and direct, 'honest' use of materials were a riposte to stylistic eclecticism and the ornamental excesses of High Victorian taste.

Simplicity, sincerity, repose, directness and frankness are moral qualities as essential to good architecture as to good men. C. F. A. Voysey

Poster for *The Studio* magazine, 1890s
Art and interior design magazines flourished in the 1890s, none more so than *The Studio*. Published in London, it was read throughout Europe and North America and acted as an important channel for the dissemination of Arts and Crafts ideals, and for informing its British readers about developments on the Continent. This poster is in typical Art Nouveau style.

whose wealth stemmed from booming trade and industry and who were eager for an art as distinctive as their way of life.

Known in England simply as the Modern Style, Art Nouveau's origins have been traced back to the Pre-Raphaelites' rediscovery of William Blake and the creation of the English Aesthetic interior, in which Japanese inspiration was vital. Bing had published a review of Japanese art in the late 1880s, and it had been introduced to England by the American painter Whistler. In the late 1870s, with the architect E.W. Godwin, Whistler created Japanese-inspired interiors in Chelsea for himself and for Oscar Wilde. Their off-white walls, gold-leaf paper panels, white lacquered furniture and occasional splashes of colour were much imitated, influencing contemporary decoration and creating a model which was taken up by Charles Rennie Mackintosh and the Glasgow School. England supplied other catalysts. The wealth of non-Western material in Owen Jones's *Grammar of Ornament* was a revelation, as were the pages by Christopher Dresser showing how to derive new ornament from plant forms – the source of most Art Nouveau ornament. Designs

such as A.H. Mackmurdo's title page of *Wren's City Churches* (1883), highly stylized, asymmetrical and freely curving, is already Art Nouveau in spirit if not name, whilst the slender columns and flat capitals of his Century Guild Stand for the Liverpool International Exhibition of 1886 were adopted by Voysey, Mackintosh and the Viennese.

The first Art Nouveau architect was the Belgian Victor Horta, who burst on to the scene in 1893 with the Hôtel Tassel in Brussels. This displayed the first use of a structural iron frame in a house, allowing the interior to be opened around a top-lit space. From there stairs lead to floors on many levels, breaking the convention of planning floor by floor. Horta's domestic style is at its best in the Hôtel Solvay (1895–1900), a remarkable synthesis of Classicism and feeling, craftsmanship and industry. In both houses a sensuous curvilinear interior presents a conventional face to the world: fantasies multiply behind the facade. In the Maison du Peuple of the Belgian Workers Socialist Party (1895–8) and the department store 'A l'Innovation' (1901–3) Horta combined iron and masonry, audaciously exposing the structure and anticipating lightweight

NORTHAMPTON COLLEGE LIBRARY

C. F. A. Voysey, *Three Men of Gotham*, design for printed velvet, c.1889
Committed to the creation of complete interiors, many Arts and Crafts architects also designed furniture, fabrics and silverware. Voysey's fabrics are amongst the finest. Rhythmic and full of life, they are also taut, economical and flat – the avoidance of any illusion of three dimensions was a matter of principle for the Victorian design reformers.

Right: Victor Horta, Hôtel Tassel, Brussels, 1893
A manifesto of Art Nouveau, spectacularly ornamented and decorated inside, the Hôtel Tassel was most remarkable for its plan. It was organized around an octagonal hall with rooms on several levels opening into each other, anticipating the *Raumplan* of Adolf Loos and the *plan libre* of Le Corbusier.

Below: Hector Guimard, Métro Dauphine entrance, Paris, 1899–1900
Guimard's astonishing ability to transform the elements of architecture into refined and highly charged images was seen to great effect in his Métro entrances which were built from a standard kit-of-parts.

curtain-walls in the handling of large areas of glass.

In Paris, the most important architectural manifestations of Art Nouveau were the new Métro entrances, built between 1899 and 1906 using a 'kit of parts' designed by Hector Guimard. They suggest strange insects, with their glass wings spreading in the sun. Organic analogies spring readily from Art Nouveau forms, and in the work of the great Catalonian architect Antoni Gaudí they are inescapable. In such buildings as the Colonia Güell Church (1898–1914), Güell Park (1900–14), Casa Battló (1905–7) and Casa Milà (1905–10) he achieved total liberation from historicism. Bones, shells, the undulating surface of the sea, an armadillo's back: all these (and many others) have been suggested as inspirations or analogies for his forms. The sense of organic energy animating the buildings is astonishing – and inimitable: what would Ruskin have made of them? Gaudí was a genius, but his style was too personal to affect the course of architecture outside Catalonia.

Glasgow was booming in the 1890s, the greatest industrial city of the wealthiest industrial power. Charles Rennie Mackintosh studied in its School of Art and his promise and independence were apparent from his first building, the corner tower of the Glasgow Herald building (1894). The following year he contributed several posters to Bing's first exhibition in Paris, introducing the linear, symbolic style of the Glasgow School to the Continent: its reputation and influence spread quickly through publication in *The Studio* and *Dekorative Kunst*. In 1897 Mackintosh began work on the Buchanan Street Tea-room and won a competition for the new Glasgow School of Art. The Tea-room furniture was specially made, and visitors were surrounded by mural decorations of tall stylized figures set between vertical lines and caught in circular waves. This manner became known through exhibitions in Munich in 1898 and the Vienna Secession in 1900, where a tiny tea-room was installed. Mackintosh and his wife Margaret (whose sister had married Herbert McNair; together they made up the 'Glasgow Four') travelled to Vienna and were received in triumph. His reputation was enhanced the following year when he won second prize in the competition for 'A House for an Art Lover', which was organized by the *Zeitschrift für Innendekoration* of Darmstadt, where a Jugendstil artists' colony flourished under the patronage of Grand Duke Ernst Ludwig of Hesse.

The School of Art posed tougher challenges, and what began as an early work of a promising young architect – he was twenty-nine when he won the

competition in 1897 –
the first major achievei   ui twentieth-cein.
architecture. Its organization followed the principles of
the English Gothic Revival, the main body of the
building which contained the studios being treated as a
loose-fitting envelope, with a regular array of large
studio windows either side of a complex entrance to the
front and a fragmented crumble to the rear. The finest
space – the library, an exquisite carpentered forest –
was designed last (in 1906) and also yielded the most
original elevation, dominated by three Shaw-inspired
oriel windows. Tall, narrow and crystalline, and divided
by a taut, square grid, there had been nothing quite
like these windows before. The Hill House in
Helensburgh (1902–3), especially its superb entrance
hall, also demonstrates Mackintosh's rare ability to
organize the flow of space and marshal all the elements
of an interior into a plastic whole. Voysey's influence is
apparent, and the plan form goes back to the Red
House; Mackintosh also drew on the Scottish baronial
and vernacular building traditions – but the synthesis
was his and his alone.

In Vienna, Art Nouveau was known as 'Secession
Style' after the *Wiener Sezession* which was founded in
1897 by a group of progressive artists led by Gustav
Klimt in rebellion against the academy. No city in
Europe offered a more challenging cultural milieu:
although deeply conservative and nervous about the
decline of the Hapsburg Empire, it played host to some
of the most radical minds of the day. Freud was busy
interpreting dreams, Mahler directing the National
Opera and Wittgenstein reducing philosophy to
language (and language to its foundations). Architecture
was much prized, and Vienna's modernization had
produced 'The Ring', a broad road on a swathe of
land formerly occupied by fortifications along which
the city's social values were carved in stone – the
Parliament, town hall, university and a series of large,
fashionable apartment houses.

The Secession's annual exhibitions were held in a
building designed in 1897–8 by Josef Maria Olbrich:
its severe, cubic mass carries the inscription 'To the
age its art, to art its freedom' above the entrance and
is surmounted by a golden openwork dome. Vienna's
major architect was Otto Wagner, who became
Professor at the Academy in 1894 and outraged his
colleagues five years later by joining the Secession.
His approach was rational and forward-looking. For
students, his recommended 'Grand Tour' was a brief
stay in Italy, followed by the study of 'the needs of

modern man' in 'the great cities where modern luxury
may be found'. He called for bright, well-ventilated
houses with simple furnishings, in harmony with the
'checkered breeches' and other leisure clothes worn in
the modern city. Wagner's lectures were published as
Moderne Architektur (discussed earlier), and his influence
was enormous. To name only those of international
importance, his students included Josef Hoffmann; Josef
Plecnik; Josef Chochol and other central figures of
Czech Cubism; and Rudolf Schindler who took
Modernism to California. Even Frank Lloyd Wright's
son applied for a place.

Wagner's work showed Art Nouveau traits around the
turn of the century, but these had largely disappeared in
his masterpiece, the Post Office Savings Bank in Vienna
(1903–12), whose top-lit banking hall with its exposed
riveted steel structure, bracketed light fittings, cylindrical
heat inlets and glass block floor, comes close to
achieving a universal style based on engineering forms.
The Secession Style is best exemplified by Wagner's
pupil Josef Hoffmann. Known as Quadrat (Right-Angle)
Hoffmann, his flirtation with the undulating romanticism
of Paris and Brussels was short-lived, and he quickly
developed the fusion of Art Nouveau and a restrained
Biedermeier style which characterized almost all his
work after 1902. In the Purkersdorf Sanatorium of 1903,
ornament is reduced to narrow checkerboard strips
around openings and along edges: the clarity and
abstraction belong to early Modernism.

In 1903 Hoffmann and Koloman Moser set up the
studios and workshops known as the Wiener Werkstätte.
Wishing 'to give comfort to all who accept the message
of Ruskin and Morris' by reviving traditional crafts, they
hoped to attract clients from the middle class 'which is as
yet very far from having fulfilled its cultural task'. The
commission for the Palais Stoclet in Brussels (1905–11)
gave Hoffmann and the Werkstätte the opportunity to
create an exquisitely opulent *Gesamtkunstwerk* ('total work
of art'), designed down to the teaspoons and replete with
mosaics by Klimt. Externally, the gilt and dark metal
mouldings which frame the edges, and the use of large,
thin sheets of stone to clad the walls, recall Wagner's
description of 'the new architecture' to come as
'dominated by slablike, tabular surfaces' – and hint at a
way of articulating space by means of planes rather than
solid volumes: its realization would await the explorations
of the Dutch De Stijl movement.

Germany was not unified until 1871, and
industrialization came late and hard: in less than forty
years, the country was transformed from a scatter of

independent states into one of the world's three major industrial powers. The so-called *Gründerzeit* (the founding period, which stretched from 1871 to 1900) was a time of intense and disruptive change; vast fortunes were amassed and the newly rich expected the decorative arts to console them with memories of the old culture. It was also a time of intense nationalism: in 1881, opening the Kunstgewerbemuseum in Berlin, the emperor declared that: 'We defeated France on the fields of battle in 1870; now we want to defeat her again in the fields of commerce and industry.' The cultural dilemmas are plain in Richard Wagner's operas, which tell of myths and of craft culture in an advanced musical language. Friedrich Nietzsche said of the overture to 'Die Meistersinger' that it 'expresses best what I think of the Germans: they are of the day before yesterday and of the day after tomorrow. Today has not yet come.'

Eclecticism was rife and the search for expressions of national identity and the *Zeitgeist* were intense: the artistic changes which in England lasted over half a century were packed into just over a decade. In 1888 Ferdinand Moser's *Ornamental Plant Studies from the Sphere of Native Flora* was published, neatly uniting the two themes of nature as inspiration and the search for a national identity. Exhibitions followed, and two years later a course of 'Ornamental Plant Studies' was established in Rome to educate teachers in Prussian craft and applied art schools. The year 1891 saw the appearance of *Innendekoration*, published in Darmstadt by Alexander Koch. It was the first magazine of the applied arts. These and other similar innovations laid the ground for the German *Jugendstil*. Architecturally the style did not make a major impact: August Endell's Elvira Studio in Munich, a frantic imitation of Horta's Hôtel Tassel interior, was essentially decorative and German architects elsewhere did not embrace the new style as enthusiastically as in its leading centres.

The 1890s saw a short but intense period of introspection, involving a withering critique of contemporary civilization and above all of industrialization. Fritz Stern has named the characteristic mixture of despair and mystic nationalism the 'German Ideology'. It sought renewal through the search for essential Germanness, and led ultimately, and not too indirectly, to Nazism. Alfred Lichtwark, the director of the Hamburg Kunsthalle and a passionate educator, was a key figure in cultural reform. He gave courses for teachers on 'the cultivation of the eyes and therefore of taste', which were intended to help create a public receptive to art. He pleaded for *sachliche Schönheit* (objective or matter-of-fact beauty), for 'smooth, polished, light forms' and 'floods of light' on fresh flowers: his words might describe a Voysey interior. In 1898 Karl Schmidt, following the Morris-Ashbee model, founded the 'Dresden Workshops of Arts and Crafts' on a heady mixture of functionalism and nationalism: they aimed to make furniture which 'serves its purpose and gives expression in its form to its purpose' and 'is prepared from German materials, created by German artists, and is the expression of German emotions and feelings'.

Opposite: Charles Rennie Mackintosh, Glasgow School of Art, 1898–1907
One of the most original early twentieth-century buildings, the design was a masterly synthesis of ideas drawn from Scottish vernacular and Baronial buildings, Baroque architecture, Japanese design and, above all, the English Free Style. The library was the last and most remarkable part of the building, its elevation dominated by three oriel windows which, although inspired by Richard Norman Shaw, were utterly original in expression.

Below: Charles Rennie Mackintosh, The Hill House, Helensburgh, 1902–3
The entrance hall of The Hill House is one of Mackintosh's outstanding achievements. The complete coordination of every element in a radically new formal language would not be seen so convincingly again until the houses of the Dutch De Stijl movement.

Right above: Gustav Klimt,
***Danäe*, 1907–8**
Never before had Zeus's
visitation as a shower of gold
been made so overtly erotic as
in Klimt's wonderfully
decorative composition. And
where else could Danäe's self-
absorbed reverie have been
painted, but in Vienna where
Freud was busy interpreting
dreams?

**Right below: Otto Wagner,
Post Office Savings Bank,
Vienna, 1903–12**
The top-lit banking hall was
the closest Wagner came to his
ideal of a new style derived
from engineering forms. The
beautifully integrated, riveted
steel structure, glazing, light
fittings, cylindrical heat inlets
and glass block floor, and total
absence of ornament, make it a
landmark in the development
of modern architecture.

**Opposite: Otto Wagner,
Project for the Interior Lobby
of Kaiser-Franz-Josef City
Museum, Vienna, 1902**
This unrealized project
illustrates Wagner's dream of
an architecture in harmony
with the 'checkered breeches'
and life of the modern city.

Hermann Muthesius returned from England in 1903
and three years later his adversary in debates about
design and industrialization, the Belgian Henry van de
Velde, arrived to head the Grand Ducal School of
Applied Arts in Weimar in a new building of his own
design (shortly after the War it was renamed 'The
Bauhaus'). The applied arts association, the
Fachverband, was unsympathetic towards progressive
artists and designers and so they went ahead and
formed the rival Deutscher Werkbund in Munich in
1907. Friedrich Naumann, a leading liberal politician
and promoter of Werkbund ideals, was convinced that
the path to German renewal depended on combining
aesthetic values and mechanical production – 'the
machine must be spiritualized', he said – and considered
the Werkbund vital to Germany's international standing.

Germany's lack of natural resources, and of colonies
to plunder, was a recurring worry, and the 'added
value' of good design was thought vital to economic
prosperity. The Werkbund was inspired by the Arts and
Crafts, but *Werk* embraced both machine- and hand-
work. 'Quality' was agreed to be the measure of
German culture, but as Muthesius pointed out, it
admitted of so many interpretations that the Werkbund
was always 'an association of the most intimate
enemies'. The internal debates were stimulating and
intensely fought, and the Werkbund rapidly became the
leading organization of its kind in Europe.

Hermann Muthesius was the most controversial figure
within the Werkbund. As we have seen, he had no time
for the 'hot-house atmosphere' of *Stilarchitektur* – of
which *Jugendstil* was the latest ephemeral manifestation.
He thought function needed no 'artistic' cladding and in
objects of use favoured *Sachlichkeit*: 'we admire a fine
surgical instrument because of its elegance, a vehicle
because of its pleasing lightness, a wrought-iron bridge
soaring over a river because of its bold use of material.
And we are right to do so, for in the muscularity of
those slim parts we confirm the triumph of technology
which has risen to the limits of mastering of materials.'

Van de Velde joined the Werkbund in 1908. He too
appreciated engineering forms aesthetically, but was
convinced that art and industry could never be united
because art – being alien to the profit motive – was sure
to be submerged. At the annual conference in Cologne in
1914, held alongside a major exhibition, Muthesius's key-
note lecture addressed the most controversial area of his
theory – the concept of *Typisierung*, or standards of good
form and taste. He was convinced these could and should
be legislated for, and then exploited in promoting German

exports – DIN standards came out of such thinking, but never engaged the value-laden issue of design-quality. Van de Velde, inevitably, disagreed. Wishing to defend artistic freedom and repudiate any subordination of art to commercial policy, he argued that true quality could only be created for a discerning circle of connoisseurs and patrons, from which a style – and aesthetic norms – might emerge. He was joined by several leading architects, including Bruno Taut, Hans Poelzig and August Endell, as well as the young designer of the model factory at the Cologne Exhibition, Walter Gropius.

Josef Hoffmann, Samovar, 1903
Hoffmann, the most sophisticated of the Viennese Secession designers, was a co-founder of the studios and workshops known as the Wiener Werkstätte which aimed to attract well-to-do middle-class clients to support their cultural vision. He was nicknamed 'Quadrat' (Right-angle) Hoffmann, for reasons that are readily apparent in this samovar.

Gropius joined the office of Peter Behrens in 1907, which had become a magnet for progressive architects – Mies van der Rohe and Le Corbusier also worked there during Gropius's time in the office. In 1910 he set up his own practice, designing motor-car bodies, a train compartment and a diesel locomotive, as well as interior schemes. His first architectural commission came the following year with the Fagus Factory, undertaken with his partner Adolf Meyer: its glass curtain-walls and glazed corners mark it out as being one of the most stylistically advanced buildings of its date. Apart from Gropius and Meyer's model factory, which combined large areas of glass and circular glass staircase towers with the *Schinkelschule* tradition, most of the buildings in the Werkbund's Cologne exhibition were in restrained neoclassical styles. The conspicuous exception was the Expressionist Glashaus by Bruno Taut – of which more in the next chapter.

The most ambitious attempt to link art and industry

just predated the Werkbund's formation, as earlier in 1907 Peter Behrens had been appointed 'artistic adviser' to the electrical giant AEG. Behrens, a designer turned architect, was given complete control over the company's visual 'image' and products, from letterheads to buildings: in effect, a 'corporate identity' programme – not common practice until the 1970s. AEG had a talented in-house design engineer, Michael van Dolivo-Dobrawolsky, with whom Behrens worked to refine products and develop new lines. Many used interchangeable parts, the best known being a range of kettles: components were produced in three shapes, three sizes, three material finishes and three surface treatments – of the eighty-one possible combinations, thirty were marketed.

In 1908, Behrens began work with the engineer Karl Bernhard on the design of a Turbine Factory in Berlin (1908–10). On the side facing the factory grounds and internally, Bernhard had a free hand: serving no representational ends, these areas could be direct expressions of utility. By contrast, Behrens clearly believed that the building's public faces should express the economic might of AEG and the role of industry in the progress of civilization. On the long street elevation he framed recessed and slightly battered glass panels between the vertical faces of pin-jointed columns – the exposed parts of a vast portal-frame structure. The gable end achieved a truly monumental character, part barn gable and part Greek pediment – a mingling of *Volk* and *Kultur* in the service of *Technik* which seems entirely apt on this gargantuan temple in the service of German industry.

Behrens believed that modern manufacturing could perform a civilizing cultural role. 'Through the mass-production of objects of use corresponding to an aesthetically refined order,' he argued, 'it is possible to carry taste into the broadest sections of the population.' And he was convinced industrialists could be persuaded of their responsibility to appoint artists and designers to ensure that their products were of 'an aesthetically refined order'. The hope was ill-founded, as apart from AEG only two shipping companies got involved with the Werkbund. But however much its members might differ on other issues, this belief was the Werkbund's common ground, and a cornerstone of the Modern Movement in architecture and design.

Both Art Nouveau and the German Werkbund faced a fierce and witty critic in the Viennese architect Adolf Loos. He observed of the Werkbund's efforts that it 'has set out to discover the style of our age. This is unnecessary labour. We already have the style of our age. We have it everywhere where the designer, and therefore a member of this very movement, has not yet interfered' – in the work of 'the cobblers, the purse-makers, saddlers, waggon builders, instrument makers' – that is, in craft traditions. Loos's vision of modernity was honed by three years in America during the early 1890s, and the newspaper articles he wrote about the 1898 Vienna Jubilee Exhibition reflect his view that genuine modernity would not come through 'design'. It was here too that he first announced his provocative views on ornament. 'The lower the culture,' he argued, 'the more apparent the ornament. Ornament is something that must be overcome. The Papuan and the criminal ornament their skin. The Indian covers his paddle and his boat with layers and layers of ornament. But the bicycle and the steam engine are free of ornament. The march of civilization systematically liberates object after object from ornamentation.' In his great essay of 1908 entitled 'Ornament and Crime' he was emboldened to castigate ornament as the creation of primitives, degenerates and criminals – but there is some uncertainty over whether he ever actually said ornament *is* crime.

Loos's critique of academic architecture went to the heart of the matter: 'The architect has caused architecture to sink to a graphic art. It is not the man who can build best who gets most orders but rather the man who cuts the finest figure on paper. And yet these two are complete opposites.' That was in 1910; Le Corbusier would soon warn architects to beware of 'the illusion of plans' and advise students to 'develop a loathing for drawings'. Loos designed a series of private houses in which he developed his idea of the '*Raumplan*', by which he meant the organization of the house as a sequence of rooms, each a clearly defined space, but each linked directly to its neighbours, often by a few steps up or down. As in Horta's Hôtel Tassel, the rooms were no longer planned on separate floors. The Steiner House in Vienna (1910) was one of the first private houses to be built in reinforced concrete, and its garden elevation was of unprecedented austerity. With its flat roofs, horizontal windows, absence of ornament, and spatial continuities within, it was as near as anyone in Europe came before the War to an unmistakably modern house.

Throughout the nineteenth century, Europeans became increasingly aware of the challenge of America. Early in the century, in his influential *Philosophy of History*, Hegel pointed to America as the 'land of the

future' where 'the burden of the world's history shall reveal itself'. And in 1856 César Daly, the leading French architectural critic, declared it 'the country to be studied as regards the advances of modern architecture'. With few entrenched craft traditions, a shortage of people and an abundance of materials and land, America was ideally suited for rapid industrialization. The use of standardized parts was advocated in the late eighteenth century by President Jefferson for the manufacture of arms, and widely applied in the nineteenth to numerous other products: in Europe the

'American system', as it was known, took many years to win out over a craft-based approach to unique designs.

The Scientific Management 'time and motion' techniques developed by Frederick W. Taylor and Frank B. Gilbreth were well known in Europe by 1914, when the influx of large numbers of women into factories during the War broke down existing work patterns and facilitated their introduction. Henry Ford's assembly-line principles were also emulated. Ford was an archetypal American, as famous and as much a hero in Europe as Charlie Chaplin – in the late 1920s Ford's autobiography sold almost as well in the USSR as Lenin's did. Americans also began the rationalization of the domestic kitchen. Catherine Beecher's and her sister Harriet B. Stowe's *The American Woman's Home* appeared in 1869, and proposed a ship's galley as a model. In 1912 Christine Frederick published articles on 'The New Housekeeping' in *The Ladies' Home Journal*, applying Scientific Management work-study to domestic routines:

Walter Gropius and Adolf Meyer, Fagus Factory, Alfeld an der Leine, 1911
The offices of the Fagus Factory are steel-framed, with a lightweight glass curtain-wall hung from the floor slabs. The fact that the wall is non-loadbearing is emphasized by the absence of structural supports at the corners, yielding an unprecedented sense of openness and continuity between inside and out. In some later Modernist buildings, even the corner mullion is eliminated or disappears when the windows are opened.

Above: AEG poster, 1910
AEG and its rival Siemens
produced everything from
power stations to light bulbs.
AEG had a history of
employing distinguished artists
to design its posters, and this
example (which features a
metal filament lamp) is typical
of the clean, modern style
promoted by Peter Behrens.

**Below: Peter Behrens, AEG
Turbine Factory, Berlin,
1908–10**
Designed with the engineer
Karl Bernhard, the temple-like
Turbine Factory's public
facades were powerful
expressions of the company's
economic might, but the
strictly utilitarian interior was
left to Bernhard. On the long
street elevation the pin-jointed
columns (right) were the only
visible parts of the vast portal-
frame structure inside.

such thinking was taken up in Germany after 1918.

In building, the balloon frame exploited the mass-production of nails and mechanized saw-mills. Invented by G.W. Snow in the 1830s, it consisted of a regular array of vertical studs linked by horizontal plates – all in two-by-four-inch timbers and held together with nails. It eliminated complex carpentry joints and slashed the cost and time of construction, and by the 1870s probably three-quarters of American houses were built this way – many still are. Architecturally what is significant about the balloon frame is that it radically separates a building's appearance from its construction since it can be dressed in any style.

By the time of the World's Columbian Exposition held in Chicago in 1893 (the 400th anniversary of Columbus's 'discovery'), America was ready to present a truly civilized face to the world. The site was planned by D.H. Burnham as a 'White City' around a lake, complete with genuine Venetian gondoliers. The style was Beaux Arts Classicism, the material plaster: Louis Sullivan predicted that 'the damage wrought to this country by the Chicago World's Fair will last half a century.' He was about right – the plaster palaces gave rise to highly durable 'mercantile classicism'.

The Exposition's importance architecturally was twofold: it attracted Europeans to Chicago, enabling them to see the early development of tall, iron- and steel-framed buildings; and it gave American architects first-hand experience of Japanese architecture in the form of the Ho-o-den temple, which had been left as a

gift to the city. The contrast between the work of skilled Japanese carpenters and the plaster palaces could not have been greater; many came and were impressed, and one seems to have seen in it the possibility of a new architecture. His name was Frank Lloyd Wright.

The perfecting of fireproof steel-frame construction around 1890, safe and efficient lifts and the telephone, combined to make the tall office building viable. By 1893 numerous examples – some of them more than twenty storeys high – could be seen in Chicago, rising above the often filthy streets of the great meat-market of the mid-West. Jacques Hermant, a French architect, wrote in his official report on the Exposition that 'astonished Europeans' would be 'forced to cross the Atlantic to witness the new expression … we are all seeking but which we have not yet found, paralysed as we are by academic tradition and the mania of the collector.' Architects invented the horizontal 'Chicago window', and studied ways of composing tall buildings – few more brilliantly than Burnham and Company, the designers of the Reliance Building (1891–5). This fifteen-storey stack of Chicago windows had only the most restrained ornament, and more glass than any other tall building would boast for many years.

Louis Sullivan was the major established talent in Chicago, and in 1892 he wrote an article entitled 'We should Refrain Entirely from the Use of Ornament for a Period of Years'. The object of this visual fast was to 'concentrate entirely upon the production of buildings well-formed and comely in the nude'. As a superlative

draughtsman and master of luxuriant plant-derived ornament, Sullivan's strictures carried weight, and it seems likely that they impressed Adolf Loos who was working (as a dishwasher, not an architect) in Chicago. In 1895, in 'The Tall Building Artistically Considered', Sullivan described the principles behind designs like the Guaranty Building which was completed in Buffalo the same year. He was the first to make a convincing aesthetic and technical whole of a tall office building, and justified his decisions by analogy with forms in nature which expressed the 'inner life' of the organism: 'Whether it be the sweeping eagle in his flight or the open apple-blossom, the toiling work-horse, the blithe swan, the branching oak, the winding stream at its base, the drifting clouds, over all the coursing sun, form ever follows function, and this is the law.' Sullivan's conception of 'Form follows Function' embraced such 'rational' principles as that 'the structural dimensions provide the real basis for the artistic formation of the exterior': his conception of 'organic architecture' was adopted and developed by his assistant, Frank Lloyd Wright.

Born in 1867, Wright was brought up in rural Wisconsin. As a child he played with Froebel's 'gifts' – educational toys which seem to have sown the seed of his love of additive and interlocking rectilinear forms. He worked and studied engineering (briefly) in Madison, and in 1888 entered the office of Adler and Sullivan in Chicago. He stayed there for five years, taking increasing responsibility for the domestic-scale work.

Wright referred to Sullivan as 'Lieber Meister' and made Sullivan's concept of organic architecture his own; he also followed his advice to read Ruskin and Viollet-le-Duc. In 1901, with several houses behind him, he published a project for 'A Home in a Prairie Town' in *The Ladies' Home Journal*: the plans were fully costed and their architect 'ready to take orders' for work in his new Prairie Style. The design applied the lessons of 'The Art and Craft of the Machine', the title of a seminal lecture Wright gave that year. Unlike most European Arts and Crafts practitioners, Wright accepted the logic of the machine as a tool; above all it demanded simplicity, he said, and could be used to bring out the beauty of natural materials such as wood.

The Ward Willitts House of 1902 is typical of a large Prairie House. The ground plan is cruciform, its asymmetrical wings reaching out into the landscape, and the roofs of the first-floor accommodation seem to float above a continuous band of glazing or solid panels. The deeply overhanging roofs (which saved on downpipes, Wright said!) create strong shadows and emphasize the horizontality of the design. The Robie House (1907–9), built on an urban site in south Chicago, marks the climax of the Prairie Style and shows Wright's ideal of 'organic architecture' fully matured. The pyramidal composition of massively overhanging roofs is masterly – the house seems to want to burst out beyond its site, yet at the same time it is defensively set back and up from a busy crossroads. Everything necessary to the house as an 'organism' has been integrated into the design –

Adolf Loos, Steiner House, Vienna, 1910
The stripped exteriors of Loos's houses give no hint of the richly finished rooms within: the contrast has been likened to that between the conscious, public persona and the unconscious inner life as revealed by his Viennese contemporary, Sigmund Freud. Loos's great innovation was the *Raumplan* or 'plan of volumes' – a complex interlocking of rooms on different levels to form a continuous living space.

Burnham and Company, Reliance Building, Chicago, 1891–5

Epitomizing the efficiency of the Chicago system of riveted steel-frame construction, the structure of this wonderfully elegant fifteen-storey building was erected in as many days. Designed by Charles B. Atwood, it featured a continuous stack of 'Chicago windows', elegantly restrained ornament and more glass than any other building would boast for many years.

to elaborating the structural rhythm of the interior. The main living spaces are in a single volume divided by the fireplace – the symbolic centre of every Wright house.

During these years Wright also completed two major public buildings. The Larkin Building (1904–5; demolished 1947) in Buffalo was a multi-storey office building organized around a central atrium. Again, his attention to the practical requirements was exemplary: because of the adjacent railway, the building was one of the first to have a form of air conditioning, with the ducts integrated into the corner stair towers. Wright also invented the hung wall for lavatories, glass doors and steel furniture – his clients stopped short of letting him redesign the telephones! He was no lover of modern cities and his urban buildings tended to be introverted;

here the atmosphere was almost ecclesiastical, a cathedral to labour – complete with biblical and other exhortations to work and good living incised around the atrium. Unity Temple (1905–7) was his first actual church, and the building, Wright thought, 'where you will find the first real expression of the idea that the space within the building is the reality of that building … space not walled in now but more or less free to appear.' You get no idea of that feeling from the outside, but inside the space is extraordinary: Wright used to speak of his architecture as a 'destruction of the box', and here he attacked the box at its strongest points – the corners, and the junction of wall and ceiling. Exploiting the structural potential of reinforced concrete, he created an almost continuous frieze of glazing. Outside, all is solid mass; inside, ineffable light and space, the like of which had not been seen before.

Unity Temple was the first building to greet European architects who acquired the first of Ernst Wasmuth's folios of Wright's work (published in Berlin in 1911), and many must surely have seen it as embodying that original 'art of construction' which had eluded European architects for so long. Wright exploited new materials to the full, yet the basic articulation of his buildings was derived from Classicism: the prominent base course, plain walls, cill, glazed 'frieze' and low pitched roofs of the Prairie Houses were derived from Classicism via the Ho-o-den temple. It is also tempting to see his work as a realization of the principles Gottfried Semper set out in his seminal book *Der Stil in den technischen Künsten* ('Style in the technical arts') of 1860–3. Semper argued that architecture was rooted in four primordial motives which gave rise to the 'industrial arts' (or 'crafts' in normal English usage): hearth-gathering (the spiritual centre, corresponding to ceramics); walling (textiles); the making of a tectonic framework (carpentry); and terracing (originally mounding, later masonry). Semper's great work is known to have been circulating in Chicago in the 1890s and his theory beautifully fits a Japanese temple such as the Ho-o-den, as well as Wright's work – the correspondence would hardly have escaped him.

The Dutch architect Berlage, a long-standing admirer of H.H. Richardson, visited America in 1910, and the following year lectured in Germany about Sullivan and Wright – that 'master who has been able to create a building which has no equal in Europe'. Wright is important to our story primarily because he arrived at a new concept of space well ahead of his European

This is the modern opportunity, to make of a building, together with its equipment, appurtenances and enviroment, an entity which shall constitute a complete work of art. Frank Lloyd Wright

Frank Lloyd Wright, Project for 'A Home in a Prairie Town', 1901
This revolutionary house illustrated an article in a series on model suburban homes published by the *Ladies' Home Journal*. The exterior was, Wright wrote, designed to accentuate the 'quiet level' of the prairie, whilst the open cruciform plan was 'arranged to offer the least resistance to a simple mode of living, in keeping with a high ideal of the family life together'. The dramatic placing of the house on the sheet reveals Wright's love of Japanese woodcuts.

Right: Frank Lloyd Wright, Larkin Building, Buffalo, New York, 1904–5 (destroyed)
All the offices in the Larkin company's new administration building looked down into the great atrium shown in this perspective. The purpose-designed furniture and exhortations to hard work and good living which ran all around it are also clearly delineated. With its destruction in 1947 America lost one of the greatest early twentieth-century buildings.

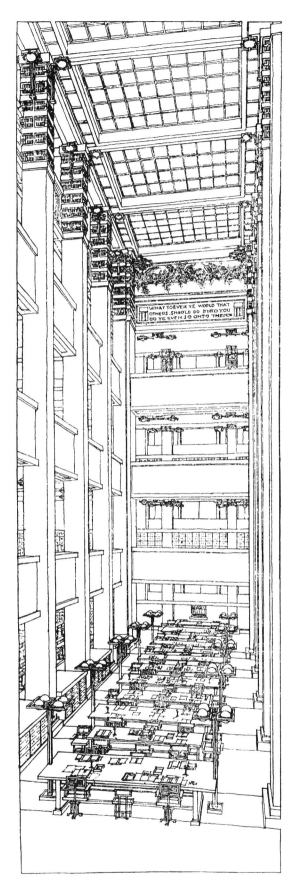

counterparts. Fiercely independent, he later presented himself as an implacable opponent of European Modernism. His work is one of the great achievements in twentieth-century architecture – but it remained on the periphery of mainstream Modernism, so much so that the American historian Henry-Russell Hitchcock could write, in his *Modern Architecture* of 1929, of the 'self-conscious fussiness' and 'self-righteous stodginess' of Wright's interiors. By comparison with the houses then being produced in Europe, Wright's work must have seemed, for all its innovations, faintly Victorian.

Greatly admired though Wright's work was in Europe, the anonymous and featureless industrial buildings of America were probably more decisive in helping European architects shed the last vestiges of 'style'. For all the modernity of Walter Gropius's Fagus Factory, for example, it still retained a Greek refinement in such details as its subtly tapered brickwork. Two years later, the 1913 Yearbook of the Deutscher Werkbund contained an article by Gropius about the 'great industrial structures' of America, followed by seven pages of photographs of factories and grain elevators. These images rapidly became known across Europe – influencing the Italian Futurists in 1914, for example – and were republished by Le Corbusier after the War. Gropius said that their forms were 'not obscured by sentimental reverence for tradition nor by other intellectual scruples which prostrate our contemporary European design and bar true artistic originality' and he considered them 'as impressive in their monumental power as the buildings of ancient Egypt'.

The *American Architect and Building News* was almost as effusive in describing a roof-lit 'Daylight factory' in 1911: 'Pure, clear, uncoloured daylight – the sunshine of roofless fields … is becoming the possession of the American factory labourer … whatever additional expenditure may have been required was fully justified in the improved health, the improved moral, physical and aesthetic conditions.' Le Corbusier soon extolled the Daylight factory's 'naked purity' as one of the 'reassuring first fruits of the new age'. This degree-zero architecture made its way to Europe in the great FIAT Factory (1915–21) built outside Turin by Giacomo Matté-Trucco, and it entered the consciousness of progressive architects as the epitome of a truly modern architecture. 'In which style should we build?' An answer seemed to be in sight, but far-reaching innovations in the fine arts needed to be assimilated as well as these lessons from America.

Left: Frank Lloyd Wright, Unity Temple, Oak Park, Chicago, 1905–7

The first building featured in Ernst Wasmuth's 1911 publication of Wright's work, Unity Temple was the design in which he thought he first made space central to the architectural conception. Wright claimed that the detailing influenced the Dutch De Stijl movement, to which it bears a surprising similarity, but it was the new conception of space which impressed the European Modernists.

Above: Frank Lloyd Wright, Robie House, Chicago, 1907–9

Although epitomizing the Prairie Style, the Robie House was built on a busy corner in south Chicago. The interior is open yet protective, and the design integrated all the latest aids to comfort – electrical light fittings and wiring, central heating, mechanical ventilation – into an organic whole of great originality and power.

2

NORTHAMPTON COLLEGE
LIBRARY

**The
Tradition of
the New**

The modern arts have a special obligation, an advanced or avant-garde duty, to go ahead of their own age and transform it.

Ezra Pound

**Opposite: Paul Citroën,
Metropolis, 1923–69**
Modernism was the art of the city, and Citroën's image of the modern metropolis combines nineteenth-century engineering, arcades, skyscrapers, overhead railways and a broad street to suggest a place of perpetual change.

**Left: Erich Mendelsohn,
Sketch for the Einstein Tower
at Potsdam, 1920**
The Tower was completed in 1921 and this dynamic sketch is typical of the Expressionist style which won Mendelsohn many admirers when his pen-and-ink drawings were exhibited in Berlin in 1919.

Modernism was born in Europe between 1900 and the outbreak of the First World War in 1914. Virginia Woolf dated its appearance with surprising precision. 'On or about December 1910,' she wrote, 'human character changed. All human relations shifted – those between masters and servants, husbands and wives, parents and children. And when human relations shift there is at the same time a change in religion, conduct, politics and literature.' December 1910 marked the end of the Edwardian era and saw the first exhibition of French Post-Impressionist art in London, and whilst a date a few years earlier might suggest itself on the Continent (1905, perhaps, in honour of the first Russian Revolution, the unveiling of Fauvism in Paris and the publication of Einstein's Special Theory of Relativity?) such precision hardly matters. What is clear is that in the decade before the First World War, artists, poets, composers and writers made concerted efforts to come to terms with the condition of modernity first identified by Marx, Baudelaire and others in the mid-nineteenth century.

The immediate pre-War years were, it almost goes without saying, a time of increasing political uncertainty and rapid change in almost all areas of life, full of promise but also deeply unsettling. The feeling that the values and institutions of traditional culture were slowly collapsing had been growing amongst artists and intellectuals for half a century, culminating in the *fin-de-siècle* decadence of the 1890s and manifesting itself in that sense of anarchy lurking just below the civilized surface of life which pervades the work of such writers as Fyodor Dostoevsky, Joseph Conrad and Thomas Mann.

Psychological and social unease would remain major Modernist themes, but the arrival of the new century also saw a renewed sense of optimism, occasioned in no small measure by the seemingly unlimited promise of nineteenth-century inventions which were then going into industrial production and beginning to make a significant difference to everyday life. Marconi's first radio signal flashed across the Atlantic in 1901, and wireless telegraphy soon combined with the telephone and telegraph to facilitate the first modern 'media explosion'. The mix of news, features and advertising, already established as the basis of the modern newspaper in the mid-nineteenth century, was transformed by the introduction of photomechanical illustrations and up-to-the-minute stories from around the world. A new sense of 'the present in its totality', as Paul Claudel put it in 1904, could now be communicated (what would he make of CNN?). Electric lighting – and with it illuminated advertising – was becoming common in major cities, thus destroying the division between day and night and instigating what the architectural historian Reyner Banham has called 'the greatest environmental revolution in human history since the domestication of fire'. The modern bicycle appeared in 1890, and industrial production ensured that cars and bicycles were an increasingly common sight. In France, for example, a mere 3,000 cars were on the roads in 1900, but by 1913 this figure had risen dramatically to around 100,000. *L'automobilisme*, promoted by a dozen specialist magazines, was all the rage. The Wright brothers' first powered, heavier-than-air plane took to the skies in 1903 and Louis Blériot flew across the Channel in thirty-six minutes in 1909, generating enormous publicity for aviation.

Sweeping technological change was matched by revolutionary new ideas in the natural and social sciences. In 1883 Ernst Mach had rejected Newton's absolute time as an 'idle metaphysical speculation', and twenty-two years later Albert Einstein published the basis of his Special Theory of Relativity which shattered conventional ideas of space and time. The German physicist William Conrad Röntgen discovered X-rays in 1895, and the following year the Frenchman, Antoine Henri Becquerel, happened upon radioactivity: not even matter itself seemed solid and reliable any more. In 1900, Max Planck announced the arrival of quantum theory, which was subsequently developed by Einstein, Erwin Schrödinger and others into quantum mechanics, the cornerstone of modern physics and harbinger of uncertainty. Knowledge, let alone understanding, of these developments outside specialist circles was not widespread before 1914, but news of them contributed to a growing realization that the world was an altogether less predictable and more mysterious affair than had been portrayed by the rational mechanisms of Classical science. The Age of Reason seemed to be giving way to a new Age of Unreason and, doubting that there could be rational answers to the big questions about life and disenchanted by traditional religion, people turned in surprising numbers to new systems of belief, amongst which Mme Blavatsky's Theosophy assumed particular importance in artistic circles. The Theosophists emphasized visual aspects of the spiritual – colour and form, like music, were said to call forth 'vibrations' which enrich the soul – and although, like today's New Age beliefs, such ideas strike the sceptical as irredeemable kitsch, they had a wide impact in Europe around 1900.

Developments in sociology, psychology and philosophy were as revolutionary as those in science, and more direct in their impact on the arts. In his *Principles of Psychology*, published in 1890, William James argued that 'reality' was not a set of objective, external facts, but was perceived subjectively through individual experience. Speaking of the mind, he said: 'let us call it the stream of thought, of consciousness, or of the subjective life'. James's 'stream of consciousness' was to become a recurring feature of Modernist literature – appearing in Virginia Woolf, Marcel Proust, James Joyce and many others. Sigmund Freud's *The Interpretation of Dreams* was published in 1900: although its immediate impact has often been over-estimated, its influence became pervasive and rippled on through the century, reinforcing and informing interest in the workings of the inner psyche and the idea that the individual is a complex of several, generally conflicting 'selves' affected by unconscious desires.

Amongst philosophers, Friedrich Nietzsche and Henri Bergson contributed substantially to the intellectual ferment of the new century. Nietzsche had famously proclaimed the Death of God and arrival of the Superman in *Thus Spake Zarathustra* (1883–5). Zarathustra declared that 'Whoever wants to be creative in good and evil, he must first be an annihilator and destroy values' and advised that 'the secret of reaping the greatest fruitfulness and the greatest enjoyment from life is to live dangerously!' Both injunctions were followed by many a Modernist. Bergson viewed life as an endless stream of 'becoming', which the intellect divides arbitrarily into fixed states, and regarded intuition – a refined form of instinct – as the key to understanding life and time. Dismissing the mathematical view of change as a series of states as 'cinematographic', he argued that true change involves the 'dynamic interpenetration' of past and present in what he called *durée* ('duration') – the essence of life, manifested in memory. Bergson was a gifted stylist and orator and gave regular, well-reported public lectures to packed audiences in Paris: his ideas became common currency and were particularly influential amongst artists and critics. Several of his favourite terms – duration, fusion, simultaneities, dynamic – became almost standard in writings on art.

Dramatic though these large-scale intellectual developments were, arguably the nineteenth century's most far-reaching aesthetic and intellectual legacy arose from the conviction that we cannot transcend a metaphorical description of the world and that even

Georges Braque, *The Bay of Leceques*, 1907
Braque came to fame as the pioneer, with Picasso, of Cubism but he first made his mark working in this vigorous Fauve style in which his mastery of colour was already apparent.

Below: Paul Cézanne,
Mont Ste Victoire, c.1904–6
The mountain dominates the
landscape around Cézanne's
home town of Aix-en-Provence
and was his favourite subject.
In this late canvas he comes
close to abstraction: almost all
traces of drawing have gone,
and Cézanne relies on small
planes of colour to create form.

Opposite: Henri Matisse,
Harmony in Red, 1908
The saturated red and
arabesques on wall and table
combine with the elimination
of detail and the picture-like
view through the window to
destroy the illusion of three-
dimensions. This emphasis on
flatness, on a shallow, non-
illusionistic pictorial space,
became a hallmark of
Modernist painting.

natural languages are inherently misleading – but also inescapable. Nietzsche again anticipated this development, arguing in his essay 'The Philosopher' that 'the drive toward the formation of metaphors is the fundamental human drive' and the basis of knowledge, and in the work of poets such as Mallarmé, Rimbaud and Hölderlin metaphor also came decisively to the fore. In *Les Illuminations* (1874, pub. 1886), Rimbaud delighted in the 'alchemy of the word' which enabled him to see 'a mosque instead of a factory, a school of drummers consisting of angels, open carriages on the roads of the sky, a drawing-room at the bottom of a lake' and explained these 'magical sophisms' by means of 'the hallucination of words', ending 'by finding the disorder of my mind sacred'. Many – from Freud to the Surrealists and beyond – would find the disorder of the mind similarly 'sacred', but more important for Modernism *tout court* is the determination, which began with Baudelaire, to use poetic language – the 'alchemy of the word' – as a means to reveal and transform the world. In the process, the mechanisms of language itself – not just its specific use in poetry or literature – assumed pre-eminence, and became the paradigm of the other arts.

The consequences of this critique and privileging of language can hardly be overstated – amongst other things it is the source of the current preoccupation with 'discourse'. In all the arts, conventions so long-established as to appear natural were questioned: perspective in painting, ornament and symmetry in architecture, tonality in music, the narrative structure of the novel and so forth. Treating the various artistic media as 'languages' encouraged practitioners to focus on the means specific to their art. As early as 1890 Maurice Denis had written that 'a picture – before being a war-horse, a nude woman, or some sort of anecdote – is essentially a surface covered with colours arranged in a certain order'. And in 1907, at the Cézanne Memorial Exhibition at the Salon d'Automne, the German poet Rainer Maria Rilke saw that no one before Cézanne 'ever demonstrated so clearly the extent to which painting is something that takes place among the colours, and how one has to leave them alone completely, so that they can settle the matter among themselves. Their intercourse: this is the whole of painting.' The pioneer of abstraction, Wassily Kandinsky, was to eliminate figurative content altogether around 1912 and concentrate on exploring colour's expressive power, whereas the Cubists worked almost in monochrome whilst focusing on the representation of three dimensions on the two-dimensional surface of the canvas without recourse to perspective illusions – the beginning of that 'road to flatness' which formalist critics such as Clement Greenberg have seen as the destiny of Modernist painting.

The new emphasis on technique, and on increasingly radical technical experimentation, is a defining characteristic of Modernism but it was not pursued as an end in itself. New techniques – free-verse, collage,

The whole arrangement of my pictures is expressive ... Composition is the art of arranging in a decorative manner the various elements at the painter's disposal for the expression of his feelings. Henri Matisse

The Tradition of the New

atonality, etc – were the means of developing new styles and forms capable of representing the experience of modernity, from the intoxication of the modern metropolis to the teeming inner life of the individual psyche. Nor, perhaps surprisingly, were their innovations seen by many of the major Modernists as representing a complete rejection of tradition – quite the contrary. For Schoenberg, the twelve-tone scale was a necessary and inevitable outcome of the trajectory of Classical harmony, and the greatest Modernist architects – Le Corbusier and Mies van der Rohe – were deeply rooted in the Classical tradition. Modernist manifestoes might proclaim a complete break with the past, but much Modernist practice grew out of the underlying principles and assumptions of traditional styles – even when appearing to turn them on their heads. Le Corbusier's 1920s houses, which we encountered in the Introduction, are a case in point.

Modernism is too varied and complex a phenomenon to be said to have had a single beginning, but the first truly avant-garde paintings since the Impressionists were those of the Fauves, first seen at the 1905 Salon d'Automne. They caused a public scandal by provoking a general feeling of 'pictorial aberration' which was caused by the vivid, 'unnatural' colours. The paintings were more provocative still the following year, when even Maurice Denis commented on 'the painful sensation of bedazzlement' which 'did not stop short of any brutality of colour'. The greatest by far of the Fauves was Henri Matisse, but it was Maurice Vlaminck

who, looking back on this phase of his career, best summed up their aspirations: 'I wanted to revolutionize habits and contemporary life – to liberate nature, to free it from the authority of old theories and classicism . . . I felt a tremendous urge to re-create a new world seen through my own eyes, a world which was entirely mine.' The overly ambitious desire to revolutionize life in general through an intensely personal artistic vision runs through Modernism: art can at best provide models of dissent and transformation, but politically committed artists from Courbet onwards have persisted in believing otherwise, and the Modernists were to be no exception.

Fauvism was radical, but for all the wildness of its colours the natural world still provided a recognizable subject-matter. The decisive break with the mimetic conventions of Western art and the consolidation of the idea of a startlingly different Modernist art came with Cubism. The movement involved the development of a radically new formal language, the dissemination of critical-theoretical texts which were essential to its propagation and reception, and a complete break with 'natural' perceptions of reality. Cubism's immediate precursor was one of the first great Modernist paintings, Pablo Picasso's *Demoiselles d'Avignon*. He began work on the canvas towards the end of April or in early May 1907, and later repainted three of the figures – following, most art historians agree, a visit to the ethnographic museum in Paris to look at African sculpture. It was seen by friends in his studio, but not exhibited until 1916, when André Salmon suggested the

Opposite: Pablo Picasso, *Les Demoiselles d'Avignon*, 1907
In this revolutionary canvas the figures seem to emerge from, rather than recede into the picture, and the violent distortions and fragmentation still shock. The painting is not Cubist, but it was the starting point from which Picasso and Braque began the quest for a new pictorial language.

Below: Henri Matisse, *Blue Nude (Souvenir of Biskra)*, 1907
Like many early Modernists, Matisse travelled to exotic locations in search of inspiration: this memory of Biskra in Algeria exemplifies his determination to make colour the essence of painting. He said of it that 'it was no longer the woman that was beautiful, but the picture'.

title – which Picasso later claimed to dislike. Although the *Demoiselles* anticipates Cubist principles, its savagery and erotic overtones reflect Picasso's social milieu and literary interests of preceding years, as do the sources on which he drew – Greek vases and Egyptian art, archaic and Iberian sculpture, Gauguin and El Greco all played their part, whilst the composition's ancestry can be traced back through Cézanne's bathers to Poussin, Titian, Raphael and the tradition of the nude. The painting may have been intended as a parody of the 'Three Graces', making its utter neglect of any canon of beauty all the more shocking. Its feel was echoed that same year by Matisse's *Blue Nude*, which, although not so violently distorted, was clearly intended as a challenge to the conventional beauties of the Venus theme in academic art. The key message of the Modernists' iconoclasm was, as Matisse said of the *Blue Nude*, that it was no longer the woman that was beautiful, but the picture – the 'colours arranged in a certain order'.

The figures in the *Demoiselles* do not appear to occupy a three-dimensional space, and their environment is painted as substantially as they are and using similar jagged forms. The viewer scans the surface of the picture because there is no pictorial space to enter – we are firmly on the road to flatness first prospected by Cézanne. Traditional perspectival space depended upon a single, fixed point of view, and Picasso also violated this convention by painting the figures from various directions: noses are shown in profile on faces viewed frontally, and the right leg of the crouching figure has been wrenched around to lie parallel to the picture plane, emphasizing its flatness. Such wilful distortions can still shock, and they horrified Georges Braque when he saw the canvas in Picasso's studio that autumn – the two painters were introduced by Picasso's friend, the poet Guillaume Apollinaire. But Braque also saw that the painting suggested a way towards a new art, and over the next few years the two worked in a collaboration of unparalleled closeness – Picasso said it was as if they were married, and Braque likened them to two mountaineers roped together.

Picasso having established the base camp, it fell to Braque to lead the first pitch. Inspired by the Salon d'Automne's memorial exhibition of Cézanne in 1907, he decided the next summer to follow in the master's footsteps and paint at L'Estaque. Braque's brilliant Fauve palette turned earthy – grey, brown and green – like Cézanne's, and he magnified the distortions of form and inconsistencies of perspective discovered in Cézanne's work, turning them to very different ends.

Piling trees, rocks and buildings on top of each other to fill the canvas, Braque eliminated the sky, atmosphere and tonal recession, and rendered lights and darks arbitrarily, unrelated to a light source. The pictured spaces were inconsistent, even ambiguous – due to the variety of lighting, cubic forms can seem alternately to 'pop out' from the canvas or recede into it: what Braque was trying to represent was an almost tactile, not optical, experience of space.

While Braque was at L'Estaque, Picasso delved further into the world of Negro sculpture, and then, impressed by his friend's work, he also turned to Cézanne. An improbable fusion of post-Cézannian space and African-inspired distortions of form guided the figure paintings made by Picasso in Horta del Ebro, Spain, during the summer of 1909, and canvases such as *Woman with Pears* (1909) have been described as the first Cubist works. But the sense of massively rounded figures in space was still too strong, and in a fully Cubist painting (Braque's *Harbour in Normandy* [1909] was amongst the first, Picasso's *Girl with a Mandolin* [1910] is more typical) the relationships between forms are more important than the forms themselves, and both are treated in terms of planes which do not fix the boundaries between them. Objects are frequently observed from several points of view, and appear to hover in an uncertain state of being – either dissolving into the space which forms around them, or materializing from it. These two possibilities have been used to define two phases in Cubism: an early *Analytical* period and a later *Synthetic* one. The Analytical works begin with a motif and take it apart, the latter 'synthesize' forms from planes, colours and other pictorial elements which begin their life with no representational role – Braque, in particular, frequently worked this way.

Cubism's classic period was during the years 1910–11, and Picasso's and Braque's ideas sometimes converged so closely that their paintings can be difficult to tell apart at first sight. As they became increasingly abstract, realistic clues were incorporated to help the viewer decipher the subject. Having trained as a house decorator, Braque incorporated such tricks of the trade as fake marbling and woodgraining, as well as stencilled letters. In 1912 came two significant innovations. In May, Picasso invented 'collage' by glueing a piece of oilcloth lithographed with chair caning on to a small oval painting entitled, naturally enough, *Still Life with Chair Caning*. Braque followed his lead and in September pasted a piece of wood-grained wallpaper on to a

Below left: Georges Braque, *Houses at L'Estaque*, 1908
Inspired by the Cézanne Memorial Exhibition held in 1907, Braque went to paint in Provence. In the intense light of the south he began to express a tactile, not optical, sense of space – the dense, layered planes were a crucial innovation in the search for new forms of representation.

Below right: Pablo Picasso, *Girl with a Mandolin*, 1910
Left unfinished when the subject, Fanny Tellier, gave up after numerous sittings, this picture gives us a glimpse of the language of 'Analytical' Cubism in the making – indeterminate forms described by faceted planes in a shallow pictorial space.

Below left: Georges Braque,
The Portuguese, **1911–12**
Below right: Pablo Picasso,
Seated Woman Playing the
Mandolin, **1911**

The stylistic convergence
between Picasso's and Braque's
work in 1911–12, evident in
pictures such as the Picasso
(below right) and the Braque
(below left), is extraordinary.
Although they begin with the
human figure, their subject is
really the contradictions which
arise in representing three-
dimensional objects on a flat
surface. Painting has become a
critique of its own language and
conventions, and nothing –
most obviously not colour – is
allowed to distract from the
emphasis on space and form.

canvas: such works became known as *papiers collés*, and bits of now-yellowing newspaper, cigarette packets, sheet-music, menus, etc soon consorted with painted planes on their canvases.

In the absence of any statement of intentions – and Braque and Picasso remained notably silent – it is impossible to know what, precisely, were their intentions. The paintings frequently evoke the smoke-filled atmosphere of the Parisian cafés they haunted, and recent interpretations by Kirk Varnedoe and others have emphasized their relationship to the Paris street-scene of newspaper stalls, Morris columns and advertising posters. The newspaper mastheads (most frequently that of *Le Journal*) incorporated by the Cubists were a ubiquitous element of the Parisian city-scene, and shortly before the War Parisian newspapers (notably *Le Journal*) began to mix editorial and advertising copy on the same pages – a development Oswald Spengler later interpreted as a sign of the decadence and impending downfall of the West. But to the Cubists – and especially to Picasso from the less developed Spain – such phenomena doubtless appeared as stimulating signs of modernity, and the newspapers themselves offered the kind of improbable juxtapositions we encounter in Cubist *papiers collés*. Words and word-fragments engaged in humorous – some decidedly schoolboy-lavatorial – interplays, and Patricia Leighten has traced in Picasso's selection of newspaper fragments compelling evidence of his continuing interest in anarchist politics, which developed in his native Spain during the 1890s. Many of the cuttings used during the last months of 1912, for example, are from accounts of the Balkan Wars. Whatever their specific meanings, it is clear that a formalist reading of Cubism does it less than justice.

Commenting many years later on his *Bottle of Suze* (1912), Picasso observed that 'if a newspaper can become a bottle, that gives us something to think about in connection with both newspaper and bottles, too. This displaced object has entered a universe for which it was not made and where it retains, in a measure, its strangeness. And this strangeness was what we wanted to make people think about because we were quite aware that our world was becoming very strange and not exactly reassuring.' A similar strategy of 'strange-making' was being advocated in Russia by the critic Viktor Shklovsky as a revolutionary task for literature, and Cubist techniques have become so familiar in advertising that it is difficult for us today to recapture the strangeness they originally provoked. Their de-centred, fragmented, all-over compositions have been seen by many as suggesting a world in which, in W. B. Yeats's famous line, 'Things fall apart; the centre cannot hold', but such interpretations do not seem to have begun until Picasso revived Cubist methods to represent the horrors of the Spanish Civil War in the 1930s – *Guernica* (1937) being the magnificent result.

By its contemporaries, Cubism was most commonly seen as having introduced the dimension of time into painting – Leon Werth, writing in 1910, thought Cubist images showed 'the sensation and reflections which we

Pablo Picasso, *Still Life with Chair Caning*, 1912
When Picasso glued a piece of oilcloth printed with a chair-caning pattern on to this canvas in May 1912, he created his first collage. *Papier collé* (cut paper) was not new, but it had never been assimilated into fine art before. It became one of the most important Modernist innovations, ideally suited to suggesting the complexities and tensions of urban industrial life.

Pablo Picasso, *Glass and Bottle of Suze*, 1912
Bold forms, dramatic contrasts and startling juxtapositions are typical of Picasso's collages, a response, he later said, to a world which was 'becoming very strange and not exactly reassuring'. The newspaper texts carried a message, often describing (as here) the tensions in eastern Europe or communist and anarchist activities.

experience with the passage of time'. Presenting the multiple facets of, say, a figure seen from several directions at once was regarded as a prime example of Bergsonian 'simultaneity', although in fact none of Braque's or Picasso's paintings does this in any remotely systematic way. More speculative writers even suggested links with multi-dimensional non-Euclidean geometries and relativistic space-time, which Picasso refuted in 1923 as 'pure literature, not to say nonsense'. For all that, it is difficult to imagine how painting could have better expressed the emerging view of reality which Alfred North Whitehead admirably described as follows: 'The misconception which has haunted philosophic literature throughout the centuries, is the notion of independent existence. There is no such mode of existence. Every entity is only to be understood in terms of the way in which it is interwoven with the rest of the universe.' Fragmented, simultaneous, interwoven: Cubist paintings could be seen as all of these – such multivalence was inherent in the works, and is part of what made them quintessentially Modernist.

Braque and Picasso inevitably attracted followers, and it was thanks to them that there was a movement called Cubism. Most talented and closest stylistically was Juan Gris, who remained faithful to Cubist principles until his death in 1927 and produced the most complex of all Cubist *papiers collés*. His approach was more theoretical, the compositions beginning with 'mathematical' drawings constructed with instruments; these helped generate a 'flat coloured architecture' which in turn might suggest a subject – or have one imposed on it. Gris' approach, not surprisingly, endeared his work to Le Corbusier and other architects in the 1920s. Acting as unofficial spokesman for Cubism, Gris introduced it to minor figures such as Albert Gleizes and Jean Metzinger, who filled the void created by Braque and Picasso's silence with Cubism's first theoretical text, *Du Cubisme*. Published in 1912, it beat by several months Apollinaire's celebrated essays *Les Peintres cubistes*. *Du Cubisme* went through fifteen printings within a year and appeared in English in 1913, a clear indication of the keen interest in this revolutionary new art, which exploded into public view in the famous Room 41 at the Salon des Indépendants of 1911. This collection consisted entirely of works by Braque's and Picasso's followers – the masters chose never to appear in group shows.

Decorative artists were not slow to capitalize on Cubism's popularity, and for the 1912 Salon d'Automne André Mare co-ordinated a team of twelve designers and decorators to create a 'Maison Cubiste'. Their initial ideas proved hopelessly over-ambitious and what resulted was a large model of the front facade and a full-size entrance leading into several brightly coloured rooms decorated with paintings by Marcel Duchamp, Gleizes and Metzinger, Roger de La Fresnaye and Paul Vera, amongst others. The house was designed by the sculptor Raymond Duchamp-Villon (a brother of Marcel Duchamp) and looks slightly ridiculous now, its 'Cubist' features no more than elements of Classical ornament fractured into multiple facets – the cornice was apparently inspired 'by the energy of the sun and its rays'. The most concerted attempt to create an architecture based on the appearance of Cubist paintings came in Prague not Paris, and was the work of Pavel Janák, Josef Chochol and others in the Graphic Artists Group. They imitated Cubist forms directly, and also attempted a Cubist reduction-to-essentials on the style of the great Slovene architect Josef Plecnik, who was then working in the city. The faceted, crystalline forms of Chochol's housing block on Neklanova Street (1913–14) are altogether more convincing than Duchamp-Villon's efforts, but Cubism's deep lessons for architecture were learnt after the War, and lay not in a superficial imitation of its forms, but in a radical concept of space.

The Cubists' leading apologist, Guillaume Apollinaire, attempted to apply some of the painters' ideas to poetic composition, constructing his poems from juxtapositions of fragmentary images in what he called a '*style télégraphique*'. In *Lundi rue Christine* (1913), for example, the familiar milieu of a Paris café is evoked by isolated scraps of description and seemingly random snatches of overheard conversation, juxtaposed in a manner modelled on collage:

> You're a crummy one
> That lady has a nose like a tapeworm
> Louise forgot her furs
> Me I have no furs and I'm not cold
> The Dane smokes his cigarette as he consults the timetable
> The black cat crosses the brasserie.

Apollinaire attempted even more literal collage-like compositions in his *Calligrammes*, where the words are organized to suggest a painterly composition – *Lettre-Océan* of 1914 is one of the most successful aesthetically. The results are intriguing, but hardly presage the revolution in thinking – from analytical-discursive to 'synthetico-ideographic' – to which Apollinaire aspired,

Juan Gris, *The Smoker*, 1913
The most theoretically inclined of the Cubists, Gris' works are much more densely organized than those of Picasso and Braque – there is no sense of improvisation here, and the forms lock together around an underlying 'architectural' framework, which was often established first with drawing instruments.

Cézanne turns a bottle into a cylinder... I make a bottle, a particular bottle out of a cylinder. Cézanne works towards architecture, I work away from it.

Juan Gris

and the Western habit of reading from left to right and top to bottom, makes attempts at such 'visual poetry' problematic.

Cubism overthrew principles of pictorial composition which had been unquestioned for almost 500 years since the Renaissance discovery – or rediscovery – of linear perspective. In the same half dozen years before 1914, the harmonic, rhythmic and formal foundations of Western music were subjected to a similarly searching scrutiny. Tonality was the first aspect to be questioned. The increasing chromaticism in the work of Richard Wagner, Richard Strauss and others had cast doubt on the power of diatonic harmony to sustain musical movement, and atonality was tentatively broached (and rejected) by the elderly Franz Liszt, Gustav Mahler and Strauss. It was finally embraced by Schoenberg in the summer of 1908 in his first Expressionist works – the last two movements of the *Second String Quartet* (1907–8) and the cycle of fifteen settings of poems from Stefan George's *Das Buch der hängenden Gärten* ('The book of the Hanging Gardens', 1908–9). For Schoenberg, the move into atonality was an inevitable consequence of the work of his immediate predecessors, but in taking it he said it felt as if he had 'fallen into an ocean of boiling water . . . it burned not only my skin, it burned also internally'. In the *Three Piano Pieces* and *Five Orchestral Pieces* of 1909 Schoenberg worked both atonally and without the support of texts, which had helped structure his first atonal works. He described the *Five Orchestral Pieces* as the antithesis of symphonic form: 'there is no

architecture and no build-up,' he said, 'just a colourful, uninterrupted variation of colours, rhythms and moods'. The intention, according to the programme notes for their 1912 performance in London under Henry Wood, was 'to express all that dwells in us subconsciously like a dream'. To Schoenberg, such intensely personal content demanded atonality and freedom from the burdens of the tradition from which it had grown.

Although Schoenberg's works baffled many of his early listeners, they never prompted the uproarious reception accorded the first performance of Stravinsky's *Rite of Spring* by Sergei Diaghilev's Ballet Russe in Paris in May 1913. Derisive laughter greeted the first bars of the prelude, and the theatre soon dissolved into chaos, the première entering Modernist lore as one of the great provocations of bourgeois taste. Diaghilev's choreography – which Stravinsky himself thought 'laboured and barren' – may have been as responsible as the score, but it was the music which became the subject of intense debate. Stravinsky turned to rhythm – regarded as the poor relation of melody and harmony in Western music since the Renaissance – as a new motivating power in the search for formal means to match the *Rite*'s pagan scenario. Nowhere was the rhythmic development more compelling than in the final 'Sacrificial Dance', in which a young girl dances herself to death, and a glance at the score makes the basic structure clear even to someone with only a passing knowledge of musical notation. The music is built from 'cells' of notes which pay scant attention to conventional bar structures and demand frequent changes of time signature – traditional notation seems to be stretched almost beyond its limits. The rhythmical structure is immensely sophisticated, but the effect is of the unleashing of primitive forces through an insistent, pounding energy: if Picasso's *Demoiselles d'Avignon* can be said to have an equivalent in music, this is surely it.

The furore over Stravinsky's *Rite* largely overshadowed the Ballet Russe's performance the same month of Claude Debussy's *Jeux*. Having announced the tentative arrival of modern music with the opening flute solo of his *Prélude à l'après-midi d'un faune'* (1892–4), Debussy now proposed a new formal structure, free of the traditional requirement of continuous evolution. The music is composed as a matrix against which the movements and evanescent emotions of a group of young people at a tennis party are represented by themes which emerge, develop and are then either reabsorbed into the background or suddenly interrupted and extinguished. Debussy had hinted at a structure akin to this in the

Is it not our duty to find a symphonic means to express our time, one that evokes the progress, the daring and the victories of modern days? The century of the aeroplane deserves its music. Claude Debussy

second movement of *La Mer* (1903–5), which was almost all 'matrix'. *Jeux* may have appeared less unsettling than Stravinsky's *Rite*, but it was every bit as radical.

Simplistic comparisons with other arts can be misleading, but in the case of Wassily Kandinsky, often credited with being the first painter to arrive at total abstraction, the parallel between painting and music was central to his work. He wrote to Schoenberg in January 1911 that 'the independent life of the individual voices in your compositions is exactly what I am trying to find in my paintings' and suggested that the way forward lay in 'dissonances in *art*'. A passionate Theosophist, Kandinsky thought art could play a vital role in preparing people for the impending millennium by teaching them to see 'spiritually'. Such beliefs were reinforced by his own synaesthesia: when he heard sounds he frequently also saw intense colours. Wagner's *Lohengrin*, he recalled, embodied 'the whole impact of the hour of dusk. I saw all the colours in my mind's eye. Wild, almost insane lines drew themselves before me.' He could have been describing one of his paintings, and a fellow Russian, the composer Alexander Skryabin, sought to present just such parallels by combining music and coloured light in *Prometheus* (1910). In his celebrated essay *Concerning the Spiritual in Art* (written in 1910, but not published for two years), Kandinsky advised against total abstraction. In the absence of 'spiritual qualities', he thought abstract art would end in mere decoration. But it was also in 1910, by his own account, that he had a revelation of its potential when, returning to his studio, he did not recognize the work on the easel: it had been turned upside-down – but was still 'of extraordinary beauty, glowing with an inner radiance'.

In the years 1910–14 Kandinsky executed three main kinds of paintings: *Impressions*, which look abstract but were reputedly based on direct experience; *Improvisations*, abstractions which apparently welled up from his inner life; and finally *Compositions*, spontaneous arrangements of colour and line fitted into a predetermined design – they may look casual, but were the result of careful planning and execution. It is anyone's guess – and quite beside the point – just when he achieved a fully abstract work, and all his best paintings of this period glow with an inner energy, neither enhanced nor diminished by the Theosophical mumbo-jumbo he wove around them. His attempts to demonstrate direct correspondences between feeling and form – a staple of Expressionist theory, as of Symbolism before it – led him after the War to try to develop a symbolic language of colour and shape, and he was no doubt encouraged in this

Left above: Pavel Janák, Design for a Facade, 1912
Left centre: Josef Chochol, Villa, Prague-Vysehrad, 1913
Left below: Josef Gocár, Dressing Table, 1912–13
Cubism had an impact throughout Europe, and Czech designers were the most energetic in trying to turn it to architectural ends. The results, however, were rarely convincing: they focused on Cubism's most obvious feature – faceted planes – but its real lessons lay in the handling of space, and were not assimilated until after the War.

NORTHAMPTON COLLEGE LIBRARY

direction by teaching at the Bauhaus. But in the pre-War years Kandinsky's articulation of an Expressionist aesthetic, based on the artist as a visionary seer who becomes the medium of change, amounted to a new religion of art. Widely shared, it was anticipated by the founders of the first modern Expressionist movement, Die Brücke, which was formed in Dresden in 1905 by four young architecture students, Ernst Ludwig Kirchner, Fritz Bleyl, Erich Heckel and Karl Schmidt-Rottluff.

The manifesto for Die Brücke, written and engraved in wood by Kirchner (who would later do the same for the Bauhaus), called on youth to join them in creating 'freedom of life and movement against the long-established older forces' and concluded with the ringing declaration that 'everyone belongs with us who, directly and without dissimulation, expresses that which drives him to create.' Expressionism is a recurring condition in German art; what distinguished the members of Die Brücke was a peculiarly modern anguish in face of the anxieties created by the industrial city and mass society, by general moral decline and the void left by the Death of God. In *The Metropolis and Mental Life*, the great sociologist Georg Simmel wrote about the 'intensification of nervous stimulation' afflicting the city-dweller, and in Kirchner's canvases we encounter images of the resulting psychological disorientation which was to loom large in the Expressionist films of the 1920s. Berlin became the focus of Expressionist art in 1910 when Herwarth Walden started the publishing

house and journal *Der Sturm*, followed by a gallery of the same name two years later. Walden's first exhibition consisted of a one-man show of the Austrian, Oskar Kokoschka, and of the *Blaue Reiter* group in Munich. In the following months he brought to Berlin work by many of the most radical artists across Europe, and his journal published Futurist manifestoes, excerpts from Kandinsky's 'Concerning the Spiritual in Art', and writings by such people as Guillaume Apollinaire and Fernand Léger. Despite Paris's prestige, the Der Sturm gallery become the liveliest centre of Modernist art in Europe.

In the immediate pre-War years there were surprisingly close links between German Expressionism and its apparent antithesis, the conservative rationalism of the Werkbund. The architect Bruno Taut, for example, acted as an advisor to the Werkbund-inspired *Deutsche Gartenstadtgesellschaft* (German Garden City Association) whilst being active in Walden's Sturm circle. In Taut's eyes both movements were manifestations of a historicist understanding of the new *Zeitgeist* – the one reformist, politically committed and practical, the other avant-gardist and idealistic. The two sides of Taut's architectural personality found expression in the Falkenberg estate (1912–14), a model development realized according to garden-city principles in which he sought to recover the 'lost tradition of coloured architecture' (brightly coloured stucco would remain a feature of his later Modernist work); and in the Expressionist Glashaus built for the 1914 Werkbund

Wassily Kandinsky,
***Dream Improvisation*, 1913**
Amongst the first to move to wholly abstract painting, Kandinsky said that his *Improvisations* were based on images welling up from his inner life, although the carefully planned *Compositions* of the same period look almost as improvised. A keen Theosophist, he believed his abstract images embodied a new language of emotion corresponding to our innermost feelings.

Exhibition at Cologne. Sponsored by the glass industry, the pavilion was inspired by Paul Scheerbart's ideas – his utopian novel *Glasarchitektur* was also published in 1914. Taut's magazine *Frühlicht* (Dawn's Light) formed a focus for Expressionist architects and in it he declared that every house should be built as 'a gown for the soul': the pavilion's form and its use of coloured glass and mosaics created a markedly religious aura, and the natural light effects were heightened by a mechanical kaleidoscope. The cupola's geometry appeared organic – pine cone or fly's eye? – and rose from a vestigial frieze into which were incised fourteen aphorisms by Scheerbart including 'Listen to my joyful sermon: / A house of glass stays free of vermin' and 'Glass brings us the new age / Brick culture only does us harm.'

Kandinsky and the German Expressionists were by no means alone in holding a quasi-religious view of art – indeed similar ideas were widespread in the avant-garde. At the *Section d'Or* exhibition of Cubism in 1912, Apollinaire identified a group he called the Orphic Cubists, and in his book *Les Peintres cubistes* he defined Orphism as 'the art of painting new structures out of elements that have not been borrowed from the visual sphere but have been created entirely by the artist himself' – like Orpheus's music, 'it is pure art'. Apollinaire's definition was so general, and the artists he included so diverse – Delaunay, Léger, Duchamp, Picabia and, probably, Frantisek Kupka – that it was not of great help in clarifying matters. But all the Orphists, in their different ways, saw the world as composed of dynamic forces rather than stable objects in static space – Bergson and modern physics both supported such a view – and Apollinaire believed this change in attitude was matched by a change in human consciousness. The Orphists, he argued, thought that man, displaced from the centre of creation, should seek fusion with a 'universal force' – the precise nature of which, however, varied. For Kupka, immersed in Eastern mysticism and modern science, it was a mystical life-force based on Theosophical ideas; for Delaunay and Léger, like the Futurists, it was the dynamism of modern life; for Picabia, it was an inner psychic dynamism (which later led him to Dada and Surrealism).

Kupka was the first of the Orphists to go fully abstract, in his *Discs of Newton* series begun in late 1911. Using a scientific colour chart, he sequenced his colours to suggest movement; the intersecting, dispersing and 'rotating' discs evoking by turns atoms, or the solar system, or the propagation of light, or ancient religious imagery. Whatever Kupka intended, they certainly look 'cosmic', and like so much abstract art, were open to many interpretations, and readily reducible to a decorative formula. Robert and Sonia Delaunay's works resembled Kupka's for a while, although it is not certain if they had met as early as 1911. Robert Delaunay began his *Sun, Moon, Simultaneous* series in 1913, with the circular radio waves from his beloved Eiffel Tower as a metaphor of the infinite expansion of human consciousness. 'Simultaneity' was an obsession of the

Below: Bruno Taut, Glass Pavilion, Cologne, 1914 (temporary)
Sponsored by the German glass industry and built for the Werkbund's Cologne Exhibition, this pavilion was one of the most remarkable examples of Expressionist architecture. Taut and his writer-friend Paul Scheerbart saw glass as the harbinger of a new civilization, and the pavilion's interior (below right) was bathed in coloured light to evoke a religious aura.

Delaunays: their aim was to express the mind's grasp of many things and thoughts at once, and they constructed their pictures from 'simultaneous contrasts' between colours. Apollinaire considered Robert's *The Cardiff Team* (1913) to be the best example of simultaneity in painting (his prize in music went to Stravinsky's *Rite*). Sonia used the idea decoratively as well – her *Simultanée* fabrics and clothes, begun in 1913, became highly fashionable in the 1920s. Robert claimed to have discovered universal principles of colour applicable to painting, clothes and interiors – the first of several systems for the design of 'total environments' based on abstract painting.

Belief in the religious role of the new art was not confined to Expressionist circles – indeed it was central to the work of that seemingly most austere and 'rational' of painters, the Dutchman Piet Mondrian. His work, too, was sustained by Theosophical thought (he joined the Society in 1909) and his belief that matter was inimical to spiritual enlightenment was one of several pointers leading towards total abstraction. In Holland he experimented with Symbolist, Impressionist and Fauve manners, and soon after arriving in Paris in 1911 took up Cubism, then at its most vigorous. His *Tree* paintings show how progressive abstractions from a more or less naturalistic starting-point (a Fauvist painting of an apple tree in this case) could arrive at almost totally non-figurative conclusions. He did the same in the *Pier and Ocean* series, with the process of abstraction going further and the paintings acquiring titles like *Composition No. 10* (1915). The pictorial elements were reduced to patches of colour and short horizontal and vertical lines, creating a field of flickering crosses uncannily evocative of the sea. As a good Theosophist Mondrian would have known that Mme Blavatsky elaborated a theory of the orthogonal, based on 'the celestial perpendicular' and 'terrestrial horizontal base line', and this juxtaposition formed the basis of his post-War development of that wholly abstract style which became one of the iconic expressions of Modernism.

For Mondrian, as for so many other painters coming to maturity either side of the First World War, Cubism provided the key to progress – so great was its influence, that it is probably true to say that virtually no serious young painter was untouched by it. But Cubism remained essentially a movement within the visual arts. Expressionism was more far-reaching but less coherent – it became a generic term for a wide range of loosely related activities and practitioners in painting, music, theatre, literature and architecture. The first avant-garde movement with aspirations to change the whole of life –

Opposite: Bruno Taut, Glass Pavilion, Cologne, 1914 (temporary)
Taut made every effort to use glass throughout his pavilion, and the marvellous glass-block stairs have been widely emulated by later designers.

Above: Sonia Delaunay, Colour plate from *Compositions Couleurs Idées*, 1931
Although Robert Delaunay envisaged his colour schemes being used on fabric and in interiors, it was Sonia who developed the idea – her *Simultanée* fabrics and clothes became highly fashionable in the 1920s.

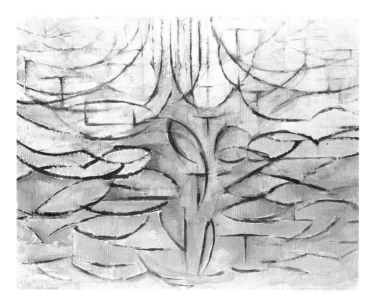

art, society, morality, religion – was conceived in Italy, and, in one of the century's greatest pieces of public relations, was born on 20 February 1909 on the front page of Europe's leading newspaper, *Le Figaro*. Among the usual miscellany of news stories, readers were confronted by a long item entitled '*Le Futurisme*' and containing details of 'The Founding and Manifesto of Futurism'. Although written in the plural, it had one author, Filippo Tommaso Marinetti. Heir to a fortune – which he spent liberally backing Futurist activities and escapades – and a brilliant propagandist, Marinetti held degrees in literature and law. In private he was apparently an obedient son and loving husband and father – but in public he dubbed himself the 'caffeine of Europe', and promoted the most provocative artistic and cultural ideas with unprecedented ferocity and ingenuity.

The *Figaro* article described in tumultuous, allegorical prose a night of 'frenzied scribbling' followed by a joy-ride in three cars, 'crushing watchdogs against doorsteps, curling them under our burning tyres like collars under a flatiron', and ending in a desperate plunge into a 'maternal ditch' to avoid oncoming cyclists. This allegory of modernity (which might well remind English readers of the speed-crazed Mr Toad of *The Wind in the Willows*) announced a movement dedicated to 'sing the love of danger' and 'affirm . . . the beauty of speed. A racing car whose hood is adorned with great pipes, like serpents of explosive breath – a roaring car that seems to ride on grapeshot – is more beautiful than the *Victory of Samothrace*.' The love of danger and speed are compounded by the determination to 'glorify war – the world's only hygiene – militarism, patriotism, the destructive gesture of freedom-bringers, beautiful ideas worth dying for, and contempt of woman.' As he had hoped, Marinetti's *coup de presse* provoked a scandal: although most people were baffled by his elaborate allegories, in Italy there was general stupefaction that the article could have appeared in such a prestigious paper, and anger at the assault on its 'museum culture', which the Futurists intended to free of 'its foul gangrene of professors, archaeologists, guides and antiquarians.' But what are we to make of this extraordinary document now?

Firstly, not even its most shocking ideas were new. In the latter years of the nineteenth century French Symbolist writers cultivated an aesthetics of violence and Georges Sorel, among others, advocated it as a legitimate political weapon; in Italy, Gabriele d'Annunzio had written in comparable terms about war, the celebration of violence and the beauty of flight. But no one had put these ideas together so forcefully and publicly. A likely inspiration for part of the manifesto was a 1907 publication by the writer and journalist Mario Morasso. Entitled 'The New Mechanical Aspect of the World', it contained similar eulogies of speed and of the racing car as 'the means for the most beautiful gesture of energy, the gesture of domination and of velocity' and (the real giveaway) it used Samothrace as an image of speed. But tracing sources does nothing to lessen the shock. Secondly, the article has to be read in

Opposite above: Piet Mondrian, *The Red Tree*, 1908
Opposite centre: Piet Mondrian, *The Grey Tree*, 1912
Opposite below: Piet Mondrian, *Blossoming Apple Tree*, 1912
This sequence illustrates beautifully how Mondrian moved from conventional figuration towards total abstraction. *The Red Tree* (top) was painted in Holland, and the later two canvases after moving to Paris in 1911 where he immediately came under the influence of Cubism.

Below: Piet Mondrian, *Composition in Black and White; Pier and Ocean*, 1915
Mondrian arrived at his *Pier and Ocean* pictures by a similar process to that seen in the *Tree* series. The results initially seem to be non-figurative and yet, once the title is known, the canvases appear as uncannily effective evocations of the flickering surface of the sea.

P. MONDRIAAN. 15.

**Cover of *Le Figaro*,
20 February, 1909**
The Italian Filippo Tommaso
Marinetti managed to publish
the Founding Manifesto of the
most aggressive of all the early
Modernist avant-garde
movements, Futurism, as a
news report on the front page
of one of Europe's leading
newspapers, *Le Figaro*. Its
readers, not surprisingly, were
bemused by this *coup de presse*.

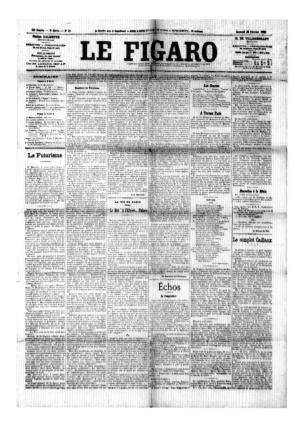

The art of becoming, the perishable, the transitory and the expendable. Filippo Tommaso Marinetti on Futurism

its Italian context. United only in 1872, Italy had achieved the fastest economic growth in Europe at the turn of the century. Vast dams and hydroelectric power stations, built to harness the Alpine torrents, symbolized this progress, but artistically there was no equivalent: the glorious past weighed heavily, and Marinetti's shock tactics were intended to drag Italian culture, kicking and screaming if necessary, into the twentieth century. But however much his attitudes can be understood tactically, there is much in the Futurist rhetoric of violence and war which remains repugnant, and later helped fuel the ideology of Fascism. Trench-warfare was hardly the heroic cleansing and 'mathematical and aesthetic intoxication' Marinetti envisaged, and the First World War claimed the lives of thirteen members of the Futurist movement. Marinetti's politics can be seen as coming from either the radical left or right, but his anarchism precluded long-term involvement with any state or party – courted by Mussolini, he moved in and out of Fascism – just as a Puritan streak prevented his being a thoroughgoing anarchist.

Marinetti already had literary allies, and among the first to respond to the manifesto were the painters Umberto Boccioni, Carlo Carrà, Luigi Russolo, Giacomo Balla and Gino Severini. The 'Manifesto of Futurist Painters' duly followed on 11 February 1910 in Marinetti's magazine *Poesia*: it was not as auspicious as *Le Figaro*, but on 18 March the piece was declaimed in Turin to an audience of three thousand – or so the Futurists claimed. The manifesto was stronger on rhetoric against dead art – 'the neurasthenic cultivation of hermaphrodite archaism which they rave about in Florence' – than on what Futurist paintings might be like. This was remedied two months later when *Poesia* carried the 'Technical Manifesto of Futurist Painting'. The key was 'universal dynamism', a synthesis of several strands of contemporary thought, above all Bergson, who had written that 'any division of matter into independent bodies with determined outlines is artificial'. The manifesto reads like a checklist of future paintings: 'a running horse has not four legs, but twenty, and their movements are triangular'; 'to paint a human figure you must not paint it, you must render the whole of its surrounding atmosphere'; 'space no longer exists: the street pavement, soaked by rain beneath the glare of electric lamps, becomes immensely deep'; 'our bodies penetrate the sofas upon which we sit, and the sofas penetrate our bodies.' The Futurists found help in formulating these from Paul Souriau's *L'esthétique du mouvement* (1889), but the problem of

actually painting a convincing image of movement, which did not end up looking like a multi-limbed Hindu god, still had to be faced.

It proved far from easy. The chronophotographs of Etienne-Jules Marey, cinematography and X-ray images provided clues, and the fusion of figure and environment had a precedent in Medardo Rosso's work, a sculptor whose reputation the Futurists revived. But their early attempts, using a Divisionist technique and Symbolist imagery, were far from convincing. In 1911 Severini returned from Paris with news of the solution – Cubism. Marinetti promptly paid for Boccioni, Carrà and Russolo to visit there in November that year to see the revolution at first hand. On their return they worked feverishly for three months preparing an exhibition, which visited Paris, London, Berlin, Amsterdam, Zurich, Vienna and Budapest: with Marinetti's backing, Futurism could travel. In Paris, Apollinaire damned with faint praise: 'The Futurists . . . will teach our young painters to have more daring, for without daring the Futurists would never have shown such imperfect paintings.' London's *Pall Mall Gazette* announced a 'Nightmare exhibition' and the *Daily Express* hailed 'The New Terror'. Marinetti promptly declared London a Futurist city and was interviewed in all the press – he understood before most that in a media-saturated world the only bad publicity is no publicity. The tour netted 350 articles and 11,000 francs

of sales: it hardly mattered if the paintings did not justify all the attention, and once the artists had time to assimilate Cubism, their work gained in strength.

Balla's famous *Dynamism of a Dog on a Leash* (1912) delightfully, if rather literally, expresses the idea of paths of movement, and Boccioni's *Charge of the Lancers* (1915) is one of many convincing images of speed – and of the aestheticization of war. Boccioni produced a succession of powerful images of the dynamism of the modern city, such as *The City Rises* (1910–11) and *The Street Enters the House* (1911), where Cubist influence is obvious, as it is in Carrà's *papiers collés* such as *The Chase* (1914) and *Interventionist Demonstration* (1914) – an outstanding work in the medium. The Futurists' representations of speed frequently came close to total abstraction and towards the end of 1912 Balla began to paint the wholly non-figurative works he called *Iridescent Compenetrations*. At first sight their interlinking triangles look like kaleidoscopic refractions of Vienna Secession decoration – to which he was undoubtedly indebted. The Bergsonian-sounding 'compenetration' was based on the Theosophical idea of 'mercurial' integration, and Balla intended the simultaneous presence and harmony of colours as microcosms of cosmic structures. It was a heavy load for a mere 'surface covered with colours arranged in a certain order' to carry, but characteristic, as we have seen, of the claims made for the first wave of abstract art. Boccioni also produced sculpture. *Development of a*

Giacomo Balla, *Dynamism of a Dog on a Leash*, 1912
For the Futurists, movement was the essence of modern life and its representation the artist's greatest challenge. This charming image by Balla is one of the most successful early attempts, although hardly typical in its gentle subject-matter.

Giacomo Balla, *Flight of the Swallows*, 1913
The challenge of representing movements through space on a static, two-dimensional canvas obsessed the Futurists. None was more successful than Balla, who progressed from pictures based on cars or birds in flight to abstract images of 'dynamism' itself.

Bottle in Space (1912) and the striding figure entitled *Unique Form of Continuity in Space* (1913) have attracted much praise, although to me the latter now looks too like a science fiction warrior and is difficult to take seriously. More radical was *Dynamism of a Racing Horse + House* – all that survives is a partial reconstruction of an unfinished work. Boccioni was aiming at 'a complete fusion of the environment with the object' by means of the 'interpenetration of planes' but its immense promise was unfulfilled. Boccioni died in 1916 after being thrown from a horse: a Futurist death of sorts.

Fine as some of the paintings and sculptures are, the historical importance of Futurism rests less on the quality of particular works than on the range of the movement's ideas and influence: it defined so much of what we now think of as 'Modern Art'. Marinetti effectively invented the avant-garde movement – with its obligation, as Ezra Pound put it, to go ahead of its age and transform it – and in this he was emulated by Dada, Surrealism and a host of others great and small. The Futurists also had ideas about seemingly everything. The painter, writer and pilot Felice Azari took choreography into the sky, inventing daring new aerobatic manoeuvres and claiming established ones for a new Futurist art which he called 'expressive flight'. Theatre being Italy's most popular entertainment, Marinetti invented the Futurist Soirée, anticipating aspects of later performance art and 'happenings'. The Soirées combined an uproarious mix of theatre, music, political rally, discussion and, with luck, riot. 'Scorn of the public' was their guiding principle, vigorous abuse the hoped-for acclaim. These evenings quickly became famous, and local greengrocers and fruit stalls did good business in ammunition. Marinetti was a brilliant public speaker, and if his words provoked arrest, all the better – there was nothing like a lively trial to ensure publicity. There was even a Futurist Cuisine, which naturally took issue with spaghetti!

Marinetti's talent for proclaiming a manifesto was matched by his lyrical prose and teeming imagination, and he had an uncanny ability to conjure up visions of absolute modernity. Here he is in 1913 describing his Variety Theatre:

> . . . we Futurists are *young gunners out for fun*, as we proclaimed in our manifesto, 'Let's kill the Moonshine', fire + fire + light against moonshine and against old firmaments war every night great cities brandish electric signs immense negro face (30 metres high + 150 metres height of the building + 180 metres) open close open close golden eye 3 metres high *smoke smoke Manoli smoke Manoli cigarettes* woman in a blouse . . . two horses (30 metres tall) roll golden balls with their hoofs *Gioconda purgative waters* crisscross of *trrrr trrrrr* Elevated *trrrr trrrrr* overhead hoo-hoo-hooting whissstle ambulance sirens and firetrucks transformation of the streets into rich corridors guide push logical necessity the crowd towards trepidation + laughter + music-hall uproar *Folies-Bergère empire crème-éclipse* tubes of mercury red red red blue violet huge letter-eels of gold purple diamond fire Futurist challenge to the weepy night . . .

It makes Baudelaire's boulevards sound distinctly bucolic – we could almost be in Tokyo or on the Las Vegas strip – and is a fine example of text-as-collage.

In the 'Technical Manifesto of Futurist Literature' (1912) Marinetti announced numerous inventions including *paroliberismo* or 'words-in-freedom', a concept refined in two further manifestoes and implemented in his novel/poem/reportage of the siege of Adrianopole entitled *Zang Tumb Tuum*, with which he apparently delighted audiences in London, Berlin and Rome. Words-in-freedom was an amalgam of ideas developed in recent French literature and dismissed by some as nothing more than an 'accelerated impressionism'. But the presentation was revolutionary, made up of a mix of different typefaces, sizes and graphic devices. The medium became the message more completely than ever before, with the layout of the poem on the page intended to give the reader an immediate insight into its meaning. In this way, words-in-freedom looked forward to concrete and visual poetry, to modern graphic and advertising design and even, in their explosiveness, to the postmodernism of such as Neville Brody.

Marinetti recruited the composer Francesco Balilla Pratella in 1910, but Pratella's musical heart lay elsewhere and it fell to the painter Russolo to write the manifesto *The Art of Noises* which advocated breaking the barrier between tempered tones and the sounds of nature and machines – Russolo determined that every 'sound-noise' had a pitch, and looked to the day when factories would become great orchestras of noise. He also invented *intonarumori*, fiendish hand-cranked machines capable of generating and modifying the pitch and rhythm of assorted exploding, crackling, buzzing, rubbing and other sounds. Demonstrated before the

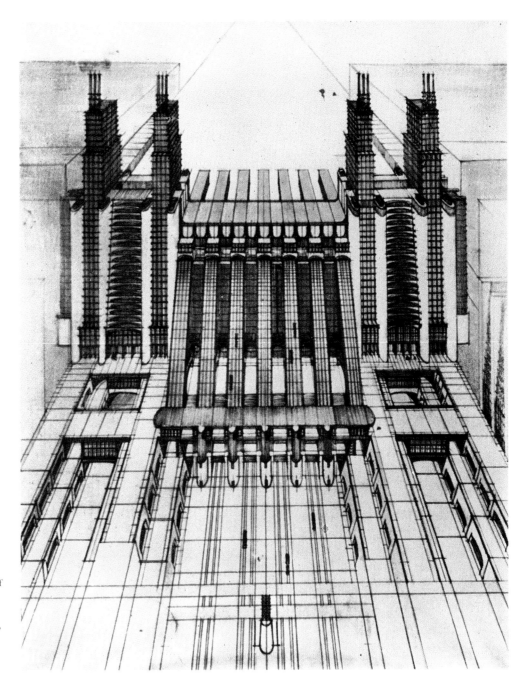

Antonio Sant'Elia, Airport and Railway Station with Elevators and Funiculars over Three-levelled Street, 1914
Stylistically, Sant'Elia's vision of the future city owed much to Otto Wagner, and functionally to drawings of Grand Central Station and 'cities of tomorrow' published in America, but the synthesis was unique and compelling.

We are no longer the people of the cathedrals and of the tribune, but rather of large hotels, train stations, of immense streets, colossal ports, covered markets, luminous arcades.

Antonio Sant' Elia

Marcel Duchamp, *Nude Descending a Staircase No 2*, 1912

Based on the French scientist Etienne-Jules Marey's sequential photographs, Duchamp's *Nude* became a canonical image of Modernism thanks to the notoriety it achieved as the focus of ridicule ('an explosion in a shingle factory' was a favourite description) when it appeared in the Armory Show in New York in 1913.

War to that mixed reaction of public ridicule and peer acclaim which the *avant-garde* relished, they were later enthusiastically received at a performance in Paris in 1921. By then machine-music was in vogue – Honegger's orchestral evocation of a train, *Pacific 231*, for example, appeared in 1923. Developments in electronics made Russolo's *intonarumori* redundant, and his ideas slipped from view, only to surface again in 1948 when Pierre Schaeffer unwittingly reinvented them as *musique concrète*.

Uncharacteristically, Marinetti failed to spot the propaganda potential of cinema, which quickly became the most popular and influential medium of the first half of the century. But there was a manifesto on cinema, signed by Marinetti and others, which declared the 'immobile book' *passéist*, the ultimate Futurist put-down, and proclaimed film to be the multi-expressive medium of the future. Only stills survive of *Vita Futurista*, the most radical of Futurist films; it included the neutralist's, interventionist's, creditor's and debtor's walks, which sound uncannily like proposals of the 'Ministry of Silly Walks' from the British cult television comedy *Monty Python's Flying Circus*. Similarly, the section entitled 'Argument between a foot, a hammer and an umbrella' was a forerunner of the Surrealists' rediscovery of the Comte de Lautréamont's now celebrated account of the 'chance encounter of an umbrella and a sewing machine on a dissecting table'.

Marinetti's Founding Manifesto contained a stirring evocation of the modern city, with its 'vibrant nightly fervour of arsenals and shipyards blazing with violent electric moons' and 'greedy railway stations that devour smoke-plumed serpents', and overhead the 'sleek flight of planes whose propellers chatter in the wind like banners and seem to cheer like an enthusiastic crowd', and he became increasingly concerned that no architect had appeared to further this vision. In 1914 this gap was filled when Carlo Carrà managed to persuade his friend Antonio Sant'Elia to join the Futurist cause. Sant'Elia shared a studio in Milan, the centre of Futurist activity, with Mario Chiattone, who followed his lead. Earlier that year Sant'Elia had exhibited drawings of a 'New City' at the Nuove Tendenze exhibition, together with an explanatory text – entitled the *Messaggio* – which amounted to a manifesto. It demanded a radically new architecture and a total rupture with past styles, stating: 'We are no longer the people of the cathedrals and of the tribune, but rather of large hotels, train stations, of immense streets, colossal ports, covered markets, luminous arcades.' The words were nothing new – but the drawings were sensational. Various sources have been tracked down: the *Wagnerschule* (Sant'Elia had a well-thumbed book of drawings by Wagner's students); a step-back apartment block by Henri Sauvage and Charles Sarazin; 'cities of the future' by Eugène Hénard and Harvey Wiley Corbett featuring multi-level streets; drawings of Grand Central Station and 'The Future Circulation and the Cloudscrapers of New York'. But Sant'Elia's synthesis was his own and was utterly compelling – remarkable for an architect in his mid-twenties. His drawings are among the first convincing images of an architecture which demands the description 'modern'. Delighted with his young architect, Marinetti republished the *Messaggio* as *Architettura Futurista Manifesto* with only minor revisions – 'futurist' replacing 'modern', 'new' etc – and a different final paragraph, which Sant'Elia thought ridiculous, but allowed for its shock value. It declared that 'the fundamental characteristic of Futurist architecture will be impermanence and transience. *Things will endure less than us. Every generation must build its own city*.' Time has proved that Marinetti was nearer the mark than any architect in 1914 would have dared contemplate – and many still choose to ignore. Sadly, Sant'Elia did not have the opportunity to realize his promise: he was another Futurist killed in the War.

The Futurist interest in the total environment culminated in the modestly titled 1915 manifesto *Futurist Reconstruction of the Universe* by Fortunato Depero and Giacomo Balla. It proposed the abolition of all disciplinary boundaries, and proclaimed a global aspiration to address all aspects of human creativity – only the Russian movements of the early post-Revolutionary period were as all-embracing. Depero and Balla go on to describe various 'dynamic plastic complexes' such as 'Futurist toys' and 'metallic animals', and a range of 'interventions' such as: 'plastic moto-noise concert in space', 'aerial concerts above the city', 'transformable clothes', 'phono-moto-plastic advertisement', 'a building in noise-ist transformable style'. Embracing the ephemeral as the inescapable condition of modernity, the images anticipate the 'electrographic landscapes' of today's great cities or the spectacular stagesets created for tours by major rock bands such as Pink Floyd and The Rolling Stones.

Futurism had outposts across Europe, and as far away as Mexico and Japan – Marinetti's influence spread widely, and he was always alert to any like-minded groups who might be co-opted. It flourished in the heady atmosphere of pre-Revolutionary Russia, where

Roger Fry and Joseph Kallenborn (Omega Workshops), Giraffe marquetry cupboard, 1916
Even the angular style of England's version of Futurism – Vorticism – proved amenable to decorative domestication. Roger Fry, an outstanding critic, became one of the leading proponents of Modernism in Britain.

NORTHAMPTON COLLEGE LIBRARY

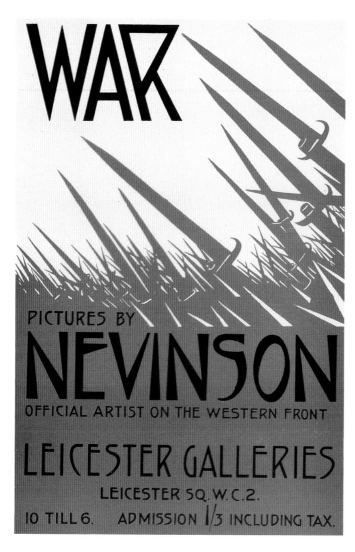

Above left: Poster for 'War Pictures by C. R. W. Nevinson', c. 1920
The work of Siegfried Sassoon, Wilfred Owen and other young war poets has become well known, that of the official war artists less so: Nevinson was one of several Modernists to serve in this capacity.

Above right: Edward Wadsworth, Poster, 1923
This poster looks back to the aesthetics of Vorticism and depicts a ship painted in the 'dazzle' style of camouflage designed to break up its profile – the technique is said to have been derived from Cubism.

Right: Cover of *Blast*, 1914
Only two issues of the magazine *Blast*, which was published to promote the ideals of Vorticism, England's version of Futurism, ever appeared. Designed and edited by Wyndham Lewis, and printed on spongy paper with dense black ink and coarse typography, it had a lasting impact on graphic design.

the painter David Burliuk organized the founding manifesto – *A Slap in the Face of Public Taste* – in 1912 and 'Futurist' came to mean any progressive art. Several painters, including the pioneer abstractionist Kazimir Malevich, designated themselves Cubo-Futurists. The best-known signatory of the first Russian manifesto was the 20-year-old writer and revolutionary, Vladimir Mayakovsky. Provocative but peaceful, he denounced the Italians as 'men of fights and fists', and was active in creating Kom-Fut (Communist-Futurism) in 1919.

In England, the Vorticists owed a major debt to Futurism. Like their Italian peers they waged war on their cultural heritage – the Victorian legacy weighed as heavily as the Classical tradition in Italy – and tried to define a role for British art as an alternative to Cubism and Expressionism. The term 'Vorticism' was coined by the poet Ezra Pound, but the movement was dominated by its most skilled polemicist, the painter Wyndham Lewis. Where the Futurists represented movement across a shallow Cubist space, the Vorticists aimed at depth – Lewis's paintings can feel almost vertiginous. He edited the only two issues of the magazine *Blast*, which was printed on spongy paper with dense black ink and coarse typography. The ambassador-at-large of Russian Constructivism, El Lissitzky, wrote of it in 1926 as a precursor of the New Typography which revolutionized graphic design in the 1920s and 1930s, but *Blast* in turn owed much to *Lacerba*, a magazine sympathetic to Futurism published in Italy from 1913 to 1915. The most disturbing of all Vorticist works, Jacob Epstein's *The Rock Drill* (1913–14), was completed only in a castrated form, the mildly menacing head and torso being deprived of their legs and phallic drill. Epstein explained its non-completion as follows: 'Here is the armed, sinister figure of tomorrow. No humanity, only the terrible Frankenstein's monster we have made ourselves into. . . . Later I lost my interest in machinery and discarded the drill. I cast in metal only the upper part of the figure.'

In 1913 Kandinsky wrote in his *Reminiscences* that 'painting is a thundering collision of different worlds, intended to create a new world in, and from, the struggles with one another, a new world which is the work of art.' Although the apocalyptic tone was alien to him, Mondrian would have agreed with the sentiment, as would almost all the Modernist artists, composers and writers – the conviction that the Modernist work of art was a 'new world' operating according to its own aesthetic laws was universal. A Modernist painting no longer sought its justification from imitation of the surrounding world, and its light, colour, form and space obeyed only the 'inner laws' of style: similar freedom in terms of content and rigour in terms of technique were, as we have seen, vigorously pursued in the other arts. Freedom lay at the heart of Modernism: artists claimed the right to be true to their inner selves, to ignore outmoded traditions and social mores, to transgress inhibiting academic conventions as they responded to the exhilarating changes around them.

After 1914 the certainties of the Age of Empire, orthodox religion and the Classical arts and sciences gave way to what Eric Hobsbawm has aptly named 'The Age of Extremes', a multivalent and increasingly secular world in which even physicists, after Heisenberg, have to accept uncertainty as a matter of principle. Modernism uncannily anticipated the cataclysmic changes which came in the wake of the Great War and, whilst many of the artistic consequences of the Modernist revolution have still to achieve genuine popularity (and many probably never will), their influence is all around us, not safely sequestered in art

Painting is a thundering collision of different worlds, intended to create a new world in, and from, the struggles with one another, a new world which is the work of art. Wassily Kandinsky

galleries, concert halls and libraries. Architects and designers were quick to embrace the aesthetic ideas explored in the fine arts, and few corners of the everyday world have been unaffected by their endeavours. And even the most inventive exponents of postmodernism depend to a far greater extent than they might care to admit on formal and technical innovations made before 1914. In forging new techniques to represent modernity and defining the role of the avant-garde, the first generation of Modernists wrought the most radical and comprehensive transformation in Western art since the Renaissance, establishing the 'tradition of the new', simultaneously creative and destructive, as a defining characteristic of twentieth-century art.

3

Modern man, who no longer dresses in historical garments but wears modern clothes, also needs a modern home appropriate to him and his time, equipped with all the modern devices of daily use.

Walter Gropius

Opposite: Le Corbusier and Pierre Jeanneret, Villa Savoye, Poissy, 1928–31
The play of sunlight across the geometric forms of the Villa Savoye's ramp and staircase epitomizes Le Corbusier's aesthetic ideal of 'mathematical lyricism'.

Left: Mies van der Rohe, Project for Brick Country House, 1923
Inspired by De Stijl but slightly predating Van Doesburg's Maison Particulière, this was the first plan in which space was defined by free-standing wall-planes, a canonical principle of much subsequent Modernist architecture.

In 1916 the young Dutch painter Theo van Doesburg was demobilized from the army. Looking back, he wrote that the moment seemed right for 'a collective and heroic act of creation', and that nowhere was 'as propitious for the gathering of renewing forces' as the neutral Netherlands. Determined to seize the moment by founding a magazine for progressive art, Van Doesburg managed to win the support of the most important Dutch artist, Piet Mondrian (then back in Holland) and several others, including the architect J. J. P. Oud and the painter Bart van der Leck. Van Doesburg called his magazine and movement *De Stijl* ('The Style'), announcing its birth on 16 June 1917. 'The objective of this little periodical,' he said in his manifesto, 'is to contribute something towards the development of a new sense of beauty.' His modesty was deceptive: Van Doesburg's ambitions could not have been greater. The De Stijl artists wanted to replace the dying 'brown world' of lyricism, vagueness and sentimentality with a brave new 'white world'. In art, this new attitude began with Cézanne, and led through

Above: Bart van der Leck, *Dock Work*, 1916
Van der Leck's experience designing commercial posters is evident in paintings such as this, whose radically simplified forms and bold use of colour greatly impressed Mondrian.

Opposite: Piet Mondrian, *Composition*, 1929
Limitations, it is often said, are the artist's best friend, and within his chosen language of vertical and horizontal lines and the primary colours, Mondrian produced a stream of taut, asymmetrical compositions for more than fifteen years. Even in reproduction, the hand-worked quality of the original can be seen.

Cubism to their own 'elementary construction' or 'neoplasticism'. Although their styles developed independently initially, the artists were united in their reactions to the devastation of the War and in 'the common need for clarity, for certainty and for *order*'.

The Netherlands – unlike nominally neutral Belgium – saw no fighting, but the pre-War optimism had been shattered. Many symbols of progress – motorized vehicles, aeroplanes, airships, radio – had turned into 'works of the devil', since they had made possible a war of unimaginable ferocity. To the members of De Stijl, the old order and its values had manifestly failed. The cult of individualism gave way to a widely felt need for collective organizations – the Netherlands, like Germany, had an attempt at a communist revolution in 1918 – and De Stijl was to be a collective style, promoting a utopian vision. As Mondrian put it: 'Let us not forget that we are at a turning point of civilization,

at the end of everything old; the separation between the two is absolute and definite.' The New Art heralded the New Life, which would eventually subsume it. By 1917, Mondrian, Van der Leck, Vilmos Huszár and Van Doesburg were painting in similar abstract styles using rectangles of colour on a white ground: each contributed to the development of the New Art, but the major creative figure was undoubtedly Mondrian.

Stranded in Holland during the war (having gone home to visit his sick father), Mondrian discovered the ideas of the popular writer Dr M.H.J. Schoenmaekers, whose book *Het Nieuwe Wereldbeeld* (The New Image of the World) became a lifelong companion. Schoenmaekers wrote about the 'plastic regularity' underlying nature – much like the order Mondrian believed he had revealed in trees and the sea. He explained his development as follows: 'Gradually I became aware that Cubism did not accept the logical consequences of its own discoveries; it was not developing abstraction towards its ultimate goal: the expression of pure reality . . . To create pure reality plastically, it is necessary to reduce natural forms to the constant elements of form, and reduce natural colours to primary colour.' Mondrian also discovered Van der Leck who, having designed posters for a company owned by Mrs Kröller-Müller, the well-known patron of modern art, had brought this experience to his painting. The subject matter of *Dock Work* (1916), for example, is represented by planes of pure colour, and has the impact of an advertisement. Inspired by Van der Leck's example, Mondrian distilled his vocabulary down to rectangular colour-planes, then to just the three primaries, plus grey and black. The lattices of colour resemble coloured draughtsboards or stained glass (Van Doesburg was designing stained-glass windows at the time) but by 1920 grey had been eliminated, and Mondrian had arrived at the spacious, asymmetrical compositions of primary colours and black lines that are instantly recognizable as his alone, and widely imitated by later designers as icons of modernity. In the 1960s Courrèges offered women the opportunity to dress as living Mondrians.

Working entirely by eye, Mondrian often took many months to complete his simple-seeming canvases, moving lines back and forth, painting and overpainting in search of precisely the right positions and widths, until they seemed to lock into place and spring to life in what he called '*a dynamic rhythm of determinate mutual relations*'. The words are cumbersome, but we can see what he means in a painting like *Fox Trot A* (1927),

The culture of particular forms is approaching its end. The culture of determined relations has begun. Piet Mondrian

Below left: Gerrit Rietveld, Red and Blue Chair, 1917–18
Although designed before he joined De Stijl, Rietveld's chair became the movement's most potent manifesto. Each element is clearly articulated and none dominates, form is independent of the material and space seems to 'flow' through it. It is less an object *in* space than a materialization *of* space.

Below right: Piet Zwart and Vilmos Huszár, Design for a chair, c. 1919
Chairs, being for symmetrical people, posed a difficult challenge to the dynamic asymmetries of the De Stijl aesthetic. Due to their use of planes rather than sticks, the symmetry of Zwart and Huszár's design is even more apparent than in Rietveld's Red and Blue Chair.

where just three lines on a square canvas turned through forty-five degrees suggest extraordinary tension and spaciousness. There is no illusory 'pictorial space' in a Mondrian: the elements and their interrelationships – what he calls 'the plastic form' – *are* the space, taut as a drumskin. In Cubism, space was as substantial as the objects, but the distinction remained; the Cubists aimed at all-over compositions, but their canvases often faded away around the edges. With Mondrian, form and space are one, the composition is all-over from edge to edge, asymmetrical and de-centred – the antithesis of Classicism, and a paradigm for much Modernist painting, architecture and design.

Mondrian's mature style exemplified the ideals of De Stijl: it was objective, concerned not with the representation of things, but with disclosing what the artists believed were the laws governing nature's basic structure – chief amongst them being the principle of 'dynamic equilibrium'. Mondrian meant this quite literally, likening the search for a universal vision in art to the project of modern science, which was revealing the unity of matter and energy. He was engaged in an aesthetic cosmology, declaring: 'Thus it [De Stijl] interprets in a stronger way the cosmic rhythm which flows through all things.' The new aesthetic order is also a glimpse of the democratic equilibrium of the New Life: 'The New Art grants an independent existence to the line and the colour in the sense of their being neither oppressed nor disfigured by the particular form, but shaping their own limitations . . . Thus society will

equally grant an independent existence . . . to every individual in the future New Life.' And when this society arrived, Mondrian foresaw 'the end of art as a thing separated from our surrounding environment, which is the actual plastic reality. . . . By the unification of architecture, sculpture and painting, a new plastic reality will be created' and 'beauty will have ripened into palpable reality'.

The first emblem of this 'palpable reality' was the Red and Blue Chair, designed and made by Gerrit Rietveld in 1917–18. Rietveld was apprenticed to his cabinet-maker father at the age of twelve, and had taken night school courses in architecture. He did not come into contact with De Stijl until 1919, when his wood-stained chair was painted red and blue, probably at Van Doesburg's suggestion. It is extraordinary that this perfect three-dimensional demonstration of De Stijl principles was produced independently and before Mondrian's mature style had crystallized. Van Doesburg recognized its importance and published it immediately: by adoption it became perhaps De Stijl's most potent manifesto. He prefaced Rietveld's matter-of-fact description with a short note explaining that its 'innovative shape' gives an answer to the question of sculpture in the new interior: 'Chairs, tables, cupboards and other commodities will be the (abstract-realistic) sculptures in our future interiors.' Almost forty years later, in 1957, Rietveld explained his attitude to the object in space as follows: 'If, for a particular purpose, we separate, limit and bring into a human scale a part

of unlimited space, it is (if all goes well) a piece of space brought to life as reality. In this way, a special segment of space has been absorbed into our human system.' Just as Mondrian saw his paintings as revelations of nature's 'dynamic equilibrium', so Rietveld came to see his furniture as the 'condensation' of a universal spatial system.

The Red and Blue Chair is often ridiculed as a three-dimensional Mondrian, a barely-sittable sculpture masquerading as a chair. Its genesis makes clear that this was not Rietveld's intention: his aims were aesthetic *and* practical, and he intended the chair to be perfectly usable, keeping the sitter firmly supported and alert – comfort, as the history of furniture confirms, admits of many interpretations. In terms of the De Stijl aesthetic, the chair's symmetry was problematic – most chairs are bilaterally symmetrical because people are. Rietveld addressed this in the asymmetrical Berlin Chair and End Table in 1923, and also applied De Stijl principles to the Hanging Lamp of 1920, three tubular lamps suspended criss-cross fashion like an advertisement for Cartesian coordinates. These pieces clearly 'work' but they are also outstanding as pure sculptures.

De Stijl acquired some ready-made architecture in the work of Robert van't Hoff and Jan Wils, both signatories of the first manifesto. The leading Dutch architect Berlage was a great admirer of Frank Lloyd Wright, and Wils's buildings were based directly on Wright's Prairie Style. Van't Hoff studied in America and worked for Wright in 1913 and, although his flat-roofed concrete villa at Huis-ter-Heide near Utrecht (1916) is heavily indebted to him, the white stucco finish and grey-painted trims make it altogether more abstract. The architect J. J. P. Oud met van Doesburg in 1916, collaborated with him in developing the De Vonk vacation house and, for the fourth issue of the *De Stijl* magazine (published in 1918), he wrote an enthusiastic appreciation of the Robie House. Wright, Oud argued, had 'laid the basis of a new plasticism in architecture. The masses shoot about in all directions . . . In the interpenetration of planes the way has been cleared for the new plasticism . . .' Despite his admiration, he made little use of these lessons in his own designs, and the extent of Wright's influence on De Stijl is difficult to determine. Through Berlage's influence, Oud was appointed chief architect of Rotterdam in 1918, and three years later broke with De Stijl, opting for the emerging international Modernist style. Several housing schemes in Rotterdam (such as that in the Hook of Holland, 1924–7, and the Kiefhoek,

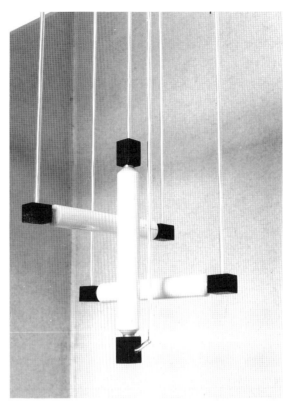

Left: Gerrit Rietveld, Light-fitting from the Schröder House, 1923–4
Rietveld designed the first version of this lamp in 1920. Like the Red and Blue Chair, it is a brilliant distillation of the De Stijl aesthetic, and altogether more dynamic than the version Walter Gropius designed for his office at the Bauhaus in Weimar in 1923 (page 134).

Below: Gerrit Rietveld, End Table, 1923
Sculpturally, this is the most sophisticated of Rietveld's designs – note how the yellow support projects beyond the top, inviting the eye to explore underneath. De Stijl furniture was to be fully three-dimensional, destroying traditional hierarchies between front and back, top and bottom.

Robert van't Hoff, Henny house, Huis-ter-Heide, 1916
Van't Hoff worked for Frank Lloyd Wright in 1913 and this house is clearly indebted to the Prairie Style. But it is far more abstract than anything by Wright, and its abstract style was important to the early development of De Stijl.

Formulating the Future

1927–30) and participation in the Weissenhof exhibition in Stuttgart in 1927 secured his international reputation.

Designing an unmistakably De Stijl building proved more difficult than making paintings or furniture, the breakthrough finally coming in 1923 when Van Doesburg met the young architect Cornelis van Eesteren. They designed two theoretical projects together that year, the Maison Particulière and the Maison d'Artiste. Plans and elevations were expunged of every trace of symmetry and ornament, and the spaces were organized centrifugally – a derivation from Wright's cruciform plans. The structure was skeletal and the non-loadbearing walls, floors and roofs were treated as boldly coloured 'floating' planes. The presentation of the Maison Particulière was especially sensational, and more influential than the design – which Le Corbusier, for one, found 'bitty'. Van Doesburg asked Van Eesteren to make axonometric drawings, seen from above and below, to emphasize the fully three-dimensional nature of the forms and spaces and to suggest weightlessness, and then produced two series of axonometric 'counter-constructions' which captured the essence of the De Stijl vision of a transparent, floating world. These images continue to haunt architects, and when they were exhibited towards the end of 1923 in Léonce Rosenberg's Galerie de l'Effort Moderne, they startled the Parisian avant-garde.

The first De Stijl building was realized in 1924 by Rietveld, working closely with his client, Mrs Truus Schröder-Schräder, who made significant contributions to the revolutionary first floor. The ground floor is conventional but on the first (called simply 'Attic' to get round regulations) the only fixed volumes are the bathroom and stairwell: the rest is one continuous space, made flexibly habitable by sliding panels and built-in furniture, including fold-away beds and tables. There was much talk in the 1920s of time as the 'fourth dimension' of architecture, but the Schröder House was the first transformable interior. Rietveld developed his ideas through intricate models before making production drawings, and the house was a thoroughgoing exercise in Dutch domesticity – down to the bench by the front door and the proliferation of shelves and broad cills – as well as a consummate piece of abstract design. Windows, for example, open only at right angles, completely dissolving corners and avoiding any conflicting diagonals. Constructionally, the house mixed steel and loadbearing construction and lacked the underlying structural discipline basic to the work of architects like Le Corbusier and Mies van der Rohe.

Left: J. J. P. Oud, Café de Unie: colour drawing of facade, 1924
Below: J. J. P. Oud, Café de Unie: vintage photograph, Rotterdam, 1924–5 (destroyed)
As city architect in Rotterdam, Oud found Theo van Doesburg's theoretical ideas difficult to apply in practice and he left the De Stijl movement in 1921. This café was his only overtly De Stijl building. Demolished in 1940, it has recently been reconstructed.

Yet within the De Stijl aesthetic it did not matter how it was made since all elements were treated as abstract coloured planes and lines, and on its completion in 1924 the Schröder House was, quite simply, the most radically innovative building in Europe.

The De Stijl artists made decisive contributions to typography, both directly and through their influence on outsiders, of whom Piet Zwart (an architect by training) was the most important. The first *De Stijl* cover was designed by Vilmos Huszár, but otherwise the magazine was undistinguished typographically. That all changed with the fourth volume, however, when Van Doesburg became interested in typography and introduced several characteristic features of modern practice: vertical as well as horizontal type; layering of words; dynamic, asymmetrical compositions; radically varied type-sizes. He aimed at 'a constructive unity of content and form' and published a series of poems, entitled 'X-images', written under one of his pseudonyms, I.K. Bonset. Drafted a few years before, they now assumed a 'concrete' form – their lineage goes back via the Futurists' words-in-freedom to the *Calligrammes* of Apollinaire. Van Doesburg's work influenced Kurt Schwitters and the Bauhaus, but innovative though it was, possibly his most significant contribution to graphic

design was the publication of El Lissitzky's children's story-book *Of 2 Squares* in 1922, which offered Europe a revelation of the vitality of graphic design in the USSR. Piet Zwart, like the Russians, made inventive use of the diagonal, an almost ubiquitous feature of Modernist typography which had been introduced by architects rather than typographers. The diagonal came naturally to architects, since they were accustomed to working with set-squares and unaware of the difficulty of securing diagonal blocks in traditional type-setting. This is one of many examples where Modernists innovated by stepping across traditional disciplinary boundaries: design superseded craft, and the consequences – especially in architecture – were frequently perceived as unsettling.

Van Doesburg had a restless, inventive mind and an outgoing personality – temperamentally he was Mondrian's opposite, always in search of new stimuli. In 1923 he visited the exhibition of El Lissitzky's *Proun Room* in Berlin and saw in it a way of refreshing the De Stijl aesthetic – this inevitably led to a dispute with Mondrian, who left the movement in 1925. The following year Van Doesburg announced the new concept of 'Elementarism'. It was born, he said, 'partly from a reaction against a too dogmatical and often narrow-minded application of neoplasticism' and 'is based on the neutralization of positive and negative directions by the diagonal and, as far as colour is concerned, by the dissonant.' The diagonal (heresy to Mondrian) represented the dynamism of the new spirit

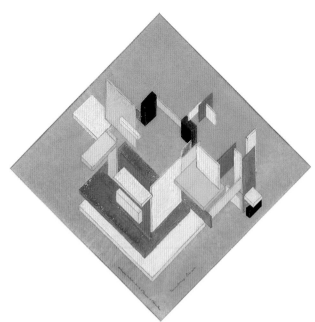

and was seen in full force in the conversion of the Café Aubette (1927–8) in Strasbourg where Van Doesburg set up counter-compositions to the existing rooms – diagonal coloured planes fold across the junctions of wall and ceiling, visually destroying the cubic enclosure.

As a movement, De Stijl was over by the end of the 1920s, its principles being combined with ideas derived from Constructivism, the Bauhaus and other international trends. Living in the Netherlands, its members had a head start and their utopian visions seem at first sight worlds apart from the movement which began in another neutral country, Switzerland.

Right: Theo van Doesburg, 'Counter-Composition', 1924
This is one of many 'Counter-Compositions' based on the Maison Particulière, which Van Doesburg designed with Van Eesteren in 1923. The house and earlier versions of this evocation of an abstract, floating world created a sensation when they were exhibited in Paris in late 1923.

Below: Cornelis van Eesteren, Perspective study for a shopping arcade with a café/restaurant, The Hague, 1924
One of the few professionally trained architects who associated directly with De Stijl, Van Eesteren produced several theoretical studies. Whilst lacking the polemical power of Rietveld's or Van Doesburg's work, this is a persuasive application of De Stijl principles.

Above and overleaf: Gerrit Rietveld and Truus Schröder-Schräder, Schröder House, Utrecht, 1923–4

The Schröder House is a major landmark of modern architecture and completely unlike any building seen before. Mass has given way to floating planes and lines, material textures to abstract coloured surfaces, enclosure to openness and continuity. The house was also eminently habitable, and very Dutch – there was even a welcoming bench by the door.

The first-floor interior of the Schröder House was conceived as a total environment of coloured planes – of painted wood for furniture, doors and windows, and of coloured felt for the floor. The space can be transformed by sliding partitions and by windows which open at right angles to dissolve the corner and change the composition.

A house has to fulfil two purposes. First it is a machine for living in, that is, a machine to provide us with efficient help for speed and accuracy in our work, a diligent and helpful machine which should satisfy all our physical needs: comfort. But it should also be a place conducive to meditation, and, lastly, a beautiful place, bringing much-needed tranquillity to the mind.

Le Corbusier

Right: Theo van Doesburg, *De Stijl* **magazine cover, 1931**

De Stijl's greatest direct impact outside avant-garde circles was in graphic design. The early issues of *De Stijl* were unremarkable, but when Van Doesburg took over he introduced numerous new ideas: vertical as well as horizontal type; layering of words; dynamic asymmetry and radically varied type-sizes.

Below: Vilmos Huszár, *De Stijl* **magazine cover, 1917**

For this, the first cover of *De Stijl*, the Hungarian painter Huszár wavers between the emerging De Stijl aesthetic of Van Doesburg and the style of Bart van der Leck. The abstract motif was printed from an existing woodcut.

Situated at the heart of Europe, Switzerland was a natural haven for intellectual refugees and it was in Zurich that the most iconoclastic of all the Modernist movements was born: Dadaism. The delivery took place in a bar called Meierei where, in February 1916, the German poet and philosopher Hugo Ball started the Cabaret Voltaire. His combined nightclub and art society proved a great success, and the hardcore of its polyglot *habitués* – the Romanians Tzara and Janco, Arp from Alsatia, the Germans Richter and Huelsenbeck – banded together to form Dada. Depending on whom you believe, the name was derived from the Romanian for 'yes', the French for 'hobbyhorse', or simply a child's first sound, which Huelsenbeck said 'expresses the primitiveness, the beginning at zero, the new in our art'.

1917 saw the opening of Galerie Dada and the launch of *Dada* magazine, which managed to reach Apollinaire in Paris during the War. Simultaneously, and independently, Marcel Duchamp and Francis Picabia were producing the proto-Dadaist reviews *391* and *Rongwrong* in New York. It was a remarkable coincidence, but as the Surrealists' leader André Breton later remarked, 'Dada is a state of mind', and one which was endemic before the War and urgent after it. The Dadaists interpreted the War as the death throes of societies based on greed and materialism: artists, they argued, were just as complicit in capitalism as their bourgeois patrons, and so undermining the aura of art was a legitimate revolutionary tactic. Although their ultimate aims differed, in this as in so much else, the

Dadaists were the heirs of the Futurists. Several of the Dadaists' assaults on art have entered the folklore of Modernism: Duchamp's pencilled moustache on a poster of the Mona Lisa and his provocative 'ready-mades' (including the notorious urinal signed 'R Mutt'); and Man Ray's menacing *Gift* – a flatiron with rows of carpet tacks glued on to it. Hans Arp explored chance by letting pieces of paper drop to the floor and pasting them where they fell, hoping thereby to reach the 'prime cause from which all life springs', and Tristan Tzara applied randomness to poetry, clipping sentences from newspapers and drawing them from a bag. Looking back on the War years Arp said they were searching 'for an elementary art that would, we thought, save mankind from the madness of these times'. He produced the most conventionally 'artistic' objects – painted wood-reliefs of sinuous biomorphic shapes, resembling children's toys. All bright colours and smooth corners, they suggest a primordial reconstruction of the world, a new Eden, free of sin.

As the War drew to a close, the Dadaists scattered to Cologne, Berlin, Paris and elsewhere. On arriving in Berlin in 1917 Huelsenbeck discovered the dispirited populace of a half-starved, nightmare city turning to Expressionist art for escape and consolation. Dadaism's task was clear – to force people to confront reality, and then try to change it. Photomontage, made with clippings from newspapers and photographs, became the weapon with which he, Hannah Höch, Raoul Haussman and, above all, John Heartfield waged war against the Weimar Republic and, in Heartfield's case, Hitler as well – his work appeared on book jackets and in left-wing magazines. Montage was akin to collage and began as a Dadaist game; its construction evoked the discontinuity and rupture characteristic of modern experience, and by collapsing different views into a single image it could suggest the passage of time. The technique soon spread to other media, notably the cinema – where Hans Richter and leading Soviet directors made frequent use of it. The disjointed selection of material exploited in montage was also characteristic of much Modernist literature in the 1920s – James Joyce's *Ulysses* and John Dos Passos's *Manhattan Transfer* being classic examples.

In Hanover Kurt Schwitters formed a one-man Dada movement, but was never accepted as a 'true' Dadaist by the founders, being insufficiently political. He dreamt of a spectacular performance-piece, a *Gesamtkunstwerk* of rubbish, but contented himself with *Merzbilder*, exquisite collages made with the detritus of the city – bus tickets, newspaper cuttings, valueless German banknotes and, later, bits of wood, a broken wheel and so on. The name Merz came from a fragment of paper showing part of the name of the 'Kommerz- und Privat-Bank'. Schwitters also created the mysterious *Merzbau*, a Cubist cave-system dedicated to private memories: it threatened to take over his house but was destroyed by Allied bombing in 1943, and Schwitters started another (a *Merzbarn*) in the English Lake District the year before his death in 1948.

Despite the depredations of war – France lost 1.4 million people – Paris became a boom town. But the social and cultural climate had changed radically: it was now austere, moralistic and suspicious of anything foreign. Modern art was seen by many as a conspiracy by Jewish-German art dealers (Bernheim, Kahnweiler, Wildenstein, etc) to corrupt French taste, and a return to the French Classical tradition was widely advocated. The Spaniard Picasso, his personal life in crisis, was amongst the first to respond. His introduction to Jean Cocteau, the writer and designer, by the composer Edgar Varèse in 1915 acted as an important stimulus. The following year Amédée Ozenfant published his critical '*Notes sur le Cubisme*', and in 1917, after being discharged from the army, Braque wrote twenty *Pensées et réflexions sur la peinture*: their tone was circumspect, and they ended 'I love the rule which corrects emotion'. Obeying that rule – the *rappel à l'ordre* as Cocteau christened it – was advocated in all aspects of life. In painting, Seurat became the new hero, and Cézanne –

Above: El Lissitzky, Page from *Of 2 Squares*, 1922
Theo van Doesburg published the Russian artist El Lissitzky's children's story-book *Of 2 Squares* in 1922 and its impact on the avant-garde was enormous. Using only geometric shapes to tell its story, it epitomized the universal visual language sought by the Modernists.

Left: Piet Zwart, Advertisement, 1925
Trained as an architect, Zwart made his name as a graphic designer. This advertisement is typical of his style in its use of machine imagery, exaggerated letter-heights, sans-serif typefaces and a vigorous, asymmetrical composition.

Above top: El Lissitzky, Reconstruction of *Proun Room*, Greater Berlin Art Exhibition, 1923
Like his book *Of 2 Squares*, Lissitzky's *Proun Room* exerted considerable influence in Europe, not least on Van Doesburg, who made the disruption of the room's stable, orthogonal geometry by strong diagonals an objective of his own work.

Above bottom: Theo van Doesburg, Café Aubette: cinema-dance hall, Strasbourg, 1927–8 (destroyed)
The impact of Lissitzky's *Proun Room* is evident in the diagonal coloured planes Van Doesburg deployed in this interior. His aim, he said, was 'to oppose to the material room in three dimensions a super-material and pictorial diagonal space'.

of all artists! – was deemed suspect. Emile Bernard, writing in 1920, thought him neither Classical nor French, and the reformed Futurist Gino Severini added that he was 'not a constructor' either. To be Classical and a constructor were *de rigeur*, and Cubism was considered dubious on both counts by many artists – and derided as *boche* by the public.

Modernism was not about to lie down and die, but it was undergoing major readjustments. The most influential vehicle for propagating Modernist ideas was the *Ballet Russe* of Sergei Diaghilev – indeed, the French philosopher Henri Lefebvre has gone so far as to speculate that without it 'France would never have had any modern art or modernity'. Diaghilev brought with him Bakst, Fokine, Stravinsky and the great dancer Nijinsky, and commissioned leading avant-garde artists to design stage-sets and costumes. The year 1917 saw the première of *Parade* and the audience was predictably scandalized by Erik Satie's dance-hall tunes, Picasso's Cubist set designs and Cocteau's strange story. Apollinaire's programme notes optimistically proclaimed it 'the point of departure of a series of manifestations of the *Esprit Nouveau*, which will not fail to seduce the elite and promises to transform arts and manners in universal exhilaration' (prophetically, the notes also included the term '*sur-réalisme*'). Apollinaire was proved right: the outrage was short-lived and by the 1920s the *Ballet Russe* was very much part of fashionable culture – after a London performance in 1925, the critic Raymond Mortimer wrote that Diaghilev 'has given us Modern Music without tears and Modern Painting without laughter'. Cocteau defined the 'new spirit' as having 'inherited from the classics solid good sense, a confident spirit of criticism, a wide view of the world and the human mind, and that sense of duty which limits or rather controls displays of emotion.'

All these qualities were to be found in the magazine *L'Esprit Nouveau* which the painter Ozenfant and the painter/architect Charles-Edouard Jeanneret (Le Corbusier) started in 1919 to promote Purism. This two-man 'movement', announced in the book *Après le Cubisme* in 1918, was intended to 'inoculate artists with the new spirit of the age'. Cubism, they said, had been 'the troubled art of a troubled era', whereas now 'we aspire to a serious rigour' and recognize that 'art must tend always to precision'. Ozenfant had perfect modern credentials: son of a builder-developer who worked with Hennebique's reinforced concrete system, he was a keen motor-racer and married a Russian painter. Jeanneret – whom I will refer to as Le Corbusier (he assumed this name from 1920 as writer, then architect and finally painter in 1928) – was Swiss by birth and widely travelled. In 1917, short of money, he took a job as the manager of a brick factory, which he described as 'magnificent: enormous gas meters, four huge chimneys to the east. I breathe proudly on my site.' This experience seems to have been a personal epiphany, because shortly before it he had written of Taylorized mass-production as 'the horrible and ineluctable life of tomorrow' whereas in *Après le Cubisme* it was embraced as the embodiment of the Modern Spirit conditioned by mechanical production.

Ozenfant and Le Corbusier were cosmopolitans who sought a universal, not specifically French, art. Ozenfant later asked: 'Can we really believe any longer in the existence of frontiers as regards ideas? Can we really go on working only for a chapel, a school, a clan, a group, a province, a nation? And not for all races, for mankind in fact? . . . Such an art is possible, because all men react unanimously to broad daylight or full night, or red or black, or love or death . . .' The introduction to the first issue of *L'Esprit Nouveau* explained where such an art should be sought: 'Neither artists nor manufacturers sufficiently realize it: it is in general production that the style of an epoch is found, and not, as is too often supposed, in a few products with ornamental aims . . . The airplane and the limousine are pure creations that clearly characterize the spirit, the style of an epoch. The contemporary arts must also proceed from it.' Adolf Loos, of course, had advanced just such an argument at the turn of the century. Yet the Purists' belief in universal aesthetic values had much deeper roots. In *Philebus* Plato wrote that: 'By beauty of shapes I do not mean, as most people would suppose, the beauty of living figures or of pictures, but, to make my point clear, I mean straight lines and circles, and shapes, plane or solid, made from them by lathe, ruler and square. These are not, like other things, beautiful relatively, but always and absolutely.' Here, laid down almost 2,500 years earlier, was the essence of the Purist aesthetic.

L'Esprit Nouveau's contents reflected its ambitions: it covered art and architecture, science and industry, politics and economics, theatre, music and literature. There were regular articles by a Dr Allendy on psychoanalysis, and even the latest sports records were reported – speed was all the rage and the training of sportsmen into efficient running, jumping and throwing machines demonstrated the new spirit in action. In a 1922 issue, a Dr Winter even suggested 'Taylorizing' daily lives 'to find time for sport, for tending to the

The best and most extraordinary artists will be those who every hour snatch the tatters of their bodies out of the frenzied cataract of life, who, with bleeding hands and hearts hold fast to the intelligence of their time. Richard Huelsenbeck

NORTHAMPTON COLLEGE LIBRARY

John Heartfield, *Zeichen der Rationalisierung* photomontage, 1927
A key figure in the Dada movement, John Heartfield used photomontage techniques to represent the discontinuity and rupture characteristic of modern life.

Formulating the Future

Left: Amédée Ozenfant and Charles Edouard Jeanneret (Le Corbusier), *L'Esprit Nouveau* **magazine cover, Paris, 1920**
The centred typography of *L'Esprit Nouveau* was traditional, in keeping with the Purists' 'call to order' which aimed to combine the spirit of the machine age with the eternal values of the Classical tradition. The immensely influential magazine (of which this is the first issue) continued to be published until 1925.

Opposite: Kurt Schwitters, *Composition,* **1922**
Far less political than the other Dadaists, Schwitters produced numerous exquisite collages made from materials which reflected his everyday life – all carefully washed before being pasted in place.

body . . . to regulate one's life is to control it and is a great source of deep joy'. *L'Esprit Nouveau* was witty, well laid-out and written in a pithy, clipped style which made telling use of juxtapositions of text and illustrations. By the fourth issue in late 1920 all the key ideas of the Purist aesthetic had been formulated. Above all, it was a plea for a collective order: in 1912, in their advocacy of Cubism, Gleizes and Metzinger had argued for forms and symbols 'sufficiently remote from the imagination of the crowd to prevent the truth which they convey from assuming a general character'; after the War, this would have bordered on treason. The Purists wanted a 'transmittable and universal language' based on the 'primary sensations' aroused by geometric forms – including Plato's 'Phileban solids' – and primary colours, and only then overlaid by the 'secondary sensations' of culture and individual experience. Purism would be 'rational, and therefore human', because the highest form of aesthetic expression is achieved 'by the clear perception of a great general law', which they described as 'mathematical lyricism' and which was best seen in architecture, because 'everything in architecture is expressed by order and economy'. The route to the new art was the Darwinian precept: 'ECONOMY is the law of natural selection', from which the Purists derived the principle of 'mechanical selection' resulting from serial mass-production, commercial competition leading inexorably to the perfection of products into *objets-types* – a similar concept to Hermann Muthesius's 'type-forms'.

Purist paintings were based on Cubism, but in place of Cubist fragmentation Ozenfant and Le Corbusier organized their planes frontally, rendering only the most characteristic aspects of objects, often shown in plan and elevation: the results sometimes resemble highly coloured engineering drawings. The Purists' paintings found few imitators, but their ideas – for which Ozenfant deserves much credit – transformed architecture. Le Corbusier elaborated them in a succession of articles in 1920–1, which were published as the book *Vers une Architecture* in 1923 and translated into English four years later as *Towards a New Architecture*. There was no 'new' in the original title, and the changed meaning is slightly misleading – his book *Urbanisme* of 1925 was similarly mistranslated as *The City of Tomorrow*. In 1929, lecturing in Buenos Aires, Le Corbusier declared: 'Today I am considered a revolutionary. I shall confess to you that I have had only one teacher: the past; only one education: the study of the past.' He was in perfect step with Cocteau's *rappel à l'ordre*, returning architecture to its Classical foundations of order and geometry. He extolled 'The Engineer's Aesthetic' of bridges, American factories and grain silos, because it was closer to the spirit of architecture, to 'the masterly correct and magnificent play of volumes brought together in light', than the academic Classicism of the Ecole des Beaux Arts in Paris with its 'illusion of plans'. And he illustrated his arguments with the same pictures Gropius had published in 1913: someone (Ozenfant later claimed responsibility) retouched the photographs to make the buildings even purer! But the Engineer's Aesthetic was *not* architecture, and the high point of the book comes in a eulogy, in words and a cinematic sequence of photographs, of the Parthenon, entitled 'Pure Creation of the Mind'.

In the chapter 'Eyes which do not see' Le Corbusier praised ocean liners, aeroplanes and automobiles, the most celebrated passage comparing the archaic temple at Paestum to a Humber car of 1907, and the Parthenon to a 1921 Delage sports car. The text argued that the process by which Doric architecture achieved perfection is similar to the 'mechanical selection' which produced the Delage, which in turn would 'evolve' towards

'Rhythmic study', illustration from *L'Esprit Nouveau*, no. 2, 1920
This extraordinary image of modern dancers resembles a living Léger. *L'Esprit Nouveau* contained articles on all aspects of modern culture, from art to sport, dance to healthy living.

perfection. Le Corbusier's examples were, however, slightly misleading: the Delage was not mass-produced, but more like a craft-made sculpture on wheels, and interestingly, many of the famous car-makers – Bugatti, Voisin, Farman and the Michelin brothers – had been art students. The comparison between industry and evolution was also misconceived: Darwin never claimed that natural forms were perfect, just that they were 'the fittest' for a given environment, and the fundamental 'force' driving industry was not the search for static

perfection, but dynamic sales – in which 'style' generally plays a very different role. But like a good advertisement, Le Corbusier's prose and images were, and still are, persuasive, and with these four images he summed up the Enlightenment belief in progress, casting pre-War Europe as the 'archaic period' before a new Golden (Machine) Age.

One widely misunderstood phrase in *Vers une Architecture* has entered the language: 'the house is a machine for living in'. To Le Corbusier, satisfying the mind's aesthetic sense was a basic 'function' of architecture, and a glance at any of his designs dispels the idea that he was purveying a utilitarian aesthetic. The book did, however, include a clarion call for 'mass-produced houses' and Le Corbusier devoted much of his early efforts to the design of standard dwellings. These ideas were cohered in 1921–2 in the Citrohan house. Intended to be industrially produced like a car, as its punning name suggests, the interior of the house was organized around a double-height living room, with a sleeping balcony to the rear and a large area of factory glazing to the front. As a universal type it seemed improbable – its closest model was a Parisian artist's atelier – and not surprisingly Le Corbusier failed to convince any industrialists to go into mass-production. Early opportunities to build came from private clients and among the first, in 1923, was Ozenfant, who commissioned a real artist's studio. Le Corbusier created a little gem, complete with Thonet chairs, metal stairs and tubular railing: *l'esprit nouveau* had crystallized in a backstreet of the fourteenth arrondissement, and *tout le monde* had the chance to see it in Paris two years later at the *Exposition Internationale des Arts Décoratifs et Industriels Modernes*.

Proposals for the exhibition went back well before the War, motivated by worries that the newly industrialized Germany threatened France's traditional dominance of the decorative arts. With its plaster pavilions symmetrically arranged down the manicured lawns of the Champ de Mars, and the Eiffel Tower newly decked out with 250,000 lights (sponsored by Citroën, whose name alternated with 'art'), the exhibition presented an image which combined Classical stability and the frisson of the new. Exhibits had to be 'artistic in character' and with 'clearly modern tendencies', and the dominant style came to be known as Art Deco – a decorative synthesis of pre-War art, which often used expensive, exotic materials and distorted, rectilinear Classical forms. Ozenfant and Le Corbusier managed to raise the sponsorship for a Pavilion of L'Esprit

Purism fears the bizarre and the 'original'. It seeks the pure elements with which to reconstruct organized paintings which seem to be made by nature itself. Amédée Ozenfant and Le Corbusier

Amédée Ozenfant,
Accords, 1922
The elements of Ozenfant's painting – guitar, jugs, glasses, carafes – are examples of the timeless *objets-types* which the Purists esteemed. Although derived from Cubism, Purist paintings presented objects in their most typical aspects as coherent wholes: the painting suggests stability and order, not flux and fragmentation.

Nouveau, much to the embarrassment of the organizers who tucked it away on a remote location in the shadow of the Grand Palais. On completion, a five-and-a-half metre high fence was erected to hide it – and only removed after the intervention of the Minister of Fine Arts, Anatole de Monzie (later one of Le Corbusier's clients). Visitors entered through a curved annex containing a display of urban ideas: the Contemporary City for 3,000,000 Inhabitants (first exhibited in 1922 at the Salon d'Automne), and the Voisin Plan for Paris which was named after its sponsor, the car-manufacturer. Le Corbusier proposed razing much of 'tubercular Paris' north of the Seine, and rebuilding it as a city of glass towers, set amidst parkland and a grid of broad avenues – a fragment of the Contemporary City transplanted into Paris. It was a drastic cure for genuine urban ills which made Haussmann look tame and it is difficult to know just how serious Le Corbusier was – his scheme was certainly intended to provoke, but he still promoted it with total commitment.

The Pavilion was presented as a unit of the blocks of '*immeubles villas*' designed for the Contemporary City. They had communal facilities – heating, restaurant, running tracks on the roof, etc – and private 'hanging gardens', beautifully realized in the exhibition by being built around an existing tree. The interior resembled the Citrohan house and was composed of a galleried double-height living area with a bent-steel-tube staircase made like a bicycle frame of which Le Corbusier was particularly proud. The interior was furnished with

Purist *objets-types* and vernacular artefacts: Thonet chairs (usually found in cafés), mass-produced armchairs, bottles and utensils, modular storage units by the office furniture-makers Remington, a Berber rug, and on the terrace, classic white Parisian park seats. For decoration there were paintings by Gris, Léger and the two Purists. By the criteria of the other pavilions, with their coordinated 'artistic' decors, this must have seemed a motley collection, being thin on 'art' and certainly not very 'decorative'. Le Corbusier, needless to say, would have nothing to do with 'the designer decorator', whom he regarded as 'the enemy, the parasite, the false brother' who dealt in 'baubles, charming entertainment for a savage'. He aimed to show that the style of today was found 'among the products of industry, articles of perfect convenience and utility, that soothe our spirits with the luxury afforded by the elegance of their conception, the purity of their execution and the efficiency of their operation', as he remarked in the book *L'Art Décoratif d'Aujourd'hui*, which also appeared in 1925. But it was a *style* nonetheless. Le Corbusier did not use just any industrial products, but only chose those of 'classic' quality. This was an act of artistic not 'mechanical' selection: he selected where others designed, but as Duchamp with his ready-mades had shown, albeit with very different ends in mind, both were ways of making art. What seemed startling, an assault on 'taste' in 1925, was to become a norm in fashionable circles during the late 1920s and 1930s, and later a commonplace of modern living.

Below left: Le Corbusier, Model of the Citrohan house, 1921–2
Its name a punning play on Citroën, the Citrohan house was intended to be mass-produced like a car. The interior was organized around a two-storey living room with a fully glazed elevation, an arrangement repeated in many of Le Corbusier's later projects.

Below right: Le Corbusier and Pierre Jeanneret, Studio of Ozenfant house, Paris, 1923
The 'new spirit' was crystallized in this studio-house which Le Corbusier designed for Amédée Ozenfant. The generous, top-lit two-storey volume, equipped with Thonet chairs, metal stairs and tubular railing, epitomized the Purist aesthetic.

Le Corbusier and Pierre Jeanneret, Pavilion of L'Esprit Nouveau, Exhibition of Decorative and Industrial Arts, Paris, 1925
A marvellous outdoor room linked the apartment interior (above) to the exhibition on urban design through which it was entered. The pavilion was designed as a unit of the 'immeuble-villas' blocks, complete with hanging gardens, as first proposed in Le Corbusier's *Contemporary City* project of 1920. It was furnished with an eclectic mix of pieces drawn from domestic, commercial and industrial contexts, and decorated with paintings by Gris, Léger, Ozenfant and Le Corbusier himself.

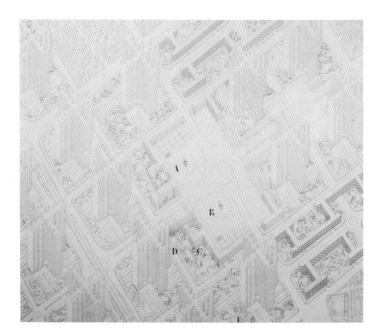

Sponsored by a car manufacturer, this provocative plan envisaged the demolition of much of 'tubercular Paris' north of the Seine, and its replacement by huge cruciform towers set in open parkland criss-crossed by vast highways.

Le Corbusier's architecture crystallized in the mid-1920s around the 'Five Points of a New Architecture' we examined in the Introduction. First demonstrated in the modestly sized Cook House of 1926, their poetic potential is seen to the full in the Villa at Garches (1926–7) and the Villa Savoye in Poissy (1928–31). Both were designed to be approached by car: at Garches you are confronted by a broad, three-storey facade which plays clever games with symmetry and forms the first in a series of planes – real, or implied by columns – which layer back towards the garden; two strips of glazing (*fenêtres en longueurs*) span from edge to edge, taut as the lines in a Mondrian. Inside, the layered spaces, terraces and balconies cut back into the volume, and sensuously curving partitions wrap around stairs or a bathtub, creating a continuous field of space in which inside and out interpenetrate. The resemblance to the frontally layered paintings of Juan Gris, woven through with diagonal and serpentine curves, is inescapable. Le Corbusier greatly admired Gris's work, and it was in these villas that the spatial possibilities of Cubism were first realized in architecture.

Standing on tip-toe in the middle of a field, beyond a screen of trees, the Villa Savoye was designed to be approached by a chauffeur-driven car steered – carefully! – through the gap between pilotis and entrance hall. The main entrance, on the central axis, is a solid metal door in a glazed screen whose slender, close-spaced mullions heighten the sense of movement as you go past. On axis is a dog-leg ramp, and next to

it a free-standing wash basin – an industrial *objet-type* for cleansing the dirt of the road and a witty reminder of Duchamp. The ramp takes you on what Le Corbusier called a *promenade architecturale* (a term he coined in *Vers une Architecture* to describe the experience of the Acropolis) up to the *piano nobile*, out and up again to the roof-top solarium, wrapped around with voluptuous pink and pale blue screens, and framing – again on axis as you approach – a view of the Seine valley. The atmosphere is unmistakably nautical – 'an architecture pure, neat, clear, clean and healthy' as he said of the liner 'Empress France' – but without a trace of kitsch. The journey through space is magical, and all around geometry stands bathed in light: here, in full song, is architecture's purest gift – 'mathematical lyricism.'

The plans of the Villa Savoye are masterpieces of clarity and sophistication, almost square and organized around the axial ramp, hinting at symmetry sufficiently to recall Classical villas, but unfolding in artful asymmetries. And the section – cars below, *piano nobile* for living, roof-top garden – makes the house a miniature of Le Corbusier's ideal city. In almost every building, no matter how small, he embodied his grand vision of a 'Radiant City' full of sun, space and vegetation. Inspired by Marcel Breuer's work at the Bauhaus, he designed bent-metal machines-for-sitting-in with Charlotte Perriand to furnish the houses, and like Breuer tried unsuccessfully to interest a bicycle-manufacturer – Peugeot – in producing them. Thonet made a small production run, exhibited in 1929, and

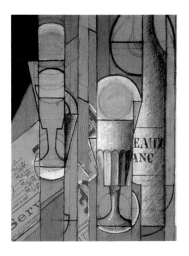

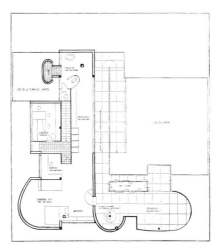

Far left: Juan Gris, detail from *Glasses, Newspaper and Bottle of Wine*
The frontally layered paintings of Juan Gris were underlain by a geometric 'architecture'. For this reason they were much admired by Le Corbusier, the plans of whose 1920s villas often recall them. The plan on the left shows the roof-garden of the Villa Savoye (below).

Below: Le Corbusier and Pierre Jeanneret, Villa Savoye, Poissy, 1928–31
Built in suburban Paris, this weekend house marked the peak of Le Corbusier's Purist phase. Organized as an 'architectural promenade' around a central ramp, the plans progress from the near-symmetry of the ground floor, dictated by the turning circle of a car, to the freedom of the rooftop garden. The colours shown here have rarely been seen: the originals are lost, and this reconstruction was short-lived since the Villa was painted white again soon after this picture was taken.

Le Corbusier and Pierre Jeanneret, Terrace and living room of Villa Savoye, Poissy, 1928–31
The terrace and living room were designed as a continuous living space, linked by a sliding glass wall. The continuous light fitting contained individual lamps, not fluorescent tubes (which were only developed during World War II).

these chairs are now produced in Italy as modern classics.

The painter closest to Purism was Fernand Léger. He owed much to Cubism, but was never truly Cubist, and had a passion for machines. The vision that inspired his art came on wartime service in the Engineers Corps where, being 'on a level with the whole of the French people', he discovered working men to be 'poets, inventors of everyday poetic images' in their creative use of slang, and 'dazzled by the breech of a 75-millimetre gun standing uncovered in the sunlight' found that 'the magic of light on white metal' was 'enough to make me forget the abstract art of 1912–13'. *Discs* (1918) suggests a complex machine, and the mural-sized *The City* (1919) evokes the vitality and restlessnes of urban life – it was inspired by the Place de Clichy, site of some of Paris's most aggressive advertising. Léger saw posters and illuminated signs as 'the new furnishing' of the urban environment: 'the ridiculous formula: *Défense d'afficher* [No posters],' he said, showed an 'incomprehension of all that is new and alive.' For Léger the human figure was no more important than any other object, but he was nonetheless a humanist who represented the machine as a friend of man; in *Three Women (Le Grand Déjeuner)* (1921) he created his image of paradise, in which the women seem to be as comfortable in their machine-age interior as the Three Graces in a Classical landscape. His last innovation, broad swathes of colour sweeping across objects and figures, was inspired by the coloured lights of New York advertising. Léger aspired to a great public art, but had opportunities only to design the occasional ballet or paint murals in mostly exclusive surroundings – nor, more surprisingly, did designers make much use of his graphically powerful images.

The most celebrated *affichiste* (poster-designer) of post-War Paris was A.M. Cassandre. He produced several hundred designs, making his debut with a four-metre-long poster for the furniture store *Au Bûcheron* (The Woodcutter). Featuring an axeman integrated into a series of stepped diagonal planes, its style was classic Art Deco. In 1925 the first of several masterpieces appeared, designed for the small-circulation newspaper *L'Intransigeant*. Cleverly organized around radiating diagonals which suggest both the despatch and arrival of news, its shouting head could almost be part of the plan of a Corbusian villa. The design is perfectly flat – no traces of graduated Art Deco planes – and it comes as no surprise to find out that Cassandre later commissioned a house from Le Corbusier. Cassandre used airbrushed images and geometrical lettering to

suggest the precision of the machine age, and the sight of a poster such as this speeding by on the side of a delivery van or pasted up around Paris could well have been many people's introduction to the Modernist aesthetic.

The new classicism was apparent in the pioneer Modernists as well as amongst the new generation – in Picasso's statuesque women, Matisse's *Odalisques* and Stravinsky's playful neoclassicism, for example – but their restraint was far from universal. Jazz and black dance rhythms were all the rage – culminating in the arrival in Paris of La Revue Nègre and the sensational Josephine Baker in 1925 – and Dada came to a climax of sorts in 1920s Paris in events which, like the Futurist Soirées, generally ended in chaos. It was in Paris that Duchamp defaced the (reproduction) *Mona Lisa* and Man Ray glued carpet tacks to his iron, and the Dadaist spirit infected the compositions of Erik Satie, who in turn became a model for the rebellious group of young composers, promoted by Cocteau, who styled themselves '*Les Six*' – Arthur Honegger, Darius Milhaud and Francis Poulenc were the leaders. It was also in Paris that the Modernist technique of allusion by citation crystallized in such works as Satie's *Parade*, Joyce's *Ulysses*, Stravinsky's *Pulcinella* and Picasso's *Vollard Suite*. Composing works as an amalgam of styles and stylistic allusions called into question the very possibility of that universal language being sought by the Purists, de Stijl and the exponents of Neue Sachlichkeit.

In 1922 the critic and poet André Breton announced

NORTHAMPTON COLLEGE LIBRARY

Le Corbusier and Pierre Jeanneret, Bathroom of Villa Savoye, Poissy, 1928–31
In keeping with the 1920s passion for 'body culture' and the Platonic belief in a balance between the moral and the physical, the Villa Savoye's bathroom was designed as a spartan shrine for the body, flooded with health-giving sunlight.

plans for an International Congress to determine 'the direction of the modern spirit'. He invited representatives of all the major modern movements including Dada, of which he was nominally a part: Dada was falling apart and Breton administered the *coup de grâce* by treating it as just another form of art. (Dada's lasting influence is still evident in contemporary art – in the artists' persistent determination to outrage public taste, and above all in the assertion, which has underpinned so much modern art, that the artist alone determines what is art.) In 1924 Breton published the *Surrealist Manifesto*, the Bureau of Surrealist Research was founded and the first issue of the review *La Révolution Surréaliste* appeared. The Manifesto dealt mainly with literature and, although the Surrealists were keen to assert their independence, they had much in common with Dada since Surrealism declared war on the bourgeoisie, used automatic techniques and, in theory at least, was against all traditional forms of art. The Surrealists preached the power of dreams and the free play of thought, seeking a 'pure psychic automatism' beyond rational control – Breton had trained as a doctor and briefly practised psychiatry before the War. Lautréamont's metaphor of the beautiful in the banal – 'as beautiful as the chance meeting on a dissecting table of a sewing machine and an umbrella' (from *Chants de Maldoror*, 1868–74) – became their ideal, an image of the random juxtaposition of different worlds born, they supposed, from the unconscious.

Surrealism was primarily a literary and poetic movement, but Surrealist ideas also had a considerable impact on all the arts, especially in the Latin countries, where their influence is still evident in the 'magical realist' writing of Latin America. The painter Salvador Dali worked with the film director Luis Buñuel to make the celebrated *Le Chien Andalou* in 1929 – its powerful, sometimes horrifying, images and use of montage and double-exposure influenced countless later film-makers. The International Exhibition of Surrealism, held in Paris in 1938, sounds like a contemporary installation: Duchamp transformed the gallery with 1,200 sacks of coal hanging from the ceiling, dead leaves and grass, a pond and several double-beds; unsuspecting dummies in his *Rainy Taxi* were showered with rain and crawled over by live snails. In painting, Dali's sickly images of impotence and decay eventually achieved great popularity, but more substantial were painters such as the Italian Giorgio de Chirico, master of eery, dream-like urban landscapes which captured what Breton called the 'irremediable human anxiety', and the Belgian

René Magritte. His deadpan technique, acquired designing advertisements and wallpapers, was used to create impossible, ambiguous images which show 'the present as an absolute mystery': precisely the kind of haunting visual puzzles many an advertising designer has exploited.

The War left Germany in chaos – physically, socially, and intellectually – but like the turbulent city-states of Renaissance Italy, this proved to be fertile ground for art. As a federation of previously independent *Länder*, Germany had numerous regional theatres and galleries, and (almost as important) wealthy families with traditions of art patronage. Following the unsuccessful November Revolution of 1918, the Weimar Republic was founded in 1919; the army chief Hindenburg encouraged the officially unofficial *Freikorps* (private armies) of disbanded soldiers to ensure revolt did not take hold, and in January 1919 they murdered the revolutionary leaders Rosa Luxemburg and Karl Liebknecht. In March 1920, the *Freikorps* staged the Kapp Putsch in Weimar; the army refused to fight, and the revolt was only defeated by a strike. Walter Gropius designed a monument to the workers killed in the conflagration: its fractured geometries came from Cubism, but the composition was decidedly Expressionist.

During the War the Activist movement in literature had been launched, and its leading spokesman, Kurt Hiller, formulated the idea of the *Literat* as a prophetic, messianic leader who could guide the people away from materialism and naturalism towards the higher, objective realm of the spirit. Whilst sharing many of the Expressionists' aspirations and aesthetic means, the Activists were outward-looking rather than introspective, determined to change society, not merely express anguish at its ills. Bruno Taut formulated the architect's 'noble, priestly, magnificent, divine calling' as a 'striving to give material expression to that which slumbers in every soul' along Activist lines, and in his *Alpine Architektur* (begun in 1917, published in 1919) he emulated Zarathustra's journey to the mountains and dreamt of reshaping and crowning part of the Italo-Swiss Alps with crystalline glass temples – a kind of 'super-technology' which he believed transcended the discredited rationalism and materialism which had led to the War. Taut was far from alone: anti-war feelings had been growing since 1916, and in 1918-19 they exploded in an outburst of utopian projects, mass theatre, temples of socialism, manifestoes and posters. They were all part of the search for a proletarian art – much the same had

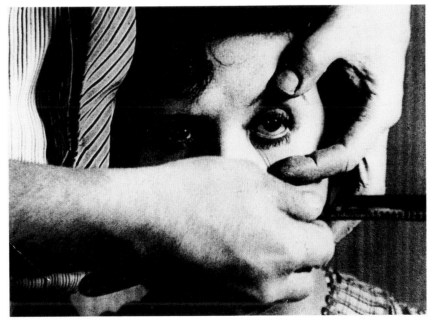

**Above: Fernand Léger,
Three Women
(Le Grand Déjeuner), 1921**
A committed Communist and
devotee of machine-culture,
Léger painted numerous
pictures of modern life. For this
image of paradise, he
transformed the theme of The
Three Graces into a vision of
heroic, machine-like women at
home in a modern interior.

**Left: Luis Buñuel (director)
with Salvador Dali, Un Chien
Andalou, 1929**
The film's short opening
sequence culminates with a
woman's eye being sliced by a
razor – the first of several
bizarre and shocking images
(such as ants crawling out of a
hand and dead donkeys being
hauled on pianos).

happened in Russia and Hungary, where Communist revolutions succeeded.

Although later renowned as a temple of rationalism, the Bauhaus espoused similarly utopian ideals. It was formed by merging the Weimar Academy of Fine Art and the arts and crafts school previously headed by Henry van de Velde, and Gropius was appointed Director in 1919. Earlier that year he had become chairman of the *Arbeitsrat für Kunst* (Work Council – or Soviet – for Art) which aimed to involve creative people in forging a new social order. Gropius's Bauhaus programme was based on the Arbeitsrat's 1919 manifesto 'Under the wing of a great architecture', which in turn was distilled from Bruno Taut's idealistic 'A programme for architecture' of 1918. Under the slogan 'The earth a good habitation' Taut advocated a return to unity in the arts 'so that every individual discipline will play its part in building . . . Everything will be one thing: architecture.' Gropius espoused similar ideals, and in his Founding Manifesto envisaged his new 'guild of craftsmen without the class distinctions that raise an arrogant barrier between craftsmen and artist' contributing to a great building that would 'rise toward heaven from the hands of a million workers like the crystal symbol of a new earth'. His vision was illustrated by Lyonel Feininger's Expressionist woodcut of the cathedal-like *Gesamtkunstwerk* of the future. Gropius's first move in this direction – the replacement of the title 'Professor' by the medieval guild's 'Master' – was not well received by the art professors, who duly formed a separate school.

Gropius appointed nine 'Masters of Form' between 1919 and 1924. Eight were painters – Feininger, Itten, Muche, Schlemmer, Klee, Schreyer, Kandinsky, Moholy-Nagy – and the ninth was the sculptor Marcks. All except the Hungarian constructivist Moholy-Nagy had an interest in Expressionism, and the rest of the students' education was craft-based. This was almost a 'Who's Who' of the central European avant-garde, but a surprising foundation for a design school. The introspective Paul Klee proved a gifted teacher, and his notes – published in 1925 as a 'Bauhaus book' entitled *Pedagogical Sketchbook*, and posthumously at greater length as *The Thinking Eye* and *The Intelligent Eye* – are among the most fascinating accounts of the creative process ever written. Of the early appointees, Johannes Itten was much the most influential. Swiss-born and trained as a primary school teacher in the Froebel system, he came with a recommendation from Alma Mahler, the composer Gustav's wife, who had a liberally indulged

The final and most pure form of a necessary item is always constructed of geometric shapes.

Jan Tschichold

Opposite: Walter Gropius, Bauhaus, Dessau, 1925–6
The Bauhaus began life in 1919 in Weimar, in a building designed by Henry van de Velde, and it moved to Dessau in 1925. The following year it occupied this spectacular purpose-designed building and quickly established itself as the focus of Modernist architecture and design.

Above: Walter Gropius, Bauhaus, Dessau, 1925–6
Sigfried Giedion influentially described the layered views seen walking through and around the Bauhaus as an example of 'space-time' in architecture. More predictably, it was christened 'the aquarium' by local residents.

**Below: Walter Gropius,
Bauhaus curriculum, 1922**
This diagram was published in
the Bauhaus statutes. Students
began with the celebrated six-
month *Vorlehre*, and then spent
three years mastering different
materials and related
theoretical studies. The target,
in the centre, was building (*not*
'architecture') which was only
offered after the move to
Dessau.

**Bottom: Walter Gropius and
Lyonel Feininger, Bauhaus
manifesto cover, 1919**
Feininger's cathedral-like
woodcut of the almost medieval
'total work of art' to which the
Bauhaus initially aspired made
clear its original commitment
to German Expressionist ideals.

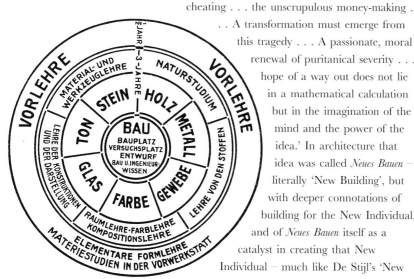

liking for artists and had been married to Gropius. Itten
followed the obscure cult of Mazdaznam, and its
physical and mental exercises and vegetarian diet soon
became the Bauhaus's most conspicuous features. After
persuading Gropius to allow him to run a six-month
introductory course – the celebrated *Vorkurs* – to release
the students' creativity, Itten all but transformed the
Bauhaus into a cross between a Zen monastery and a
hippy commune.

Itten's idealism took strange forms, but the
introspection and other-worldliness were understandable
and widespread, given the difficulties of daily life. A
dispirited Peter Behrens wrote in 1920 that: 'what is
most depressing is not the scarcities we have to face, not
the inflation, not the neglect of the streets and means of
public transport, but the demoralization of broad
sections of the population. The stealing, lying and
cheating . . . the unscrupulous money-making . .
. . A transformation must emerge from
this tragedy . . . A passionate, moral
renewal of puritanical severity . . .
hope of a way out does not lie
in a mathematical calculation
but in the imagination of the
mind and the power of the
idea.' In architecture that
idea was called *Neues Bauen* –
literally 'New Building', but
with deeper connotations of
building for the New Individual,
and of *Neues Bauen* itself as a
catalyst in creating that New
Individual – much like De Stijl's 'New
Art, New Life'.

In 1921 Van Doesburg made a timely appearance in
Weimar. The perfect counterpoint to Itten, his black
shirt, white tie and monocle created a very different
image to the mystic's bald head and monk's robe. Van
Doesburg decided to publish *De Stijl* from Germany, and
became a sympathetic but severe critic of the Bauhaus.
The September 1922 issue contained an article
condemning its lack of progress, signed by Vilmos
Huszár but instigated by Van Doesburg. He offered free
classes to Bauhaus students in the principles of De Stijl
composition, and in 1922 drew the avant-garde to
Weimar for a Constructivist and Dadaist Congress.
Gropius was dissuaded from giving him a post, but
knew the criticisms were valid: changes were already
afoot. In the autumn of 1921 the school adopted a new
seal by Oskar Schlemmer – comparison with the first,

neo-primitive design by Karl Peter Röhl gives a hint of
how radical the transformation would be. Early in 1922
Gropius issued a memorandum criticizing Itten's
romantic belief that individual creative work was
antagonistic to industry: the pre-War Gropius had
returned and the memo even sang the virtues of grain
silos and factories! Itten was persuaded to resign in
October, and left the following spring. He was replaced
by László Moholy-Nagy.

Moholy-Nagy epitomized the New Man – 'the type
of individual,' as Charlotte Perriand wrote, 'who keeps
pace with scientific thought, who understands his age
and lives it: the Aeroplane, the Ocean Liner and the
Motor are at his service; Sport gives him health; his
house is his resting place.' Moholy-Nagy was machine-
mad, and dressed in industrial overalls and nickel-
rimmed spectacles to project an image of sober
rationality. Self-taught, he made significant contributions
to painting, kinetic sculpture and photography;
produced films, designed sets and costumes, and was an
outstanding graphic and exhibition designer. He was
also a prolific theoretician and a brilliant teacher: one
student described him as 'a pike in a pond full of
goldfish' – just what the Bauhaus needed. He
revolutionized the *Vorkurs*, introducing students to basic
techniques and the properties of materials – in the
metal workshop steel replaced silver, and electric light
fittings supplanted 'spiritual samovars'. Moholy-Nagy's
assistant was Josef Albers, who became a noted theorist
of colour: he presented students on their first day with
a pile of newspapers, told them to make something
respecting the material, and left them to it. It was a
quintessentially Modernist assignment – working 'in the
nature of materials' being basic to the Modernist
aesthetic – and similar tasks are still set in art and
design schools. The best responses were made without
glue or tools – the way the sculptor Andy Goldsworthy
now works with natural materials – and later exercises
involved making structures from a single sheet of thin
card by cutting and folding, with results that could be
highly ingenious and elegant.

Feeling the need to promote the Bauhaus's work,
Gropius decided to hold an exhibition and a week of
events in the late summer of 1923, despite continuing
worries that too many problems remained unresolved:
some workshops were continuing to produce pseudo-
sculptures rather than usable objects, and there was
little cooperation between disciplines. But he need not
have worried. Six months of advertising paid off and
the event proved a triumph, drawing 15,000 visitors

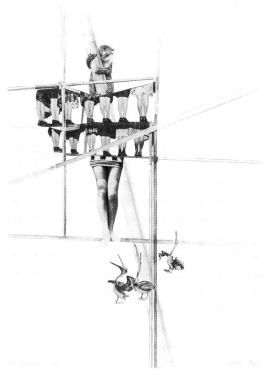

**Left: László Moholy-Nagy,
The Structure of the World,
1927**
Moholy-Nagy was a master of
many media, not least
photography and montage, and
this visual conundrum combines
figurative and abstract elements
in a dynamic composition
which also seems to owe
something to the circus.

**Above: Oskar Schlemmer,
Costumes for the 'Triadic
Ballet', designed 1922;
photograph 1926**
This photograph appeared in
the *Wieder Metropol* review
following a performance at
Berlin's Metropol Theatre. The
'Triadic Ballet' was the most
celebrated of Schlemmer's
performances at the Bauhaus;
he saw the marionette-like
figures as metaphors for perfect,
innocent human beings.

from all over Europe. The specially built experimental Haus am Horn, designed by the painter Georg Muche, was unadventurous architecturally, but the furnishings were exceptional. Moholy-Nagy designed some lamps, and a brilliant student, Marcel Breuer from Hungary, produced much of the furniture – including bent-metal pieces. He also designed the revolutionary kitchen, the first in Germany to have a continuous run of worktops and wall cupboards, designed in accordance with the 'work-study' principles pioneered in America.

The Bauhaus exhibition happened to coincide with the most vicious economic inflation – the Deutschmark rose by 8,000% to 160 million per dollar during its six-week run. Currency reforms were implemented in November 1923 and the following spring the Dawes Plan gave hope of a stable economic climate in which industry could prosper. The shift from Expressionism to rationalism – Itten to Moholy-Nagy – was apparent throughout German culture, and in architecture can be seen in the work of Ludwig Mies van der Rohe in Berlin. His 1919 competition project for a corner-building on Friedrichstrasse with its all-glass skin, soaring dramatically at the corner and faceted to dramatize the reflections between surfaces, clearly echoed the utopian ideas of Taut and Scheerbart. So, to a lesser degree, did his 1920–1 project for a glass tower, in which the architecture was reduced to a glass skin, structural bones and a service core. Both designs were published in 1922 in Taut's Expressionist magazine, *Frühlicht* ('Dawn'), which promoted a characteristically bizarre mix of solar energy, 'ancient wisdom' and 'total frankness in sexual matters'. Mies's library included numerous books on fringe science and he was an active member of the Novembergruppe, founded in 1918 and named after the month of the attempted revolution. Mies directed its architectural section from 1921 to 1925, and helped launch the magazine *G* (for *Gestaltung* – 'creative force'), to which he contributed a series of aphoristic articles, containing a number of lapidary statements such as:

Architecture is the will of an epoch translated into space; living, changing, new.

We refuse to recognise problems of form, only problems of building.
Form is not the aim of our work, only the result.

Essentially our task is to free the practice of building from the control of aesthetic speculators

Left above: Marcel Breuer, Kitchen in the Haus am Horn, 1923
Designed for the Bauhaus Exhibition of 1923, the Haus am Horn included many novel ideas for living, including this kitchen – the first in Germany to have separate floor and wall cupboards, and a work surface in front of the window, not in the middle of the room.

Left below: H. Bayer and J. Maltan, Bauhaus Exhibition entrance, 1923
The banner and lettering form a striking contrast to Van de Velde's Jugendstil building in Weimar. The exhibition was a great success, drawing visitors from all over Europe.

Opposite: W. Wagenfeld, Coffee pot in German silver and (right) W. Rössger and F. Marby, Jug in German silver, both 1923–4
Designed whilst precious materials were still in favour at the Bauhaus, both designs nonetheless show the reduction to simple geometric forms which quickly became synonymous with 'Bauhaus'. Wagenfeld went on to become one of Europe's outstanding designers of tableware in the 1930s.

NORTHAMPTON COLLEGE LIBRARY

**Right: Mies van der Rohe, Glass Tower on Friedrichstrasse, Berlin, competition project, 1919
Far right: Mies van der Rohe, Glass Tower, project, 1920–1**
Glass was established as one of the preeminent modern materials well before the War and Mies's Friedrichstrasse project, designed in angular facets to exploit inter-reflections, was in the exuberant, Expressionist spirit of Bruno Taut, albeit without the mystical baggage. The later, calmer tower used an undulating plan form to create similarly elusive elevational effects.

Opposite: Mies van der Rohe, Project for Concrete Office Building, 1922
This prophetic project was amongst the first to use the ribbon-window, a leitmotif of Modernist architecture. Mies's Classical education is still evident in the entasis produced by the progressively increasing cantilevers of the upper floors – a feature clearly visible in the 2.7-metre long original drawing.

and restore it to what it should exclusively be: building.

The glass towers showed what he meant, and were soon followed by projects in concrete and brick from which every trace of Expressionism had disappeared. First came the Concrete Office Building in 1922, a grid of columns with cantilever beams and slabs turned up to form continuous parapets, infilled with ribbon windows supported by slender steel mullions; the corners swelled slightly outwards – a refinement symptomatic of Mies's lifelong oscillation between Modernism and Classicism. The Brick Country House of 1923 shows his familiarity with De Stijl and Wright, but unlike De Stijl is grounded in a specific material: to drive the point home he drew in every brick. Slightly predating the Maison Particulière, this was the first design in which the placing and shaping of free-standing walls generated the plan – a consummate expression of the Modernist conception of space as a continuous 'field'. Finally, in 1924, Mies produced the Concrete Villa, a pin-wheel plan on several levels which again looked back to Wright but also forward to developments in the 1930s.

None of these celebrated 'Five Projects' was built, but each was pregnant with possibilities: few architects invent anything original, and in a mere five years Mies had integrated new structural and aesthetic principles with astonishing clarity. Curtain-walled towers, ribbon-windowed office and apartment blocks, open plans with 'flowing space', and compositions of functionally zoned volumes are all around us – and were all anticipated in these designs.

During the 1920s Modernist architecture was pioneered in Germany, Holland and Paris, but it was also practised by architects scattered across Europe. An early and important Modernist enclave was formed in Switzerland, thanks to its celebrated fresh air and numerous sanatoria. Late in 1923 Russian Constructivism's travelling salesman, El Lissitzky, contracted tuberculosis and repaired to Locarno in search of a cure, calling in at Zurich where a friend, the Dutch architect Mart Stam, was working. Whilst recovering, Lissitzky formed a group and planned a magazine – *ABC Beiträge zum Bauen* – whose first issue appeared in 1924: the Swiss members included Emil Roth, Hans Schmidt, Hannes Meyer and Hans

Less is more. Mies van der Rohe

Wittwer. ABC were radical, left-wing Modernists who became the major advocates of Constructivism outside Russia. They demonstrated their vision of a technologically advanced, socially relevant modern architecture in Meyer and Wittwer's 1926 Petersschule project in Basle, a steel-framed school of uncompromising severity – the proposed finishes included steel windows, aluminium doors, rubber floors and asbestos-cement cladding. Stam returned to Holland in 1925 to work on the Van Nelle factory (a masterpiece of Constructivism), Meyer left for the Bauhaus in 1927 and El Lissitzky resumed his travels: the hard edge of the ABC group quickly softened.

In the move from Expressionism to rationalism apparent throughout German culture, exposure to Soviet art played an important part: exhibitions, exiles and El Lissitzky's excursions around Europe helped spread the news. The new sobriety became known as *Neue Sachlichkeit* (New Objectivity) – a name coined by the critic G.F. Hartlaub in 1924. In art, matter-of-factness generally proved less memorable than in other fields, and the Social Democrats placed a considerable emphasis on design, seeing it as a means of cultural engineering – several Modernists occupied important positions. In Berlin, for example, Bruno Taut (who adopted the *sachlich* spirit) was appointed principal architect to the main building society, and in Berlin-Neukölln in 1927 he built an open-air, open-plan school which greatly influenced English school design after the Second World War. In Frankfurt Ernst May started a ten-year plan of major house-building and research in 1925, adopting systems of prefabricated construction and developing the famous 'Frankfurt kitchen' as part of the *Existenzminimum* (low-wage earner's) dwelling. Regular reports of progress were given in the magazine *Das Neue Frankfurt* (1926–33), but May left for the USSR in 1930 when the socialists lost power, having completed 15,000 housing units.

Commercial graphics (*Gebrauchsgrafik*) were stimulated by the influence of El Lissitzky and De Stijl, and flourished in the hands of some outstanding typographers and designers. Jan Tschichold was the leading spokesman of the New Typography which transformed the look of printed materials and his *Die neue Typographie* of 1928 became the bible of the field. It was written whilst teaching under Paul Renner (designer of the Futura typeface) at the Munich printing school, which in this area was even more influential than the Bauhaus. There, Herbert Bayer nonetheless made significant contributions to the typographic revolution,

Opposite: Brinkman and Van der Vlugt, Van Nelle Factory, Rotterdam, 1926-30
One of the great industrial buildings of Europe, the Van Nelle cigarette factory's Constructivist character owed much to Mart Stam's collaboration following his return from Switzerland.

Above: Grete Schütte-Lihotzky, Frankfurt kitchen, 1926
Following Ernst May's appointment as City Architect, Frankfurt became a centre of avant garde, functionalist design. The celebrated 'Frankfurt kitchen' was designed to make the most of the small rooms inevitable in *Existenzminimum* public housing.

Herbert Bayer, Design for a newspaper kiosk, 1924
After studying at the Bauhaus, Bayer became a noted graphic and exhibition designer. The seeds of his approach to exhibition work are already apparent in this student design.

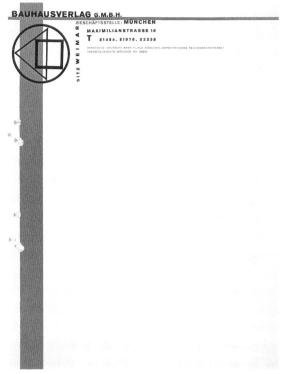

waging war on serif typefaces and upper-case letters – in the 1920s much German printing used Gothic, let alone Roman, typefaces, and German orthography still requires the upper case for the initial letters of nouns. Moholy-Nagy proved himself to be a superlative graphic designer, exploiting his facility with photographic processes to stunning effect – he designed most of the 'Bauhaus books' which helped spread the school's ideas. El Lissitzky formed an advertising agency in 1924, and Kurt Schwitters, the master of *Merz*, also took up graphic design, forming the *Ring neuer Werbegestalter* (Circle of New Advertising Designers), which had a dozen members by 1930, including Tschichold and the Dutchman Piet Zwart. Schwitters had earlier launched a one-man movement with its own journal named, inevitably, *Merz*. The fourth issue (July 1923) included El Lissitzky's 'Topography of Typography', which began 'Words on the printed sheet are seen, not heard' – what the Modernists were creating was a new, international 'language of vision'. A vivid example is provided by Cassandre's 1932 poster for Dubonnet. Its three images show a geometric man filling with colour and glowing with satisfaction as he drinks, with the name Dubonnet also appearing in stages: unsophisticated by late twentieth-century standards, perhaps, but ommunicating its message visually in a way which had few precedents. The Dubonnet man became an icon of his age.

The utilitarian spirit even spread to music and literature: Hindemith and his friends sought opportunities to compose for films or with mechanical instruments, Brecht wrote for the high-brow sports magazine *Arena* and Ernst Krenek created a boxing opera. Germans emulated aspects of Anglo-American culture such as jazz (the Bauhaus had its own band, and the staff had themselves photographed with a symbolic saxophone), sport, humour and down-to-earth respect for facts. The craze for sport was reinforced by the pre-War *Wandervogel* movement's promotion of physical emancipation, later taken up by the youth divisions of political parties of left and right. As in France, the culture of the body – exercise and sun – was part of the *sachlich* way of life. Gymnasia appeared in private houses and apartments: Van Doesburg and Van Eesteren's Maison Particulière was organized around a small gym on the top floor, and Modernist flat roofs were equipped for outdoor exercise. The modern Olympics movement, launched by Baron Coubertin in 1896 to 'give renewed vigour to a young generation grown flabby and anaemic', was in full swing and the games were held in Paris in 1924. In 1929 the German artist Willi Baumeister published *Sport and the Machine*, a eulogy of the athlete as machine. Diaghilev created a Sporting Ballet, Cocteau praised the 'wonderful value of sport', German intellectuals frequented boxing matches, soccer

Above left: Herbert Bayer, Design for a Bauhaus exhibition catalogue cover, 1923
By filling the space with the letters and using unusual contrasting colours, Bayer achieves tremendous graphic impact with admirable economy of means.

Above right: László Moholy-Nagy, Bauhaus Press letterhead, c. 1920
Moholy-Nagy was perhaps the most original graphic designer at the Bauhaus and this typography for the Bauhaus Press's letterhead was in his vigorous Constructivist style.

became a mass spectator-sport, rugby was imported to France and became a passion in the south, and tennis enabled the two sexes to meet free of traditional constraints, the functional new shorts also affording women unprecedented freedom in dress – Sigfried Giedion included a picture of an American model wearing the 'new practical tennis-wear' in his book *Liberated Living*. And for the Classically minded it was all, of course, in keeping with Plato's ideal of a 'perfect moral balance' between the physical and intellectual – 'a harmony more perfect even than the harmony produced by the strings of a lyre'.

In Weimar the term after the 1923 Bauhaus exhibition was exceptionally productive, but faced with the Nationalist victory in the regional elections the following February, attacks by the right-wing press and antagonism from local craftsmen fearful of the students' interest in industrial production, Gropius decided to look for alternative funding. The best offer came from Dessau, a larger town in a coal-mining area governed by Social Democrats, and with modern industries. The Bauhaus recast itself as a *Hochschule für Gestaltung*, the Masters became professors again and Gropius started designing its new home, which opened in October 1926. Planned as a three-winged pinwheel, with a two-storey bridge across a road containing his own studio and shared facilities, it was the first time the new architecture had been realized on a large scale. Here were Mies's ribbon windows and a vast glass curtain wall flowing effortlessly around the volume of the workshop block – earning it the nickname of 'the aquarium' amongst bemused local residents, and offering layered views through glass planes which Giedion later

declared, dubiously but influentially, as both Cubist and an example of Einsteinian 'space-time' in architecture.

With the new building came the architecture department which many thought the Bauhaus was supposed to have had from the start. To run it Gropius appointed Hannes Meyer, whose *Neues Bauen* rationalism and uncompromising left-wing views quickly antagonized Kandinsky and Klee. He then fell out with Moholy-Nagy – who should have been an ally, but soon left. Wearied by internal discontents and external sniping, Gropius resigned as Director in 1928. Mies refused the job and Gropius – to many colleagues' consternation – recommended Meyer. He accepted, and immediately made architecture the 'master discipline' but also surprised his colleagues by bringing in a stream of distinguished lecturers who broadened the students' horizons to take in sociology, political theory and the sciences. A photographic workshop was set up under Walter Peterhans: it concentrated on photojournalism, advertising and display work, not 'art' photography. Ludwig Hilbersheimer, designer of some of the most extreme 'rational' cities, arrived to teach town-planning and, thanks to the strong German economy, the links with industry and outside commissions increased.

Marcel Breuer, who was amongst the first Bauhaus graduates in 1925, was appointed to head the carpentry workshop. He acquired a bicycle to get around and, fascinated by its strength and lightness, approached the manufacturers Adler about producing furniture. They said no, but he bought some tube anyway and the Wassily Chair (1925), named after Kandinsky who was the first to buy one, was the result. The chair's leather straps do not so much support as suspend you in space,

Cassandre was the outstanding French poster designer, and this celebrated advertisement communicated its message in a way which was both amusing and unmistakable – not always the case with more abstract forms of visual communication.

NORTHAMPTON COLLEGE
LIBRARY

sutnar

žijeme 1001 1931

obrázkový magazin dnešní doby

první ročník ● sešit 4-5 ● str. 97-160 ● červenec-srpen 1931

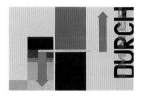

Above: Bauhaus graphic 'Raumgestaltung einer Durchfahrt', c. 1925
This elegant and slightly mysterious image shows the side walls and ceiling of a service route under a building. The graphic treatment is intended to indicate which direction has priority.

Left: Ladislav Sutnar, *For Life*, magazine cover, 1931
Modernist design flourished in the new Czech Republic, and this cover characteristically linked fit bodies and a dynamic lifestyle with pieces of Modernist furniture and graphic design.

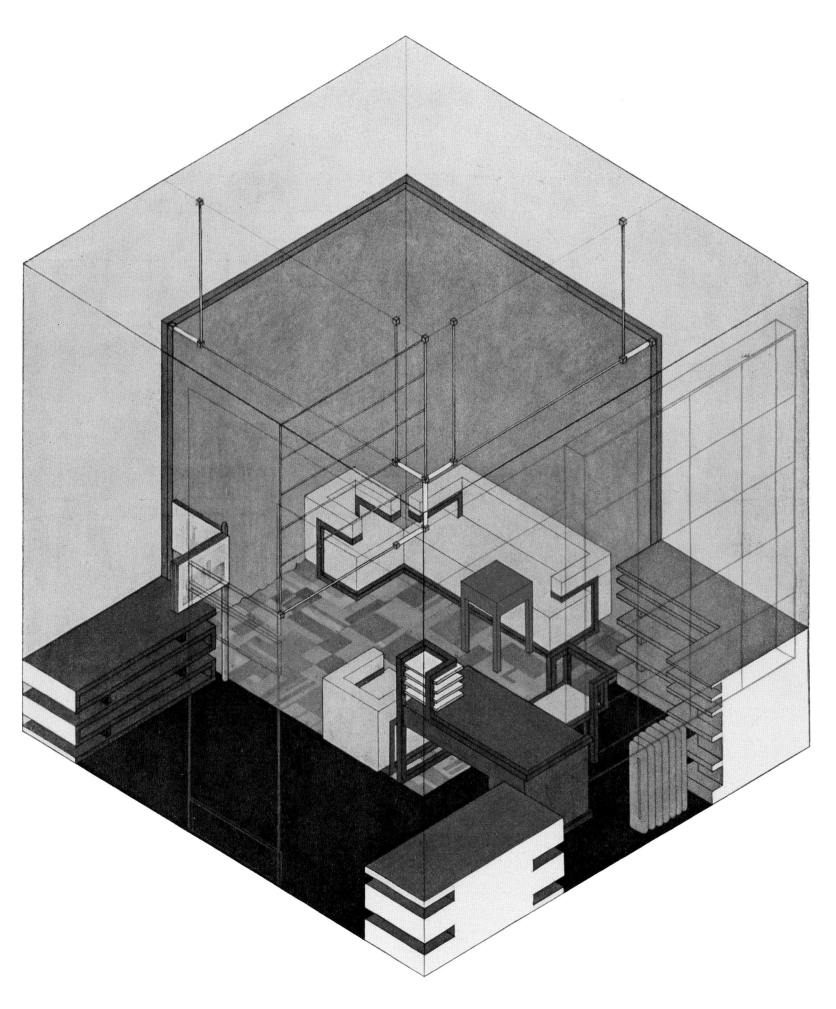

Formulating the Future

Left: G. Guévrékian, 'Salle d'Exercices et de Massage' from Répertoire du Goût Moderne, vol. IV, 1929
In deliberate contrast to the bourgeois norm, a preoccupation with health and fitness was characteristic of the 'modern' life, and the cleanliness and clarity of Guévrékian's exercise and massage room drew a familiar equation between health and logic. The *Répertoire du Goût Moderne* was one of several publications of designs intended to disseminate the new aesthetic.

Opposite: Herbert Bayer, Isometric drawing of Walter Gropius's design of the room for the director of the Bauhaus in Weimar, 1923
The design and presentation were a manifesto for the Bauhaus. The isometric projection stresses the machine-like precision and 'total design' of the interior, and every element – from the overall shape, to the furniture and lamps – is developed from a square. The lamps were derived from Rietveld's 1920 Hanging Lamp, but were not as dynamic in their composition.

Gropius's study shows many of
the features first developed four
years earlier in Weimar. The
chairs, which had solid
cherrywood frames, were
designed in the early 1920s and
treated as three-dimensional
sculptures, not machine-like
products.

and, as Breuer said of all his metal chairs. 'They do not encumber space with their mass'. 'Originals' and cheaper versions are still in production. The year 1926 saw the Cantilever Chair, inspired by a slightly earlier design by Mart Stam and made from a continuous tube to exploit the springiness of the material – it was the model for innumerable later designs. Breuer designed matching bent-metal tables and stools, and their manufacture was taken over by Thonet in 1929. Breuer's chairs were available in several lacquered colours – not just 'natural' metal as has often been supposed. Early Modernism was *not* all white walls, shiny metal and black leather – anything but, in fact! Breuer himself moved to Berlin in 1928 to begin a new career as an architect, and whilst it was to be many years before metal furniture became generally acceptable in living rooms, cantilever chairs on the lines he pioneered were made in huge numbers in the USA during the 1930s, and used mainly in 'functional' areas such as barbers' shops and kitchens. And as stacking chairs, cheap derivatives of the 1920s prototypes were eventually found all over the world in school- and church-halls and other such multi-purpose spaces.

Another of the talented 'Young Masters' who helped shape the Dessau Bauhaus was Gunta Stölzl, the only woman on the staff. She ran the weaving workshop and excelled at both craft-made pieces and designing for machine production, much of her work emulating the qualities of abstract painting. The Bauhaus published its own journal (1926–31), actively sought manufacturers for its prototypes and designed an experimental housing programme in Dessau's Törten district. But many of the designs which later became models for modern taste attracted no interest from industry, and the Törten development was dogged by administrative and constructional problems. Despite these difficulties, the Bauhaus succeeded in developing a language of design entirely free of historicism, applicable to everything, and many of the designs produced during the 1920s later entered production, or were closely copied and came, as we shall see, to define the image of 'modern design' over thirty years later. In founding the Arbeitsrat für Kunst, Bruno Taut expressed the hope that 'henceforward, the artist alone, as the one who gives form to the people's sensibility, is responsible for the visible part of the new state. He must determine the design, from the city to the coin and the postage stamp.' The Bauhaus demonstrated how such an all-embracing design programme might be developed, and whilst no state ever exerted such control over design, the new

world-rulers in the 1950s and 1960s did, design becoming a key weapon in promoting the image and interests of multinational corporations.

The most public expression of Bauhaus ideals came in 1927 when the Deutscher Werkbund presented the state-of-the-art in house-building, furniture and equipment in Stuttgart. A large exhibition, *Die Wohnung* (The Dwelling), was held in the city centre, and on its outskirts the permanent Weissenhofsiedlung was built (literally 'White House Settlement'), the Siedlung, or planned settlement, being the Social Democrats' preferred form of public housing. The Weissenhof featured twenty-one structures by seventeen architects, with interiors by a further fifty-five designers. *Die Wohnung* showed projects from all over Europe, including the work of thirty Czechs – the highest number after the Germans. The Weimar Constitution stated that 'reconstruction could take place only on a basis of total equality', and the Weissenhof was originally intended to be entirely for workers. As realized, it included middle-class housing as well, in which familiar social hierarchies were still going strong – the maid's room in a typical house was tiny, and she was expected to wash in the laundry. To the politically committed, the Modernists were merely 'Salon Marxists', more interested in New Form than New Life; to the rising Nazis, however, they were 'Bolshevik Builders'.

There were genuine innovations at the Weissenhof: Mies, the overall Artistic Director, designed a block of flats which showed the flexibility of layout possible with frame construction, and J. J. P. Oud planned a terrace of very compact low-income houses. Le Corbusier was asked to design for 'the educated middle class' and produced a semi-detached pair of dwellings, and a free-standing Citrohan-type which Mies, rightly, considered 'the most beautiful and best thing at the Weissenhof'. Only a corner-house by Hans Scharoun departed significantly from the 'cubic constructional style' which Muthesius criticized as having 'nothing to do with practicalities'. All the buildings were rendered and most were painted white, with just a few vivid exceptions. Taut, finally having an opportunity to put his 1919 *Call for Colourful Building* into practice, painted the front of his house bright red, one side wall a vivid yellow and the other blue. The interior apparently made this look restrained, Taut explaining that 'it is part of the task of architecture to regenerate the human eye'. The geographical range of houses shown in the *Die Wohnung* exhibition confirmed that by 1927 Modernist architecture was truly international – only Britain and Scandinavia

P. Martiniere, Outside terrace design published by Editions de Bonadona, 1920s
Sport was all the rage in the 1920s, and in Germany the pre-war Wandervogel movement's promotion of physical emancipation was taken up by political parties of left and right. Culture of the body – exercise and sun – was part of the modernist way of life and many houses and flats featured exercise and sunbathing terraces.

Below: Walter Gropius, Hall I of the Werkbund exhibition in Paris, 1930
Gropius's contributions to the exhibition were recreation rooms for a block of flats, including a library with reading alcoves, sports and rest areas, and the 'Cafébar' with its adjacent dance floor.

Bottom: Josef Albers, Dismountable chair, 1929
An early example of knock-down furniture, Albers' design exploited to the full the possibilities of machine production of metal components – unlike many examples of metal furniture which still required craft techniques.

Below: Bauhaus wallpapers, 1920s
Students were invited to submit designs for wallpapers, the best of which went into production. At the time they proved to be the most popular of the Bauhaus products.

Bottom: Marcel Breuer, Model B33 chair, 1930
Breuer was the outstanding furniture designer at the Bauhaus and pioneered the use of bent-metal whilst still a student – bicycle frames and the nearby Junkers aircraft factory were sources of inspiration. Several chairs, including this cantilever model, were manufactured by the Thonet Brothers in Austria.

Opposite: Gunta Stölzl, *Schlitzgobelin rot-grün* rug, 1926–7
A former student and the only woman on the Bauhaus staff, Gunta Stölzl was one of the century's great weavers, equally at home designing for machine production or, as here, on a hand-loom.

NORTHAMPTON COLLEGE
LIBRARY

Above left: Mies van der Rohe, Flats at the Weissenhofsiedlung, Stuttgart, 1926–7

The Weissenhof exhibition was the first major presentation of Modernist architecture to a wide public and attracted numerous, often bemused, visitors. Mies was the artistic director and also designed these flats, whose varied internal plans demonstrated the flexibility of layout possible with frame construction.

Above right: J.J.P. Oud, Workers' Houses, Weissenhofsiedlung, Stuttgart, 1926–7

Oud's small houses were masterpieces of economical, functional design for the *Existenzminimum*.

Right: Paul Klee, *Italian Town*, 1928

The introspective Paul Klee proved to be one of the most influential teachers at the Bauhaus. The interlocking transparent cubes of this typically playful composition have much in common with the interpenetrating spaces of Modernist architecture.

were conspicuous absentees – but beneath the apparent uniformity ran a divide between those to whom it was a problem of *form*, and those who saw it as a question of *building*. Hannes Meyer, in his manifesto 'Building' published in 1928, declared that 'all things in this world are a product of the formula: (function times economy)' and that 'all life is function and is therefore unartistic'. To Le Corbusier, architecture began where Meyer's 'building' ended.

These fault-lines within Modernism were crucial to its future, but to most of the 20,000 people per day who came to wonder at the new architecture of the Weissenhof they were of no concern. To them, the houses must have looked both uniform and uniformly strange. Ernst Bloch thought they had 'the charm of a sanitary facility' and Bertolt Brecht – as iconoclastic in literature as the architects were in building – blamed them on the filth and trauma of the trenches of Arras and Ypres, which he thought had left the soldiers with a desire to live in tiled bathrooms. Against this background of public incomprehension, what united the Modernists was more important than what divided them: they believed in a radical new architecture, in bringing industrial mass-production to bear on the housing problem and in a visual language that was universal both as a matter of principle (humanity had to transcend divisive individualism and nationalism) and because modern science was revealing the basis for a common, abstract language of form. In retrospect these ideals may seem misguided or naively optimistic, but they were born of an understandable passion to change the world irrevocably and for the better.

With the rise of Nazism, Modernism in all its manifestations came under increasing pressure in Germany, and as Hannes Meyer moved the Bauhaus inexorably to the left external attacks grew and he was forced to resign in 1930 as head of an apparently flourishing institution – he had doubled its income and there was keen competition for places. Mies van der Rohe agreed to come to the rescue and tried to de-politicize the courses, facing a near riot in the process – many students considered him a right-wing formalist. In 1931 the Nazis gained control of Dessau, and Mies faced an even more vigorous onslaught than had confronted Gropius in Weimar: the Bauhaus was cosmopolitan and therefore anti-German, Modernist and therefore Bolshevik and, inevitably, Jewish – the architect Paul Schultze-Naumberg had declared the Weissenhof a 'Jerusalem suburb' on account of its white walls and flat roofs, and the Nazis even had a postcard made showing

it by the sea and populated by Middle Easterners! The Bauhaus closed in 1932, and the building itself was only saved by an international campaign. Mies reopened the school as a private institution in Berlin but this was shut down by the police on 11 April 1933, three months after Hitler's accession to power.

By the end of the 1920s, the basis of an 'International Style' in architecture and design was established, some of the most radical manifestations of Modernism in the arts had been assimilated into mainstream culture and Modernism was beginning to shape daily life, most obviously through graphic design. It would be wholly misleading, however, to suggest that public knowledge of, still less appreciation for, the works we have discussed was widespread. The commonly accepted signs of modernity were American rather than European, and those wishing to prove themselves cultured and up-to-date typically professed a passion for Duke Ellington and Charlie Chaplin, not Picasso or the Bauhaus, of which most knew little or nothing. And although Modernism was a thoroughly international phenomenon amongst its producers, it was far less so for its audiences. Even, let us say, a well-informed English admirer of French modern art would be unlikely to know of the leading German Expressionists and still less of what was for many years one of the twentieth century's best-kept secrets, the Russian revolution in art, to which we now turn.

Below: 'Arab Village' postcard, 1940
This postcard, showing the Weissenhofsiedlung transported to the Mediterranean and populated by Arabs, would be amusing but for its racialist overtones: it was produced by the Nazis to ridicule the Modernists' 'Jewish', 'anti-German' ideas.

1940 Stuttgart. Weissenhofsiedlung, Araberdorf

4

We do not need a dead mausoleum of art where dead works are worshipped, but a living factory of the human spirit – in the streets, in the tramways, in the factories, workshops and workers' homes. Vladimir Mayakovsky

Opposite: Gustav Klutsis,
Electrification of the Entire Country, **1920**
Klutsis was the outstanding exponent of the propaganda poster and a pioneer in the use of montage. This study is for one of his finest posters. Its intention was to promote Lenin's plan to electrify Russia, as memorialized in his declaration that 'Communism equals Soviet power plus electrification'.

Left: Alexander Rodchenko,
Coloured typographic designs, 1924
Rodchenko was a masterly graphic designer, producing numerous film and other posters, advertisements, book cover and even sweet-wrappers.

Aesthetic and political revolution were inextricably linked in Russia, and both were fermenting well before the 'ten days that changed the world' brought the overthrow of the Tsar and bourgeois culture in October 1917. The first stirrings of a rebellious modern spirit came in 1863, when a group of young Moscow artists challenged the authority of the St Petersburg Academy of Art – much as Courbet was doing in France. Their hero was Tolstoy, their art Realist and Russian and thus as free as possible from the European influences represented by the Academy. Determined to take their work to the people, the young painters founded the Travelling Exhibitions Society in 1870 and became known as 'The Wanderers'. In 1898 Sergei Diaghilev started *The World of Art* magazine which promoted interest in progressive Western art movements such as Art Nouveau, and also covered developments such as the Nabis, Cézanne and Gauguin. Following its closure in 1904 *The Scales*, a Symbolist literary magazine, *The Golden Fleece* (1906–9) and *Apollon* (1909–17) carried the torch of modern art, organizing exhibitions and publishing the latest (mostly French) ideas. René Ghil, the French correspondent of *The Scales*, wrote regularly about synaesthesia, inspiring the poet Velimir Khlebnikov and the composer Alexander Skryabin, whose *Prometheus* (1910) was scored for piano, orchestra, organ, wordless chorus and a '*clavier à lumières*' ('light-piano'), with keys wired to produce coloured light. Following Skryabin's example, Wassily Kandinsky composed an amalgam of music, movement and light

entitled *Der gelbe Klang* ('The yellow sound').

Two of the wealthiest and most enthusiastic collectors of early modern art lived in Moscow, Sergei Shchukin and Ivan Morozov. Between them they amassed over 350 paintings, including several dozen Picassos and what remains the world's finest collection of Matisses. Morozov opened his house to the public on Sunday mornings, and artists and critics could visit on any day except Mondays; Shchukin was similarly accommodating, and Moscow artists thus had freer access to Europe's most radical art than many of their counterparts in Paris or Berlin and they made good use of it. With revolution in the air – a serious attempt was made in 1905 – it is no surprise that Futurism also found eager followers. Russian Futurism was launched in 1912 by the three Burliuk brothers with the manifesto *A Slap in the Face of Public Taste*. David, a poet and painter, was the natural leader and in 1911 convinced the young Vladimir Mayakovsky (who had already been imprisoned twice for revolutionary activities) that he had poetic talent. Frenetically energetic and with a massive ego, but also generous-spirited and at heart peace-loving, Mayakovsky personified the Russian Futurist spirit.

In collaboration with the painters Mikhail Larionov and Natalia Goncharova, the Burliuks organized the 'Jack of Diamonds' exhibition which ran from December 1910 to January 1911. It was the first landmark Modernist show in Russia. At the same time in St Petersburg, the painter-composer Mikhail Matiushin and his painter-poet wife Elena Guro formed the 'Union of Youth'. They organized exhibitions in 1910-11 which brought together the Moscow and St Petersburg circles and marked the emergence of the 'Cubo-futurists' Olga Rozanova and Vladimir Tatlin. The involvement of women in leading roles was already a notable feature of the Russian avant-garde and was perpetuated into the 1920s. Many of the artists also practised more than one discipline, and literature and the visual arts were so closely linked as to be almost inseparable, the Futurist writers often having their books illustrated by their painter-friends.

David Burliuk, Mayakovsky and the writer, painter and aviator Wassily Kamensky began a long tour of recitals in 1913 and, in the heady air of pre-revolutionary Russia, Futurism proved contagious. The artists spiced such familiar provocations as outrageous dress and painted faces with novelties like pouring tea over their audiences and ringing church bells. The same year Matiushin joined with the painter Kazimir

Matisse Room in Sergei Shchukin's Moscow mansion, photographed in 1913
Shchukin was one of the major patrons of Modernist art and built up the world's finest private collection of Matisse (now in the Hermitage in Leningrad). His mansion was regularly opened to the public, enabling Russian artists to see the latest European ideas.

Malevich and the writers Kruchenykh and Khlebnikov to create the experimental science-fiction opera *Victory over the Sun*. The curtain featured a single black square (which became Malevich's emblem) and Kruchenykh's libretto bemused listeners with pronouncements like 'We have pulled out the sun with fresh roots, it smelt of arithmetic. We are free. Long live darkness.' Following this 'victory', the actors found themselves in the '10th Country', where normal perceptions of space and time had been destroyed, because darkness ruled and gravity had ceased.

Larionov's early work was Primitivist and deeply rooted in Russian tradition, so it was not surprising that he split from the Burliuks' circle in 1912, condemning them as inveterate 'Cézannists'. He was joined by Goncharova, who believed that 'all art comes from the East . . . In the West there was civilization; in the East, culture' – but added that 'our having to fight against Cézanne, Picasso and occidentalism does not mean that we do not need their works.' The tension between Western (generally French) culture and supposedly native and therefore 'authentic' Russian traditions was longstanding, and in his *Neo-Primitivism*, published in 1913, Alexander Shevchenko sided emphatically with all things Russian, writing that 'the primitives, icons, lubki, trays, signs and fabrics of the East – these are authentic models of plastic beauty.' The year 1913 also saw the publication of Larionov's manifestoes on *Rayonist Painting* and *Why We Paint Ourselves* – he appeared in public with his face covered in hieroglyphics and radial markings, hoping to start a new collective art. Rayonism proceeded, he said, from 'the following facts':

1. The radiation caused by reflected light forms a sort of chromatic dust in space between objects.
2. The theory of radiation.
3. Radioactive rays, ultraviolet rays, reflection.

The ideas were probably worked out by Goncharova in 1909-10 and were certainly indebted to the Italian Futurists, as well as to an enthusiasm for (more than an understanding of) modern science. The Rayonist, according to Larionov, saw and painted 'the new shapes created between tangible forms by their own radiation, and it is them alone he captures on canvas'. Or in other words, the Rayonist painted the 'space' the Cubists treated as 'material'.

Having made a modest appearance in the first 'Jack of Diamonds' show and designed the sets for *Victory over the Sun*, Malevich was still unknown outside avant-garde

Kazimir Malevich, *An Englishman in Moscow*, 1913–14
Painted in what was known in Russia as a Cubo-Futurist style, this early work by Malevich confirms his mastery of the principles of Cubism. The underlying symmetry sets it apart from Parisian prototypes, however, and is reminiscent of an icon.

Above: Kazimir Malevich, Backcloth for the opera *Victory over the Sun*, 1913–14
Created by the composer Mikhail Matiushin and writers Kruchenykh and Khlebnikov, the experimental science-fiction opera *Victory over the Sun* was a celebrated avant-garde event. Malevich's backcloth marked the first appearance of his black square motif.

Right: Kazimir Malevich, *Black Square* in '0.10' exhibition in Petrograd (St Petersburg), 1915
Malevich's *Black Square* created a sensation, not least because it was hung diagonally across the corner of the room in the manner of an icon, surrounded by works in his familiar Suprematist style.

circles, but his ambitions became apparent in the '0.10' exhibition held in Petrograd (the new name for St Petersburg, since 1914) in 1915–16. Advertised as the 'last Futurist exhibition' (although Futurism had by no means delivered its last slap in the public's face), Malevich used the occasion to announce the arrival of a new art. His manifesto was republished in 1916 under the title *From Cubism and Futurism to Suprematism: The New Pictorial Realism* and began by staking his claim to have invented abstract art: 'All painting of the past and prior to suprematism (sculpture, verbal art, music) was in thrall to the form of nature and awaited its liberation in order to speak in its own language.' He exhibited thirty-nine wholly abstract works, and the real manifesto of Suprematism was hung across a corner of the exhibition room looking down on the visitors – it is instantly noticeable in photographs, standing out amid the cluttered hang. To any Russian, Malevich's intentions would have been immediately apparent: the painting occupied the place reserved for an icon. And what was this icon of the '10th Country'? A black square, framed in white and titled, naturally enough, *Black Square*. It was painted in 1915 – although Malevich later tried to re-date it to 1913 to help his claims in the race-to-abstraction stakes.

The *Black Square* bordered on the sacrilegious and caused the sort of scandal any Futurist would have been proud of – and amongst supporters of modern art as much as the general public. But Malevich could not have been more serious: he declared *Black Square* 'the face of the new art', the square itself 'a royal child full of life . . . the first step of pure creation in art.' Looking back he said that 'this was no "empty square" which I had exhibited, but rather the feeling of non-objectivity'. He was advocating 'the supremacy of pure feeling in creative art' and the black square became his symbol of artistic revolution. Malevich projected himself as a sage-like figure, declaring: 'I transfigured myself into the zero of forms and went beyond that to the zero of creation, that is to say towards suprematism, towards the new pictorial realism, towards non-figurative creation. Suprematism is the start of a new culture: the savage is conquered as was the ape.' His vision was expanded in paintings of geometric forms floating or soaring in a white, universal space, free of gravity: photographs of early exhibitions show them hung 'upside-down' or on their 'sides' – whether these were mistakes or indications that there was no longer a correct way up is not clear. Malevich believed that his art was the first fruits of a new age in which form would finally triumph over

Kazimir Malevich,
Dynamical Suprematism,
1924
Coloured geometric forms floating or soaring free of gravity in a white space were Malevich's expression of his belief that his art, Suprematism, was the harbinger of a new age in which form would triumph over brute material. His vision was shared by the similarly utopian members of De Stijl in the Netherlands.

Suprematism is the start of a new culture: the savage is conquered as was the ape.

Kazimir Malevich

Rosta Posters, c.1918–19
The State telegraph (Rosta) offices displayed large, brightly coloured propaganda posters. The idea of Mikhail Cheremnykh, a political cartoonist, 1600 were produced in the two years after the Revolution. Many were designed by Cheremnykh himself, and some of the most celebrated were by the poet Mayakovsky.

nature and brute material, and where intuition, not reason, was the only guide. He was an inspiring figure and other artists – Kliun, Rozanova, Popova, Puni and his wife Boguslavskaya, and later El Lissitzky – were not slow to rally to the Suprematist cause.

The year 1915 also marked the arrival of Vladimir Tatlin, who two years earlier had been in Paris where he had met Picasso and seen the latest developments in Cubism. He was familiar with Cubism before he left, but would not have known about collage and *papier collé*, or Picasso's three-dimensional constructions/sculptures, which clearly inspired the polychrome reliefs he made on his return. Wishing to emphasize that Russian inspiration was just as important, Tatlin later told the architect Berthold Lubetkin how, 'inspired by the icons, he started to drill his boards, mounting on them rings, screws, bells, marking and screwing the background, gluing abacus beads, mirrors, tinsels and arriving at a shimmering dangling and sonorous composition.' There was an exhibition of icons in Moscow in 1913, and Tatlin said that without them he would 'have remained preoccupied with water-drips, sponges, rags and aquarelles'. His constructions do not recall icons (although the *Corner Counter-reliefs* occupy the icon's place) but Tatlin may well have been thinking of their elaborate frames, encrusted with precious stones and metals, more than the pictures themselves. What is not in doubt is the primacy of materials in Tatlin's art. He fashioned it from the proletarian stuff of the workshop – wood, scraps of iron and copper, wire and rope, string and nails – and made his love of materials the method and subject-matter of his art, giving pride of place to what in Russian is called *faktura* – the English 'facture' ('the manner of making something, esp. a work of art') is not in common usage. Tatlin published far fewer manifestoes and theories than Malevich, but he was a key figure in the move from art towards design and 'construction': what interested him were real materials in real space. In many ways Tatlin was Malevich's antithesis, and younger artists tended to be drawn to one or other of these poles. This opposition between dematerialization and 'truth to materials' has formed a conspicuous and recurring theme of Modernist art – De Stijl and Cubism presented similar polarities – and finds its roots, ultimately, in the opposition between idealist and materialist philosophies, between religion and 'the world', between the spirit and the body. In Russia, where the mystical traditions of the Orthodox Church were about to be challenged by the revolutionary materialism of Karl Marx, the opposition

not surprisingly took a variety of extreme forms.

The desire to renew the world inspired all the progressive artists and they eagerly embraced the Bolshevik Revolution of October 1917. Tatlin later observed that 'the political events of 1917 were prefigured in our art in 1914', and as artistic revolutionaries who had conquered exhausted bourgeois traditions, they welcomed the challenge of forging a revolutionary, proletarian art. New organizations and groupings proliferated, and several avant-garde artists assumed key positions in the cultural administration: Tatlin, for example, ran the Moscow branch of the Department of Fine Arts (IZO) and Alexander Rodchenko, his most talented follower, became director of the Museums Bureau and Purchasing Fund. Not all agreed with the alliance of art and State, however, and Burliuk and Mayakovsky, in true Futurist spirit, issued the *Manifesto of the Flying Federation of Futurists* in March 1918, calling for 'the separation of Art and the State' and 'the transfer of control of institutions to the artists themselves'. Their words fell on deaf ears and Anatoly Lunacharsky, the Commissar of Education and Culture, only valued the avant-garde's support in the aftermath of the Revolution because no-one else would collaborate with him.

In the chaotic aftermath of the Revolution the Red Army and Agitprop (Agitational propaganda) were equally necessary: the one to fight the Civil War which dragged on into the spring of 1921, the other to sustain revolutionary fervour and win converts to the Bolshevik cause. Where European Modernists had pioneered a 'language of vision' which soon found use in advertising, their Soviet counterparts faced the challenge of helping to sell the Revolution to a vast population, many of whom were illiterate. There were several traditions of visual communication in Russia, including the '*lubok*', an illustrated broadsheet; icons, intended as biblical commentaries; and graphic designs in newspapers. But even knowing that the Red Communists were fighting the counter-revolutionary White Army, the abstract language of El Lissitzky's famous Civil War poster *Beat the Whites with the Red Wedge* (1920) would surely have baffled most unless they could read the title – and many even then.

Every opportunity was taken to promote revolutionary zeal: major holidays, anniversaries of the Revolution and large congresses were marked by elaborate decorations and settings. For the first anniversary of October 1917, for example, artists conceived vast, city-wide spectacles for Moscow and

Left above: Oleg Lialin and Igor Fomin, Installation on the Equality Bridge, Leningrad, 1927
Many avant-garde artists designed large-scale public projects to celebrate significant events and anniversaries in post-Revolutionary Russia. This installation marked the tenth anniversary of the October Revolution.

Left below: El Lissitzky, *Beat the Whites with the Red Wedge*, 1920
Intended as propaganda, this poster's message (the Red Army's impending victory over the anti-Revolutionary White Army) was probably lost on most viewers; as a piece of Suprematist graphic design, however, it remains stunning.

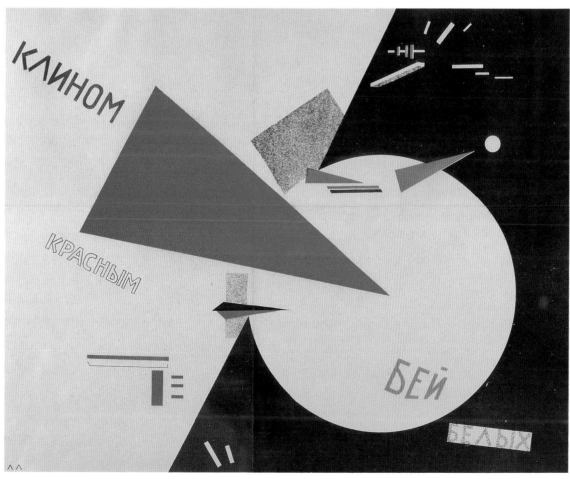

Petrograd, covering them with diagrams and huge coloured panels, punctuated by flags and mottos. One commentator remarked that abstract works which 'seem so acutely revolutionary at exhibition' did not work out-of-doors, and photographs suggest that most struggled to make their presence felt. Size mattered, and in 1921 Alexander Vesnin and Liubov Popova proposed a spectacular setting for a military pageant on Khodynskoe Field for the Third Communist International: two airships supported banners (some the size of a football pitch) above a decaying 'City of Capitalism' and a visionary 'City of the Future'. The idea came to nothing, but the ambition was dazzling

Agitprop trains, boats and lorries roamed the country, taking trained agitators and Communist Party representatives to distribute leaflets and show propaganda films to bemused peasants. The trains had a library, bookshop, printing press, gramophone for broadcasting Lenin's speeches and a coach for meetings and cinema, and carried posters to be displayed by the State telegraph (Rosta) offices. Printed in bright colours on cheap paper, these Rosta posters could be up to four metres high. Many were originated by Mikhail Cheremnykh, a political cartoonist responsible for almost a third of the 1,600 produced in two years – including, it is said, fifty in one night. Despite regular reports of the demise Futurism kept bouncing back, and reservations about too close an alliance with the state were quickly forgotten: the Futurists claimed the Revolution as their own, and threw themselves wholeheartedly into agitprop. Mayakovsky declared, 'Let us make the squares our palettes, the streets our brushes!' and turned his pen to writing texts for Rosta posters – he also drew the illustrations for several hundred. Most were cartoons or in representational

Above: Vladimir Tatlin, Monument to the Third International, on exhibition in Petrograd, 1920
'Tatlin's Tower', as it became known, was to be 400 metres high and straddle the River Neva in Petrograd. Intended to be built of steel and glass, its leaning double-helix symbolised collective effort and aspiration, and was to house vast rotating volumes past which visitors would be moved mechanically, surrounded by flashing messages and a giant screen showing the latest world news.

Right: Replica model of Tatlin's Tower being paraded through Leningrad on May Day, 1925
The Tower became a symbol of the Revolution and made occasional appearances at festivals, when it might, as here, be paraded through the streets like a modern-day relic.

styles, although Malevich contributed a Suprematist image far more baffling than El Lissitzky's 'Red Wedge'. Kom-Fut (Communist-Futurists) was formed in 1919, but was bitterly opposed by Lenin and Lunacharsky who, wanting to preserve the cultural heritage, were horrified by the 'anarchizing, destructive' nature of Futurism. Lenin said he could not understand 'this nonsense that seeks to destroy and reject what is beautiful purely on the grounds that it is old. We must . . . *develop* the finest traditions of our existing culture instead of trying to *invent* a new culture at all costs.' After 1921 the term 'Futurist' was invariably used as a slight, later as an insult, and finally as a pejorative catch-all for the avant-garde.

Few pre-revolutionary institutions survived, but Proletkult (the Proletarian Organization for Culture and Education) was successfully re-formed. Founded in 1906 and revived at the end of 1917, it was the only cultural organization to escape Lunacharsky's control. Its members' Marxist credentials appeared impeccable: they denied the autonomy of art, and advocated a collectivist class art to help in the struggle against the bourgeoisie. But they also believed in the artist's autonomy, prompting Lenin to accuse them of offering 'bourgeois philosophical ideas' under 'the cloak of proletarian culture'. Nor did they find favour with most of the Futurists who considered them 'addicted to the past'. Despite this, the writer and Futurist Osip Brik formulated Proletkult's artist-proletarian ideal, arguing that where the bourgeois artist seeks to please the masses, the true proletarian 'fights against their stubbornness and leads them in a direction that will steadfastly advance art' – much like his Western avant-garde counterpart. The following year he wrote that 'in the Commune everyone is a creator – not in dreams but in life' and the 'artist must know how to do the job of art, how to execute the work . . . (and) carry out specific, socially useful tasks.' Brik became the founder of production art, and many of his precepts were later followed by the Constructivists.

In 1919 Tatlin was asked by IZO to propose a monument to the Revolution and this turned into his visionary *Monument to the Third International* – generally known as 'Tatlin's Tower'. It was conceived as a critique of Lenin's 1918 'Plan for Monumental Propaganda' which envisaged replacing monuments to the 'Tsars and their servants' with sculptures of sixty-six father-figures of the Revolution – even Cézanne was on the list. The tower was to be built of steel and glass – Tatlin called them 'the materials of modern Classicism'

– and the constructional language came straight from the 'Engineer's Aesthetic': a banner hung above the model proclaimed 'Engineers create new forms'. One aim, almost certainly, was to surpass Eiffel – and, by implication, capitalism: in 1918 the great engineer Vladimir Shukhov had proposed a 350-metre radio tower specifically to outdo Paris, a half-size version of which was under construction. Intended to straddle the River Neva in Petrograd, Tatlin's Tower was a leaning double-helix, diminishing as it spiralled up to 400 metres high, from where the inevitable radio antenna transmitted revolutionary propaganda to the world. Three glass volumes were suspended inside the steel framework, each intended to rotate: first, a vast cube for the legislative council of the International, meetings and congresses, turning once a month; next, a pyramid, housing the executive and rotating once a week; and finally, a domed glass cylinder for news media and propaganda offices – the 'spin doctors' appropriately revolving once a day. Dynamism was of the essence – visitors would be moved around mechanically, past flashing messages and a giant screen showing the latest world news, whilst overhead, projections on to clouds would relay messages to the city.

Tatlin's Tower was well beyond the technological capability of the 1920s, let alone backward Russian industries, but like Eiffel's it had a memorable form and quickly became famous. A large wooden model was exhibited in November 1920 in Petrograd and in December during the Eighth Congress of Soviets amidst a mass of other propaganda. Students carried copies in

Alexander Rodchenko and the Stenberg brothers, Obmokhu exhibition, Moscow, 1921
Rodchenko's *Spatial Constructions* and the Stenbergs' *Standing Spatial Constructions* (seen here) are examples of the 'laboratory experiments' with which the Constructivists began their move away from fine art towards architecture and design.

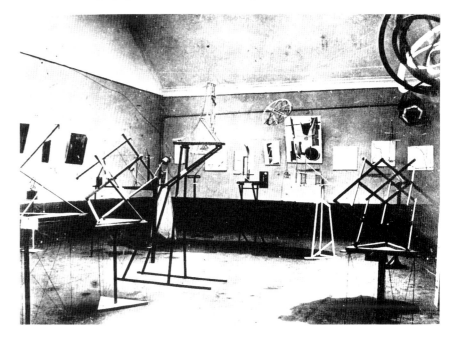

El Lissitzky, Project for Lenin Tribune, 1920–4
El Lissitzky combined the floating planes of Suprematism with a Constructivist lattice structure to create a memorable image of a dynamic, revolutionary aesthetic in the service of the Revolution.

triumph through the streets, and it was debated in the press. Lenin did not like it – he said he would prefer the Eiffel Tower! – nor did El Lissitzky or the sculptor Naum Gabo. Mayakovsky, however, enthused about its 'engineering art', and declared it, with typical wit, 'the first monument without a beard'. Adopted by artists as an emblem of the new artistic consciousness, it soon transcended its original association with the Third International.

The avant-garde exhibited together for the last time at the Tenth State Exhibition in 1919. It turned into a face-off between Suprematism and the emerging Constructivism: in the white corner was Malevich with his first *White on White* square, and in the black corner Rodchenko with several black-on-black paintings, which proved to be the hit of the show and the 'rage of the season' according to his wife, the painter Varvara Stepanova. Their truth-to-materials *faktura* was particularly admired: 'Those shiny, matt, muddy, uneven and smooth parts of the surface result in an extraordinarily powerful composition,' Stepanova noted in her diary. Tatlin had led the way towards this

conception of art, but the outgoing Rodchenko was acclaimed as the leader of the Moscow avant-garde – he likened his discovery of black *faktura* to Columbus's discovery of America.

Rodchenko and Stepanova declared themselves 'the smallest possible creative collective' and took 'The future is our only goal' as their motto. The black-on-black paintings were part of a series Rodchenko called *Concentrations of Colour*. Canvases were prepared with an even, coloured ground, into which geometric forms were inscribed and then distinguished texturally, by *faktura*: the art was in the handling – which Rodchenko called 'the very essence of painting'. After the black-on-black paintings, he moved on to a series based on lines, producing dozens of pencil studies and then ten black and white paintings. Of these he wrote: 'Colour has died in black and become irrelevant, let the brushstroke die too', suggesting a move away from painterly *faktura*. In 1920 he made constructions using a repeating unit – such as a short length of square wood – or by repeated operations: several *Spatial Constructions* were made by cutting rings from a regular figure of silver-painted plywood (circle, hexagon, etc) and then fixing the rings inside each other. Initially thought of as works of art (they are *very* appealing), later the term 'laboratory experiment' was coined to describe such studies: their resemblance to the exercises Albers ran at the Bauhaus is striking, as is the gulf between them and Rodchenko's painterly *faktura* of a few months before. Anonymous, repeatable structures had replaced the unique products of the hand – and the materialist foundations of the Constructivist aesthetic had been laid.

Numerous artists made a similar shift around this time. In a manifesto of October 1920, Stepanova had rejected Osip Brik's idea of the artist-proletarian as 'anathema' and praised the individual 'creative impulse'. Lecturing a year later, she said that in Constructivism 'the intellect is now our point of departure' replacing 'the soul of idealism' and leading to 'the negation of art'. The artists were responding to indicators of significant political changes: in late 1920 the government newspaper *Pravda* published a letter in which 'futurists' were bracketed with 'decadent elements' and 'followers of an idealistic philosophy hostile to Marxism'. The state was tightening the central control of cultural policy, and what had been primarily a political and social transformation had to become an industrial revolution. In 1920 the government began the key programme of the electrification of the country: this prompted Lenin's celebrated pronouncement that

'Communism equals Soviet power plus electrification' – even the British *Daily Express* featured it. Electrification was on everyone's lips and artists projected visions of the new utopia, such as Gustav Klutsis's 1920 photomontage (later turned into a poster) entitled *Electrification of the Entire Country*.

With the Western capitalist system stabilizing after its post-War crises and the immediate prospects of world revolution receding, in 1921 the Soviet government launched the New Economic Policy (NEP) to get production moving again by encouraging private entrepreneurship. Such compromises were deeply unpopular with many of the avant-garde, who wanted a continuation of the atmosphere of the October Revolution. They formed Lef (Left front of arts) and started a journal, edited by Mayakovsky: in effect Lef was the cultural counterpart of the political Left Opposition led by Trotsky – but it was never embraced by the Trotskyites.

Malevich gave up painting in 1918 for several years, preferring to concentrate on theory and teaching. With his rivals in the ascendancy in Moscow, he moved in November 1919 to Vitebsk, where El Lissitzky was head of the graphics and architecture studio at the school of art, recently reorganized by the painter Marc Chagall. Malevich's next theoretical treatise, entitled *On New Systems in Art*, became both the embryo of El Lissitzky's invention of the visual book, and the basis of the lectures with which Malevich won student disciples. He was then at his most charismatic, and the commission to paint decorations for a local anniversary soon after he arrived provided an ideal opportunity to galvanize the school into a collective Suprematist work. The following February a new grouping called Unovis (Affirmers of the New Art) formed around Malevich, dedicated to the principle of collectivity, and in June they received a rapturous reception for an exhibition of work at the First All-Russian Conference of Teachers and Students of Art in Moscow. Unovis was constituted along the lines of a Masonic lodge, with its own password (the 'transrational' U-el-el-el-el-te-ka), rules and symbols and special clothing. As the grand master, Malevich wore white clothes and a white hat symbolic of the 'purity of man's creative life' and his passage into the white world of Suprematism, whilst all the members wore a small black square on their cuffs. With an eye on the wider world, perhaps, El Lissitzky preferred a red square and was never a totally committed member of Unovis. Despite this he always referred to his Lenin Tribune of 1924 as his 'Unovis project'. Based on a 1920 project made with one of his Vitebsk students, I'ia Chashnik, the Tribune combined the floating planes of Suprematism with the industrial elements beloved of the Constructivists: it was never built, of course, but it is difficult to think of a single image which more clearly sums up the idea of a revolutionary aesthetic in the service of the Revolution.

Malevich's ideas had developed significantly after 1917,

Below left: Kazimir Malevich, *Horizontal Arkhitekton*, 1925–6
Malevich's *arkhitektons* were intended as more concrete embodiments of the 'new world' than his Suprematist paintings. Based on the cube (the three-dimensional counterpart of his iconic square) and made of plaster, they influenced the designs of young Soviet architects.

Below right: Nicholas Suetin, Suprematist inkwell designed as a *Planit*, Lomonosov factory, 1929
The ceramic wares designed by Malevich's students were amongst the most successful attempts to get avant-garde ideas into industrial production. The *planits* were a form of *arkhitekton* – the intended connotations are obvious.

NORTHAMPTON COLLEGE LIBRARY

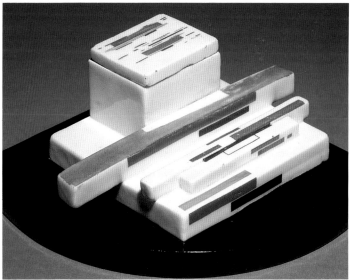

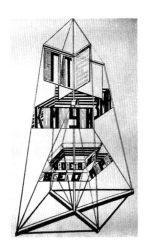

Gustav Klutsis, Demountable agitational stand, 1922
Klutsis designed fourteen agitational stands, 'radio-orators' and 'cinema-photo stands' in an exuberant Constructivist style. This one, painted red and black, bore the slogan 'Agit-propaganda for Communism. Proletariat of the whole world.'

and were embodied in white plaster constructions of a rudimentary new architecture he called *Planits* (probably derived from 'planets') and later *Architektons*. Integral to his vision of utopia was a technology which could overcome gravity: the weightlessness he projected in his paintings became the ideal state of a truly revolutionary architecture, towards which the *Architektons* were a first tentative step. Like the De Stijl artists, Malevich thought that in this New World 'the harmonization of architectural forms . . . will necessitate the replacement of existing furniture, crockery, clothes and posters.' He developed a theory that all matter was a product of 'rotating energy', writing that 'the universe or the cosmos seems to me to be an infinite number of fields of force turning around their centres of excitation'. El Lissitzky took this literally and made some paintings which were designed to be rotated.

Malevich's ideas of a weightless architecture also inspired El Lissitzky's *Prouns* and *Sky-hooks*: he saw 'flying man' as the ultimate product of evolution, and as early as 1922 Ernst Kállai mentioned the 'relationship to the spatial feeling of flying' when commenting on the *Prouns*. The name is a contraction of the phrase 'Projects for affirming the new' and Lissitzky defined them as 'interchange stations' to architecture. Resembling an aerial view of a group of buildings, they were invariably positioned on the paper or board diagonally – the diagonal being dynamic, as opposed to the 'passive' horizontal and 'the authoritarian' vertical. El Lissitzky was sent to Berlin in 1921 by Lunacharsky, following the decision at the second Communist International in 1920 to form an international Proletkult. Most artists assumed he was simply there to promote Russian art – which he did – but the real purpose was to help prepare for a Communist takeover: Lenin had decided that a cultural invasion should precede military action. Lissitzky became a Russian ambassador-at-large and spent a considerable amount of time travelling around Europe, seeking converts and making contacts with left-wing artists. In 1923 he installed the *Proun Room* in an exhibition in Berlin, which greatly impressed Mies van der Rohe and Theo van Doesburg, amongst others, and his graphic design work became influential throughout Europe – he was perhaps the outstanding innovator in the field.

Two key art and design institutions were established in 1920 in Moscow: Inkhuk (Institute of Artistic Culture) and Vkhutemas (Higher State Artistic and Technical Studios). Inkhuk was a research centre for contemporary art directed first by Wassily Kandinsky – who resigned the following year, his idealist spirituality having fallen out of favour – and then by Rodchenko. Vkhutemas was as experimental and innovative an art school as the Bauhaus; within it, Obmas (United Architectural Studios) became the focus of a Rationalist architecture led by the influential teacher Nikolai Ladovsky, who also founded Asnova (Association of New Architects) in 1923. Ladovsky's Rationalism was based on theories of psychology rather than the more familiar form-follows-function rationalism of use, structure and materials. He wanted to find scientific methods applicable to design, and believed it should be possible to measure the psychological effect of architecture on the viewer – much as Pavlov extrapolated from salivating dogs to human behaviour. This emphasis on spatial perception, despite its materialist foundations, set him apart from the more functionally and technologically minded Constructivists. Ladovsky developed inventive introductory projects which found their way into the school's basic studies programme, the equivalent of the Bauhaus's *Vorkurs*. Drawn studies of historical architecture were replaced by analyses of abstract shapes and architectural elements using models, and the results were remarkable: many of the student projects would look quite at home in schools of architecture today – as would Georgy Krutikov's 1928 Diploma design. Having studied 'mobile elements' in architecture, Krutikov designed a 'cosmic city' whose 'site' was the Solar System – embodying the ultimate dream of 'Flying Cities', and very much in the spirit of Malevich's expansive thinking.

A theoretical base for a constructive art was first laid out by the brothers Gabo and Pevsner in their *Realist Manifesto* of 1920. They argued that artists should forsake past art 'and like an engineer building a bridge construct . . . our objects with the precision of a pair of compasses' – an ideal captured in El Lissitzky's masterly montage self-portrait *The Constructor* (1924), in which hand and head are united in the act of drawing a perfect circle. Rodchenko, Stepanova and Alexei Gan formed the First Working Group of Constructivists in 1921, and by the end of the year Rodchenko's Inkhuk group had concluded that 'genuine construction appears only in perfect, utilitarian products . . . The prospect of participating in the organization of life by organizing objects, buildings and institutions was inspiring.' Encouraged by Osip Brik, Alexander Vesnin, Rodchenko and others made their 'last' paintings and sought opportunities to get involved in real production in industry designing anything from sweet-wrappers to

Every form is the petrified snapshot of a process. Therefore, work is a station in evolution and not its petrified **aim.** El Lissitzky

El Lissitzky, *The Constructor*, 1924
A composite photographic image fusing the artist's head and hand (holding a pair of compasses) against a ground of graph paper, personal letterhead and large stencil letters. The result is a brilliant image of the artist-constructor-typographer whose work combines hand, eye and mind.

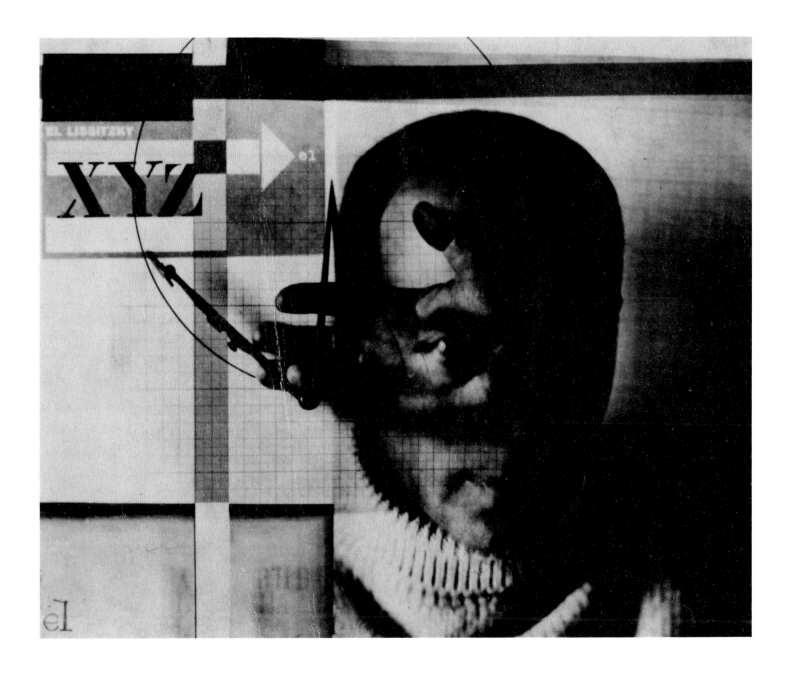

**Top: Nicholas Suetin, Small Suprematist plate, c. 1920
Centre: Soviet propaganda plate 'Long Live the Third International', c. 1920
Bottom: Soviet propaganda plate 'Land to the working people', c. 1920**
The Imperial Porcelain factory in Leningrad had an outstanding tradition of finely decorated wares, which was successfully turned to serve propaganda ends. Most of the production was stylistically unadventurous, but a few members of the avant-garde such as Suetin succeeded in getting designs into production.

buildings. The '5x5=25' exhibition of 1921 marked the point of no return: Rodchenko's five canvases included three in monochrome (red, blue and yellow) which seemed to spell the end of painting. The Constructivists saw themselves as the heirs to Tatlin's ideas – exemplified in his Tower – and believed there should be a direct link between revolutionary ideology and construction.

Alexei Gan's *Konstruktivizm* of 1922 was a highly polemical combination of aesthetics and ideology calling for a revolt against the cult of 'pure beauty' and denouncing traditional art as inextricably linked to 'theological, metaphysical, and mystical premises' which were inimical to the emerging materialist culture. All that could usefully be learnt from past art, Gan argued, was its accumulation of skills and knowledge about techniques – beyond that, 'We declare unconditional war on art.' Or, as one of the Productivists' slogans proclaimed, '*Down with Art! Long live Technology! Long live the Constructivist Technician!*' Trying to develop the role of 'Constructivist Technician' in industry as opposed to in theory, however, proved fraught with difficulties. Quite apart from the desperate state of most industries, both managers and workers were prejudiced against any contribution by artists – let alone true collaboration.

Tatlin's forays into industry produced nothing, and Popova and Stepanova met with only limited success working in the First State Textile-printing Factory in Moscow in 1923–4. They began with the basic weaving techniques, rather than supplying 'designs' to be 'applied', and sought to rationalize the patterns into simple geometrical forms of unmixed colours. But their interventions, which were intended to achieve a maximum economy of means, seemed to matter little in practice, and the factories soon reverted to traditional designs after they left. Clothing appeared more promising because the October Revolution had ushered in the idea of 'mass clothing for the workers' – from which, Stepanova argued, 'all decorative, prettifying aspects of clothing are swept away by the watchword of comfort and suitability for the given form of production.' In the theatre, the new men and women appeared dressed in her bold, geometric sportswear, and Rodchenko worked in his own artist-engineer's outfit – but their clothes did not make the transition from stage or studio to street. Most of the 'agitational crockery' produced by the famous Imperial Porcelain factory near Petrograd was relatively traditional but with the addition of uplifting slogans such as 'Science Must Serve the People' and 'We shall set the World Ablaze with the Fire of the Third International'. Many members of the

avant-garde submitted proposals but relatively few were put into production. Amongst those that were were Nikolai Suetin and I'ia Chashnik's Suprematist motifs and a cup and saucer by Kandinsky. Not content with mere decoration, Malevich produced prototypes for a Suprematist cup and a surprisingly complex teapot.

Rodchenko set to work with his students at Vkhutemas making prototypes to demonstrate the Constructivist credo, central to which was the idea that objects should be 'constructed throughout' or, in the words of his friend Alexander Vesnin, they should be 'materialized energy, possessing dynamic properties (movement, direction, weight, speed) and determined according to their purpose' – a kind of dynamic (i.e. Revolutionary) form follows function. Gustav Klutsis drew fourteen demountable agitational stands ('radio-orators', 'cinema photo-stands', etc) in this spirit, to be made from readily available materials such as wood, wire and canvas. The vehicle Rodchenko chose was multi-purpose furniture, such as a combined bed, chair and desk, or a table that folds away after use, and he saw them as making the most efficient use of space and materials, but they were often not as practical as he hoped. Their ideological charge was just as important, and like Rietveld's Red and Blue Chair, they were intended as prototypes of a new reality. The past culture of solid objects and monumental buildings would be replaced by transformable structures in space; ponderous, static masses of stone (the old Classicism) by dynamic, gravity-defying frames of steel and moving parts and volumes (Tatlin's modern Classicism). This dynamic new functionalism was a major addition to the Modernist vocabulary, and radically different from the Platonic beauties of the International Style. It is only now, since the rediscovery of Russian Constructivism and the development of affordable technologies, that its possibilities are being explored in practice – although fairground rides have long offered analogous delights, as free of revolutionary zeal as the current formalist revival of the Constructivist aesthetic.

In 1923 Mayakovsky asked Rodchenko and Stepanova to work with him on a Soviet commercial advertising campaign to compete with the private companies resurgent under the NEP. In two years they produced over a hundred advertisements, Rodchenko winning a silver medal in the 'Street Art' exhibition in Paris in 1925. Mayakovsky later looked back on this as some of the most useful work he had done, and his friend Blaise Cendrars – who declared 'Poetry = Publicity' – envied him the opportunity to reach the masses. Recalling a

Alexander Rodchenko,
***Kino-Glaz* poster, 1924**
The radical film-maker, Dziga
Vertov, founded the magazine
Kino-Glaz in 1924. He
advocated Constructivist
principles, from the
revolutionary content to the
'construction' of the film and
what he called the 'geometrical
extract of each shot'.

slogan for the state department store, Mayakovsky wrote: 'I believe that *Nowhere / Like at Mosselprom* is poetry of the highest order', which sounds a tall claim until it is heard in the rhythmic, cleverly phrased Russian original: *Ni-gdye kromye/ Kak v Mosselpromye*. To complement Mayakovsky's words, Rodchenko developed a bold graphic style designed to grab attention and be cheap to print, generally requiring only two colours and black. Combining large exclamation marks, arrows and lines, with stylized pictures and hand-drawn sans-serif lettering, he frequently organized the words symmetrically, with colours reversed either side of a central axis. In addition to display material, Rodchenko and Mayakovsky designed sweet-wrappers on themes like 'Leaders of the Revolution' and 'Industrialization', many of which found their way to rural areas.

In pictorial art, the Constructivists followed the Dadaists away from easel-painting (which was regarded as 'bourgeois' and unrelated to industry and the needs of mechanical reproduction) and into experiments with photographic material. Klutsis claimed that his *Dynamic City* (1919-20) was the first photomontage by a Soviet artist, and he developed into a master of the medium which became the favoured vehicle for revolutionary propaganda. Klutsis called photomontage 'the art of socialism's construction' and its appeal was obvious: it combined two of the most characteristic tendencies in

modern visual culture – abstraction and photo-realism – into an effective means of mass-communication. The formal structure of *Dynamic City* was probably derived from one of El Lissitzky's Proun paintings, with abstract elements replaced by a skyscraper (volume) and facade (plane): the rotational composition was intended to suggest the dynamism of the new Communist world.

At the Cologne *Pressa* exhibition in 1928, El Lissitzky drove home the idea of total revolutionary transformation by engulfing visitors to the Soviet pavilion in a three-dimensional montage of images, some fixed to enormous belts, like a rotary printing press – a homage to the technology of news propaganda. Klutsis worked for several organizations during the 1920s, but it was in promoting Stalin's first Five-Year Plan (1928–33) that he produced his finest work. The poster *Development of Transport: The Five-Year Plan* (1929), for example, effortlessly combines graphic and photographic elements, uses relative size to represent both importance and numbers, and communicates its essential meaning by the design alone – words only reinforce or supplement the message. Unlike Rodchenko's work in which the 'design' elements were conspicuous, Klutsis seems to achieve pure communication – nothing is extraneous. Like most Soviet designers, he made frequent use of the dynamic diagonal and in *Let's Return the Coal Debt to the Country!* (1930) a slight tilt turns a photograph of three miners walking towards the viewer into a powerful expression of the onward march of industry and the proletariat. The avant-garde energy evident in the posters of Klutsis and many other Soviet designers was finally suppressed by Stalin, and little work of merit appeared after 1932. Familiar in the West through exhibitions and publications, Soviet graphic design was widely admired for its fusion of a revolutionary aesthetic with radical social needs, and remains one of the major achievements in the search for a machine art expressive of a mass society which Russian artists shared with their Western counterparts.

Cinema was well established in Russia before the Revolution, and as early as 1913 Mayakovsky expressed doubts that theatre could survive this new competition. Shortage of film-stock in the aftermath of the Revolution (when it was hidden by companies unsympathetic to the Bolshevik cause) meant that there was little activity until the NEP brought a more stable economic climate. In 1922 a group of 'film-constructivists' started the magazine *Kino-Fot*, and in their October issue Mayakovsky advocated the cinema

Gustav Klutsis, 'Workers, Everyone Must Vote in the Election of Soviets' poster, 1930
Trying to build consensus in a country as vast and disparate as the Soviet Union was a formidable task, and with illiteracy still common in rural areas, posters needed to be as visual and direct as possible. For this memorable image Klutsis used his own hand, repeated many times.

as 'a way to understand the world'. This was the aspiration of Dziga Vertov who developed a highly original documentary method based on sending out roving correspondents to shoot footage around the country, which Vertov and his assistant, Elizaveta Svilova, then edited. Vertov aimed to follow Constructivist principles in all aspects of film, from its revolutionary content to the 'construction' of the film and what he called the 'geometrical extract of each shot'. In a 1924 manifesto he said that cinema was 'the microscope of time, the possibility of seeing without boundaries . . . it means tele-eye, ray-eye, . . . EVERYTHING that might serve to seek out and show forth the TRUTH.' Using a host of innovative cinematic techniques – slow motion, superimpositions, dissolves, montage, sound in counterpoint – Vertov aimed to replace direction by documentation, acting by real life. Echoing Marx's judgement of religion, he condemned conventional dramas as 'the opium of the people' and made a series of picture-poems – *Stride, Soviet!*, *The Eleventh Year*, *Symphony of the Donbas* – in which his determination to innovate cut him off from the mass audience he wanted to reach – the familiar fate of the avant-garde.

The second half of the 1920s proved to be the golden age of Soviet cinema, yielding almost 800 films and seeing the emergence of several outstanding directors. The leading figure and greatest innovator was undoubtedly Sergei Eisenstein, who established a national and international reputation with *Strike* in 1924. Adapting the theatrical principle of a 'montage of attractions' learnt in the theatre under the great director Meyerhold, he used a flood of details and events to shatter conventional photographic realism, the montage technique enabling him to assemble a new reality from images which ceased to operate as simple reflections of objects, but became bearers of emotion and thought. *Strike* changed Soviet cinema and exerted an influence worldwide, as did his masterpiece *Battleship Potemkin* of 1925 – the unforgettable Odessa Steps sequence ranks amongst the great moments in world cinema. *October* (also known as *Ten Days that Shook the World*) appeared in 1928. A dramatic reconstruction of the Bolshevik revolution to mark its tenth anniversary, it signalled Eisenstein's position as, in effect, the State's 'official film-maker', a role he relinquished in 1930 to join Paramount in Hollywood – only to return, disillusioned, five years later.

There were few opportunities to build anything in the early 1920s, let alone the kind of innovative projects the avant-garde architects envisaged. Constructivist architecture was first realized as cinema- and stage-sets, and in films, much the most spectacular example being Yakov Protazanov's film *Aelita* (1924), which featured scenes on Mars using a gigantic Constructivist set and costumes by Alexandra Exter and Isaac Rabinovich. In the theatre, Meyerhold was applying Taylorist principles to acting, modernizing it through a system of 'biomechanics' intended to remove superfluous movements and leave only 'constructive gestures'. For Meyerkhold's staging of *The Magnanimous Cuckold* in 1922 Popova created a simple wooden machine-for-acting-on, and for *The Earth in Turmoil* the following year, she used a striking machine-assemblage (made of car, tractor, bicycle and weapons) around a kind of gantry crane. It was through his stage-sets that Alexander Vesnin emerged as a major force in Constructivism, and these culminated in his 1923 design for *The Man Who Was Thursday*, a miniature modern city of cross-braced frames, skeletal towers – and a crane to add the necessary hint of dynamism.

The three Vesnin brothers, led by Alexander, quickly became the recognized leaders of Constructivist architecture, making their mark with a third-prize-winning entry in the competition for the vast Palace of Labour (1922–3). In 1924 they produced two more outstanding competition projects: the Offices of the Leningradskaya Pravda (2nd prize) and the Arcos Building. The tiny newspaper tower, set on a site six metres square, featured lifts and stairs in glass shafts, a large plate-glass window for back-projections of news and advertising, a clock and a loudspeaker. At night it would become a truly dynamic miniature city – like the views of New York which probably inspired it – and it was technically feasible, unlike the winning design by Konstantin Melnikov whose 'architecture that is alive' featured floors rotating around a circular core – dynamism as literal and almost as technologically improbable as in Tatlin's Tower. The Vesnins' Arcos project was much larger but simpler, an elegantly proportioned skin-and-bones building presented with immaculately rendered coloured drawings.

The competition for the Soviet pavilion at the 1925 Paris Exhibition of Decorative and Industrial Arts brought the twin challenge of representing revolutionary ideals and doing so in double-quick time – France was slow to recognize the official formation of the USSR, so the invitation arrived late. Melnikov's winning project was designed to be prefabricated in wood and composed as a long rectangular box, slashed open by a diagonal staircase and walkway, roofed with inclined planes flipping back and forth – dynamism through static means. Rodchenko organized the displays, which included a model of Tatlin's Tower and a small purpose-designed 'Workers' Club', full of ingenious furniture including a 'spatial construction' lamp which had a short production run in Italy in 1974 – and won a medal for 'originality' at the Milan Triennale fifty years after its first appearance. The rigour of Melnikov's design – a constructional necessity arising out of the demands of prefabrication – greatly impressed the European avant-garde, and with Le Corbusier's pavilion for *L'Esprit Nouveau* it was the only Modernist architecture to be seen at the exhibition. Henri Lefebvre (who saw it when he was in his mid-twenties) later recalled that its aggressive originality not only 'scandalized the bourgeoisie' but also brought home to the radical young the idea that abstract art 'was synonymous with cultural revolution'.

The Soviet Union was seen as a promised land by several leaders of the Western avant-garde, and developments in Europe were equally keenly followed in Russia. *Vers une Architecture* was reviewed soon after publication, and knowledge of the original *L'Esprit Nouveau* articles was apparent in Moisei Ginzburg's *Style and Epoch* (1924), a systematic treatise setting Constructivism in a historical context. When Le Corbusier made his first visit to Moscow in 1928, he thought he had entered 'the promised land for technicians'. His ideas being already well known, he was accorded a warm reception, and his enthusiasm no

doubt also reflected the fact that he had just won the competition for the Tsentrosoyuz building and was hopeful of securing further commissions in a country where it seemed that social and aesthetic experimentation could go hand in hand.

One of the new building types being thrown up by the Soviet system was the Workers' Club, where people of all ages could 'be educated into becoming collective human beings', as El Lissitzky put it in 1930 in *Russia: An Architecture for World Revolution*. With the population largely illiterate, still highly religious and ignorant of what the new regime was trying to achieve, workers' clubs, usually attached to the workplace, were places where basic re-education was combined with some entertainment and the building of a more collective mentality. Clubs quickly proliferated in disused palaces and houses – 7,000 were established during the first two years of Soviet rule, but some were showpieces of the new architecture. Melnikov built several around Moscow, of which the Rusakov Club (1927–9) was the most striking, thanks to its dramatically projecting auditoria – a feature which led to its becoming one of the most widely published of all Soviet buildings in the West. Mass bakeries – most bread was still baked in the home – and kitchens ('communal cooking laboratories' as Lissitzky called them) were established with the intention of freeing women from cooking, and the traditional (i.e. 'bourgeois') idea of the family was questioned. Architects were asked to study alternative, communal, forms of housing, and the first OSA (Union of Contemporary Architects – the Constructivists' alternative to Asnova) Congress in 1929 backed a model for socialist housing based on communal facilities, including collective eating and raising of children, with only sleeping accommodation provided on an individual/family basis.

Alexander Vesnin argued that architects 'must engage in the active construction of the new life and share in the formulation of original architectural requirements' and noone relished the freedom to invent the future more than Ivan Leonidov, a prodigiously talented student of the Vesnins at the Vkhutemas – 'a poet, and the hope of Russian Architectural Constructivism' was Le Corbusier's assessment. Leonidov achieved recognition with a project for the *Izvestia* newspaper offices in 1926 made as a student in Alexander Vesnin's studio in Vkhutemas architecture department, and broke new ground in 1927 with his Diploma project for a Lenin Institute of Librarianship. This started as part of the student phase of the Lenin Library competition,

Liubov Popova, Stage-set for *The Magnanimous Cuckold*, 1922
The set – or 'acting apparatus' – was designed for a production by Meyerhold, who later acknowledged that 'much in the tone of the performance was taken from the constructive set'. The idea of a skeletal framework was originated by the Stenberg brothers and proved to be highly influential.

but Leonidov changed the brief and site, and produced a design which broke completely with traditional ways of conceiving buildings, offering a seductive vision of a new urbanism based on volumes in space organized around communication links. In 1929–30 Leonidov designed a competition project for a House of Industry which rethought office work: he envisaged open-plan working, with periodic breaks in landscaped areas, and exercise facilities on the roof of a forty-storey glass tower – it would have fitted seamlessly into the 1980s. For the 1930 competition for a Palace of Culture to serve a southern district of Moscow he produced his purest Suprematist composition: four squares for sports arranged around a pyramidal gymnasium, and all part of a comprehensive proposal for the leisure facilities of the district. The design provoked a storm of criticism – 'petit-bourgeois', 'cut off from reality', 'profoundly individualistic', 'irrelevant experimentalism' – and offered a pretext for criticizing the avant-garde as a whole.

By 1930 the political and cultural climate had changed dramatically. The Left Opposition were defeated in 1927, and Stalin and his apparatchiks had tightened their grip on power: Trotsky was in internal exile, and opposition became a crime. During the late 1920s the leading avant-garde artists came under attack from two directions: firstly, from members of the younger generation, often their own students, who were strongly committed to Marxism and the ideal of production art; and secondly from officials, politicians and workers suspicious of their ideas. All media were now expected to communicate a clear ideological message: the geometric fabrics designed by Popova and Stepanova, for example, failed this test since if there was a 'message', it was certainly not one the average worker could respond to. The younger designers argued for 'agitational' designs with motifs based on electrification, machinery, aeroplanes and other industrial themes. These were elegantly designed, but proved as unpopular as the earlier abstract designs: the workers wanted traditional floral patterns. The young designers responded that this was because they were still in thrall to feudal values, proving the need for more, not less, agitational designs. The younger generation had a tight grip on the relevant union, and stocks of unsold agitational fabrics mounted up – the policy was only reversed in 1933 at the start of the second Five-Year Plan, when the Council of Peoples' Commissars, no less, banned the agitational designs.

Every medium was debated in these terms. In architecture, the Rationalists' association, Asnova, was taken over by young architects whose devotion to functionalism was so fanatical that the older Constructivists were considered ideologically suspect. In 1928 Rodchenko turned to photography as his main medium, and managed to achieve his dream of obtaining a Leica camera. He developed a style of reportage based on multiple snapshots, many taken from unusual angles or close up, reflecting his literary friend Viktor Shklovsky's idea of 'making strange' as a means of opening people's eyes. This was opposed as 'bourgeois subjectivism' by a group advocating 'photo-

Above: Alexandra Exter, Puppet, 1927
One of the first Constructivists, Exter was a gifted painter who produced her most innovative work in the theatre. Her 1917 sets for the Kamernyi Theatre's production of Oscar Wilde's *Salome* were revolutionary, as were those for the 1924 film *Aelita*, which were amongst the largest executed Constructivist designs.

Below: Alexander Rodchenko, Workers' Club at the Soviet Pavilion, Exhibition of Decorative and Industrial Arts, Paris, 1925
The Soviet Pavilion, designed by Melnikov, was an outstanding success and included this model Workers' Club by Rodchenko. It features purpose-designed furniture and light fittings and was donated to the French Communist Party.

NORTHAMPTON COLLEGE LIBRARY

The modern engineer has created works of genius: the bridge, the steam locomotive, the aircraft, the crane . . . The modern artist must produce objects equal to them in strength, tension and potential, organising principles in terms of their psychophysiological impact on human consciousness. Alexander Vesnin

Right: Vesnin brothers, Competition project for Pravda Tower, 1924
This seminal project won second prize in the competition for the Moscow offices of the Leningradskaya Pravda newspaper. The scale is tiny, but the Vesnins still managed to evoke a dynamic city in miniature (note the lifts in a glass shaft) in an image which has entered the Modernist canon.

Opposite: Ilia Golosov, Zuev Club, Moscow, 1926–7
One of several clubs erected to mark the tenth anniversary of the October Revolution, its bold and brilliant resolution of the corner was emulated almost immediately in Italy by Giuseppe Terragni in his Novocomum block of flats in Como.

Ivan Leonidov, Diploma project for the Lenin Institute of Librarianship, 1927
Highly acclaimed at the time, this has become one of the seminal Modernist projects. It broke radically with traditional ways of conceiving buildings and offered a powerful vision of a new urbanism based on volumes in space organized around communication links.

Aspirations of the Constructivist and Rationalist architects to see modernism predominate in the Soviet Union were dashed in 1931–2 when Party preferences in architecture were unequivocally manifest in the competition to design the Palace of the Soviets, an updated version of the Palace of Labour first mooted in 1922–3, whose hall was now to seat 15,000 people. Several leading European Modernists – including Gropius, Mendelsohn, and Le Corbusier – were invited to take part and Le Corbusier produced a *tour de force* of a project. But none of the entries found favour and the competition was re-run. Lunacharsky explained that what was needed was an expression of 'the grandeur – that is, the power, simplicity, and joyful attitude toward life – of the proletariat' and gave the helpful advice that 'a nearly classical allure, much as in Greece, displaying grandeur, stability, harmony of proportion, light, and extensive use of sculpture' would be appropriate. Three equal first prizes were awarded in the main, open competition and one of the authors, Boris Iofan, went on under guidance of the Palace Committee to produce the ultimately approved scheme, an astonishing neo-classical wedding cake of a building surmounted by a vast statue of Lenin intended, one suspects, to outdo the Statue of Liberty.

In his determination to catch up with the industrially advanced West, Stalin pursued the single goal of economic growth with ruthless efficiency – Soviet economic output at least tripled between 1929 and 1940 – and through the exercise of absolute power. In April 1932 the Central Committee of the Party issued a decree dissolving all the separate groups and associations and created single official 'Unions' for artists and writers – the same fate befell architects in July. Art was to be socialist in content and realist in execution; in architecture, public buildings should be monumental in character and draw upon appropriate historical styles, ideally incorporating mural paintings and sculptures on revolutionary themes. Avant-garde art became a crime against the state. Several leading artists had left during the early 1920s – Chagall, Kandinsky, Pevsner, Gabo; a few (the most notable was Klutsis) became victims of Stalin's purges. The poet Mayakaovsky had already committed suicide in 1930. Tatlin and Malevich reverted to realism, and Rodchenko eliminated unusual perspectives from his photographic repertoire. He spent more than a year documenting the building of the White Sea Canal – one of Stalin's great set-piece projects – for a special issue of *SSSR na Stroyke* (USSR in Construction). The pictures were superb, not

pictures' which showed the world 'whole': Marx, they said, wanted to 'connect the disconnected' whereas Rodchenko's approach was based on deliberate fragmentation. He, in turn, saw theirs as banal, calling it 'flag-waving patriotism in the form of spewing smokestacks and identical workers with hammers and sickles.' To Rodchenko photography was the modern medium par excellence and, in his seminal article 'Against the Synthesized Portrait, For the Snapshot' published in 1928, he asked: 'Tell me honestly, what should remain of Lenin: a bronze statue, oil portraits, etchings, watercolours, his secretary's diary, the reminiscences of friends – or a folder of photographs taken when he was working and relaxing, an archive of his books, writing pads, notebooks, shorthand notes, film-clips, gramophone records?' Rodchenko's grasp of the power of the new media was remarkably farsighted: but the Russian tide was turning emphatically in favour of 'bronze statues'.

Alexander Rodchenko, *The War of the Future*, 1930
Images change meaning according to their context. What Rodchenko presents here is an evocation of the future, presumably heroic, war against capitalism (represented by American skyscrapers) and not a chilling vision of the inhumanity of mechanized warfare.

Rationalism in architecture is an economy of psychic energy for the sake of perceiving the spatial and functional properties of an edifice. Nikolai Ladovsky

Le Corbusier, Competition project for the Palace of the Soviets, 1931–2
Several Europeans were invited to compete in this prestigious competition, and Le Corbusier produced one of the finest projects of his career. However, a Modernist design stood no chance of winning as the ideological tide had turned decisively against the avant-garde.

one even hinting at the suffering in what was, in effect, a mobile forced labour camp which cost tens, probably hundreds, of thousands of lives.

Of all the developments we have examined, it was undoubtedly Constructivism that was the most radical, both in its formal innovations and its challenge to traditional conceptions of art. No longer to be the province of a cultured few, art must become part of, and reflect, everyday life – not represent, beautify, idealize or criticize it. In seeking to eliminate the distance between art and life the Constructivists redefined the artist as an artist-engineer who could be an integral part of economic production. In retrospect, the aspiration of a tiny urban avant-garde to formulate a visual language which could represent Soviet society as a whole may seem hopelessly naive – especially in the light of the USSR's predominantly peasant population – but it was sustained by the conviction that the artist was afforded special insight into the historical processes underpinning the Revolution itself. Many artists and designers in the West had a similar sense of destiny and, with the consolidation and spread of the International Style in the 1930s, Modernism began to permeate everyday life through the work of 'artist-engineers' – industrial designers, graphic designers and architects – albeit with consequences that would ultimately have horrified their Russian counterparts.

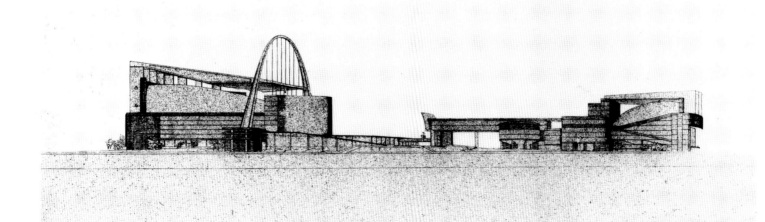

**Above: Iakov Chernikov,
Architectural fantasy, 1930**
Chernikov entertained no
illusions about his 'architectural
fantasies' ever being realized. As
free explorations of architectural
form, however, they are
remarkable: more playful than
earlier Constructivist work, and
uncannily anticipating some of
the characteristic forms and
compositions of 1980s Hi-Tech.

**Right: Iofan, Shchuko and
Gelfriekh, Competition
project for the Palace of the
Soviets,1931–4**
This wedding-cake of a building
was officially approved early in
1934 but it was never built. The
result of a protracted and
fraught competition, it was one
of the first projects in the
eclectic socialist-realist style
favoured by Stalin.

5

NORTHAMPTON COLLEGE
LIBRARY

When the concept of new times will be relevant, when contemporary harmony will be grasped, exalted by a new mentality, conquered by the decision to move forward and not backward, when we shall be turned toward life and not congealed in death, times will be oriented unanimously toward clarity, toward joy, toward limpidity. The hour is near, believe it. It sounds simultaneously in all countries, in Argentina as in France, as in Japan. Le Corbusier

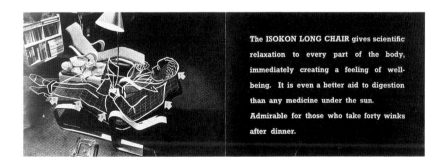

The ISOKON LONG CHAIR gives scientific relaxation to every part of the body, immediately creating a feeling of well-being. It is even a better aid to digestion than any medicine under the sun.

Admirable for those who take forty winks after dinner.

Opposite: John Somerset Murray, 'Glass Age Train' bathroom, 1937
Created for the glassmakers Pilkington Brothers, the train visited forty towns. With its delight in transparency and light, the sparkling functionalism of this bathroom epitomized the International Style.

Left: Isokon chair leaflet, c. 1936
Designed by Marcel Breuer, this chair became an icon of Modernist design in Britain, and its form (as the leaflet made clear) was healthy as well as beautiful.

167

Introducing the first Bauhaus Book in 1925, Walter Gropius wrote that 'architecture is always national and is also always individual. Of the three concentric circles – individual-nation-mankind – the contents of the last are greater than the two others: hence the title "INTERNATIONAL ARCHITECTURE"!' As the Weissenhof and the 'Die Wohnung' exhibition at Stuttgart made clear, Modernism had spread through most of Europe by 1927 – but its roots were shallow and, in terms of building production, its contributions insignificant. To set against the success in Stuttgart, 1927 also saw a dispiriting reverse in the competition for the new League of Nations headquarters in Geneva. Le Corbusier's masterly project appeared to be the winner – only to be disqualified for being drawn in the wrong ink! The setback confirmed the strength of official opposition and helped focus the widely felt need for an organization to represent the Modernist cause internationally. In 1928, after consultation with Le Corbusier and Sigfried Giedion, leading architects were invited by the patron, Mme Hélène de Mandrot, to her Swiss château at La Sarraz, where they resolved to found the *Congrès Internationaux d'Architecture Moderne* (CIAM).

CIAM's founding declaration was signed by twenty-four architects from France, Switzerland, Germany, Holland, Italy, Spain, Austria and Belgium, and addressed the links between architecture and 'the general economic system' – declaring rationalization and standardization, industrially based building and land-reform to be prerequisites for town-planning. The hard-line functionalists, led by Ernst May and Hans Schmidt, won a battle with Le Corbusier's faction to determine the agenda of the second congress, which was held in Frankfurt in 1929 and focused on *Die Wohnung für das Existenzminimum*, or 'Workers' Housing'. The fourth took place in 1933 on board the *SS Patris* sailing between Marseilles and Athens. Its theme was 'The Functional City', and the discussions were dominated by Le Corbusier, who later published the conclusions (anonymously) as *The Athens Charter*. In typically passionate style it committed CIAM to reductive town-planning principles based on functional zoning and 'high widely spaced apartment blocks' as the only form of high-density housing. These dubious ideas assumed the power of statutes and proved widely influential after World War II – most large European cities were affected, few if any for the better.

The uniformity of the Weissenhof had begged the question 'Is this a new style?' – indeed, *the* new style, the long-awaited expression of the industrial *Zeitgeist*. Walter Curt Behrendt, for one, was in no doubt – it featured on the front cover of his pamphlet *Der Sieg des neuen Baustils* (The Triumph of the Modern Style), published in 1927. And it was as a style that the new architecture became widely known in the English-speaking world, thanks to the famous – some thought infamous – exhibition held at New York's Museum of Modern Art (MOMA) in 1932. The show was actually entitled 'Modern Architecture: International Exhibition', but in addition to the catalogue, the historian Henry-Russell Hitchcock and the young director of the Department of Architecture and Industrial Design (the first in the world), Philip Johnson, published a book entitled *The International Style*. It featured almost a hundred buildings from sixteen countries, and the title caught on: without it the show's impact would have been modest – it travelled to eleven other cities, but attendance levels were relatively low, as they had been in New York where it was seen by only 33,000 people.

Hitchcock and Johnson identified three stylistic traits: treating the building as a *volume* defined by surfaces, not as a mass; formal *regularity*, resulting from proportional control and an orderly structure; and the *avoidance of applied decoration*. They said nothing about the social, economic and technical issues which preoccupied many Europeans, and the reader gained little idea of the complex interplay of space, enclosure and structure which was the glory of the new aesthetic. The narrowness of Hitchcock and Johnson's definition blinded them to the outstanding early Modernist building in America – the Lovell Beach House (1925–6) in Los Angeles by Rudolf Schindler, a Viennese emigré. Schindler very much wanted to be included and sent his work to MOMA, explaining 'I am not a stylist, not a functionalist, nor any other sloganist. Each of my buildings deals with a different architectural problem, the existence of which has been forgotten in this period of rational mechanization.' Johnson replied that his 'work would not belong in the Exhibition'. Schindler's house was a masterpiece, but Johnson was right – it was not an example of *his* International Style. Nor was the work of Frank Lloyd Wright, which featured in the exhibition – national honour demanded it – but not in the book. Hitchcock and Johnson even had to acknowledge that the major Modernists, Le Corbusier and Mies, were not bound by their rules either.

The Europeans had no desire to see their ideas packaged as a new style. In the British *Architectural Review* in 1935, Marcel Breuer wrote that 'we reject the traditional concept of "style"', and explained that 'there is no hard and fast formula for doing this or that in the New Architecture'. His former colleague, Oskar Schlemmer, was similarly dismissive of the tendency to label anything geometric and in primary colours 'Bauhaus', saying: 'The Bauhaus style which sneaked its way into the design of women's underwear; the Bauhaus style as "modern decor", as rejection of yesterday's styles, as determination to be "up-to-the-minute" at all costs – this style can be found everywhere but at the Bauhaus.' What the Modernists were after was a style in the sense the critic John Berger uses the word – 'a way of working', not a set of visual prescriptions. The Bauhaus contained several such ways of working – how could it not, under the direction of such different personalities as Gropius, Meyer and Mies – and add to them the aesthetic systems of De Stijl, of Le Corbusier and of the Constructivists, and you have a complexity which Hitchcock and Johnson's reduction to 'The International Style' could hardly encompass. However, the universal 'style without a style' in which Gropius believed proved elusive, and in practice the functionality of many a Modernist design was compromised by the *stylistic* insistence on 'pure' geometric forms. The labelling of a new style fitted the needs of a young, campaigning museum, and was part of history as much as an adequate writing of it. And for all its shortcomings, 'International Style' did describe a recognizable phenomenon: variously adapted, buildings akin to those at the Weissenhof appeared throughout the world during the late 1920s and 1930s. The triumphalism it suggests, however, is misleading. Buildings in the International Style were a small – generally vanishingly so – proportion of total production, and Modernists rarely won the major commissions: in that sense, Classicism remained the real international style of the 1930s, favoured by democracies, dictators and Soviets alike.

'International Style' could just as well refer to architecture and the applied arts as a whole, because an all-embracing style which built on the innovations of the mid-1920s had clearly been consolidated by the beginning of the new decade. How to characterize it? Precise, logical and unsentimental; sensitive to materials, respecting their intrinsic qualities or 'nature'; a meticulous attention to details, which were reduced to a minimum; a delight in transparency and light – in light-filled interiors, the luminous play of light on undecorated surfaces, the sheen and shine of reflective materials; and light also in the defiance of gravity and appearance of ease. This refined and restrained aesthetic is apparent everywhere in the early 1930s – in the clothes photographed by Edward Steichen and Cecil Beaton, the villas of Le Corbusier, the posters of Cassandre and Herbert Bayer, the glassware of Wilhelm Wagenfeld (a former Bauhaus student and teacher) and the Orrefors company in Sweden, and in cutlery, ceramics and industrial design. Its classic, if not entirely typical expression, came early – in Mies van der Rohe's German Pavilion for the Barcelona International Exhibition of 1929. The pavilion contained only Mies's celebrated calfskin and chromium-plated steel 'Barcelona' chairs and stools, and a statue by Georg Kolbe and was the most sophisticated Modernist architectural composition yet seen, its open, asymmetrical spaces flowing between partition-walls of green Tinian marble and onyx, through subtly tinted glass screens and around a regular grid of cruciform columns which supported the 'floating' roof. In retrospect it seems strangely poignant that this supremely confident expression of the new era should appear as the Weimar Republic – and the world economy – were about to be thrown into turmoil and depression by the Wall Street stock-market crash.

The International Style was hardly a populist aesthetic, but contemporary photographs confirm that simple, functionally designed furniture, lamps and utensils came into widespread use during the early 1930s, albeit more often in places such as hospitals, railway stations and post offices, than in homes or offices. The Continent led the way: the British *Studio*

M. D. Silva Bruhns, 'Carpet Design', Two images from Plate 3 of *Modernes Tapis* by Maurice Matel, 1930
Modernist formal innovations, notably Cubism, proved eminently adaptable to decorative ends and by the end of the 1920s designs such as these were becoming widely available as models.

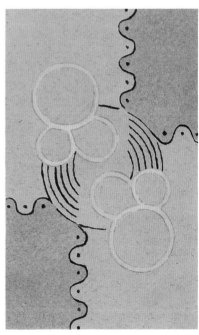

**Above: J.-C. H. Moreux,
'Desk in study with spiral
staircase' from *Répertoire
du Goût Moderne*, Paris,
1929**
With its spiral staircase,
transformable table and built-in
cupboards, Moreux's design is
almost a caricature of the
'functional' interior – note the
adjustable lamps on the
strangely contorted arms of the
easy chairs.

**Opposite: Mies van der
Rohe, Barcelona Pavilion,
1929 (destroyed;
reconstructed 1986)**
Built for the Barcelona
International Exhibition, the
Pavilion contained only Mies's
celebrated calfskin and
chromium-plated steel chairs
and stools, and a statue by
Georg Kolbe. The green
Tinian marble and onyx walls,
tinted glass screens and
chrome-covered cruciform
columns created an atmosphere
of remarkable opulence. Mies
was inspired by De Stijl and
Suprematism, but the synthesis
was uniquely his; it was
proclaimed by many who had
only seen photographs and
drawings as the century's most
beautiful building.

Year Book noted in 1931 that 'on the Continent dinner services are getting simpler and simpler' and the previous year the Berlin State Porcelain Factory had conducted a poll to assess public preferences using 150 cups and saucers of all periods. The most popular, by a substantial majority, was a simple white cup from the mid-eighteenth century – the result would have been very different in Britain, where decorative excess and floral motifs were still ubiquitous.

Modernism was an intellectual and aesthetic contagion, not just a taste for simplicity, and it spread like an epidemic during the 1930s. Contact with emigrés from Nazi Germany and the Soviet Union was the surest source of infection – several passed through Britain and later assumed key positions in American universities and colleges. International travel and work offered opportunities for direct contact, and the germ also migrated through professional journals, popular and specialist books, and major exhibitions such as the Paris and New York World's Fairs of 1937 and 1939 and the Milan Triennali. For the general public, the mass media – radio and later TV, cinema and lifestyle magazines such as *Harper's Bazaar* and *House and Garden* – were unreliable but important sources of information. The new architecture generally met with ridicule and resistance from the public and architects alike, and Modernist ideas spread more freely in fields where attitudes were less entrenched and sensibilities less easily offended. Despite the economic depression, the development of credit-purchasing schemes and the

emergence of a new middle class laid the foundations for the consumer societies of the 1950s, prompting the growth of advertising, the proliferation of special-interest magazines and the need for clear identities for products and companies. To service these needs, the 1930s saw the emergence of the independent professions of industrial and graphic design which largely created the image of a modern, international culture.

The cultural climate was almost everywhere markedly more conservative than in the 1920s, and in Germany, the Nazi *Kampfbund für Deutsche Kultur* (KDK or Fighting League for German Culture) was briefed to suppress all manifestations of Modernism – its efforts culminated in the notorious exhibition of Degenerate Art in 1937. The Nazis have commonly been presented as rejecting Modernism outright, but in reality the situation was more complex. Hitler thought 'today's tasks require new methods' and a 'crystal-clear functionalism', and considered the new architecture admirably suited to industrial buildings. There even seems to have been a moment, after the appointment of Hans Weidemann to a post in the Propaganda Ministry, when it was contemplated as the official style of the Third Reich. Most of the leading Modernists fled – only Mies hung on, not leaving for America until 1938 – but some of those who stayed were able to work. The prestigious interior of the Hindenburg airship was in the International Style, as were some buildings for the railways and the new autobahns, aeroplane and car factories, and those associated with sport and health – burgeoning industries everywhere in the 1930s, and nowhere more so than in Germany, thanks to the 1936 Berlin Olympics. The rational, orderly approach to recreation promoted by the KdF (*Kraft durch Freude*; Strength through Joy) was in tune with Modernist ideals, and reflected in the design of cruise ships for group tours and the elegantly streamlined Volkswagen touring car designed by Ferdinand Porsche and first produced (for military use) in 1936–7. Wagenfeld continued to design his geometric machine forms for several glass manufacturers during the 1930s, including the beautiful 'Kubus' modular containers, and Hermann Gretsch (who led the Werkbund division of the KDK) similarly produced Modernist ceramic designs for Arzberg and Villeroy and Boch. The Nazis may have opposed Modernism in principle, but in practice they produced more in the International Style than most European countries.

The Italian Modernist architects campaigned under the banner of Rationalism and were convinced that

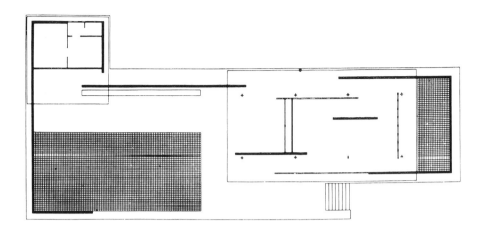

Architecture is the will of the age conceived in spatial terms. Mies van der Rohe

NORTHAMPTON COLLEGE
LIBRARY

Below: Fritz Breuhaus, Dining room with cushioned aluminium chairs, Hindenburg airship, 1935
The Nazis accepted Modernist design in appropriate contexts, which included an interior as prestigious as that of the Hindenburg where economy of materials and an aesthetic of lightness clearly belonged.

Bottom: Wilhelm Wagenfeld, Kubus (Cube) glass containers, 1938
Although no friend of the Nazis, the Bauhaus-trained Wagenfeld continued to work throughout the 1930s without obvious stylistic compromises, producing outstanding Modernist glassware.

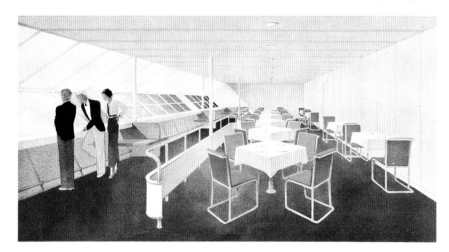

their synthesis of Classicism and the machine age would find official favour. In 1930 they constituted themselves as the *Movimento Italiano per l'Architettura Razionale* (MIAR), and the following year the Milanese gruppo 7 held an exhibition in Rome. It was opened by Mussolini, and accompanied by a pamphlet claiming that Rationalist architecture was the only true expression of Fascism – a view which appeared to find the Duce's favour, although the National Union of Architects thought differently and eventually won the day with its stripped Classicism. The outstanding Rationalist building, and one of the best built anywhere in the 1930s, was nonetheless designed specifically for the Fascist party – Giuseppe Terragni's Casa del Fascio in Como (1932–6). Terragni took Mussolini's statement that 'Fascism is a house of glass into which all can look' as his guiding metaphor, and the square plan and elegant proportions are reminiscent of an Italian palazzo, with the cortile transformed into a top-lit, double-height meeting hall surrounded by galleries and offices. Terragni's sophisticated composition was highly esteemed, but the most influential Italian design of the 1930s internationally was Persico and Nizzoli's Medaglia d'Oro room at the first Italian Aeronautical show held in Milan in 1934, a mesmerizing labyrinth of images suspended on a square grid hovering in space – a major influence on exhibition design for at least the next twenty years.

In 1935, the visionary industrialist Adriano Olivetti commissioned a Swiss Bauhaus graduate Xanti Schawinsky to work with his Modernist architects, Figini and Pollini, on the design of what became the Studio 42 typewriter: they established the basic form which survived into the 1970s. Marcello Nizzoli was employed as Olivetti's chief consultant designer from 1936, and the company committed itself to presenting a modern image in every aspect of its operations – the seeds were sown for the post-War policy of employing painters, sculptors and designers to work on the products, publicity, showrooms and worldwide travelling exhibitions which did so much to promote not only Olivetti's, but also Italy's, pre-eminence in industrial design.

Paris played a pivotal role in the 1920s, but patronage was confined to a small circle and France offered surprisingly few opportunities in the 1930s. André Lurçat and Gabriel Guévrékian built some interesting houses, and the steel and glass construction and wonderfully inventive details (from the bookcase balustrades to the steel-framed doors, everything was rethought) of Pierre Chareau's Maison de Verre (constructed in 1928–32 with Bernard Bijvoet) offered a unique and poetic vision of the 'machine for living in'. The rise of tourism opened up opportunities in the south, and several Modernist hotels were built, such as Lurçat's Nord-Sud at Calvi on Corsica (1930). Although several leading Modernists had marked left-wing sympathies, Socialist local authorities could by no means be relied upon to commission Modernist designs. A few notable public buildings were built, however, including two by Beaudouin, Lods and Prouvé – the Open Air School in Suresnes (1932–5) and the Maison du Peuple at Clichy (1937–9). The latter featured an external steel structure, large areas of glass, and sheet-metal cladding panels, articulating a radical new expression of the separation of structure from enclosure which anticipated High-Tech – as did Prouvé's use of 'technology transfer', his innovations in buildings and furniture frequently owing more to automobile production than to conventional architecture or design. Having trained as an art-metalworker, Prouvé had a craftsman's understanding of materials and was the first, in 1934, to develop a workable curtain-walling system.

Surrealism was the liveliest art movement in 1930s Paris, but it was more influential outside France, with French designers still favouring Purist geometries and Cubist imagery to present an image of chic modernity. Cassandre continued along this path, and Jean Carlu, Paul Colin and Charles Loupot produced work in a similar vein, although rarely matching Cassandre's inventiveness. More modernistic than Modernist, their work eschewed the rigours of German typography – a point made clear in a book by the Paris printer Alfred Tomer. Entitled *Mise en Page; The Theory and Practice of Layout*, this book was published (in English) in 1931. For

Tomer, the essence of layout was in its 'free use of processes . . . combined with the hand of the designer and an unprejudiced eye': very French.

It is typical of Le Corbusier that as soon as the style he had pioneered was gaining acceptance, he began to question its foundations. Between 1932 and 1933 he completed four major buildings: the Maison Clarté in Geneva; and in Paris, the Swiss Pavilion in the Cité Universitaire, the Salvation Army Building and the Porte Molitor apartments (in which he had a penthouse). All featured machine-age modular steel and glass facades, but in the Swiss Pavilion this was counterpointed by muscular concrete pilotis and a wall of random rubble masonry with deliberately crude pointing. Similar combinations of seemingly 'primitive' and advanced technology appeared in smaller projects: the turf-covered concrete vaults of the Weekend House in suburban Paris (1935) recalled Mediterranean vernacular buildings and were set against glass bricks and plywood, and the Pavillon des Temps Nouveaux at the 1937 Paris World's Fair was made of canvas and aeronautical steel cables. The last of his great urban projects, the Obus Plan for Algiers, appeared in 1930. It was a vast, sinuous motorway megastructure on which, he said, families could build what they liked: the numbing repetitiveness of the Immeubles-Villas gave way to a collage of 'participatory design' within an open frame – an idea which resurfaced in the 1970s in Nils Habraken's 'Support Structures'. Having been one of the most effective advocates of the International Style, Le Corbusier began to challenge it with a less technocratic view of the future, in which industrialized and traditional techniques combined to respond flexibly to different situations and needs.

In the Netherlands the post and telephone service PTT became a major public patron of modern design, thanks largely to one man, Jean François van Royen, who joined as a clerical assistant in 1904. During the 1930s he commissioned stamp designs from such leading Modernists as Piet Zwart, Paul Schuitema and Gerard Kiljan, and a new telephone kiosk from Willem Gispe. Van Royen died in a Nazi concentration camp in 1941, but his policies continued until the PTT was fragmented by privatization in 1989. After their considerable achievements in the 1920s, progressive Dutch architects found few opportunities in the 1930s. Traditional styles were revived, and the Delft School led by Granpré Molière became vigorous and influential opponents; the only major Modernist buildings were Duiker's Handelsblad-Cineac cinema, completed in 1934 in

Illustration from *Der KdF-Wagen von A bis Z* handbook, 1939
The Volkswagen car is shown against a 'streamlined' petrol station which combines Modernist ribbon windows with a stepped Art Deco facade.

Giuseppe Terragni, Casa del Fascio, Como, 1932–6
Designed as the headquarters of the local Fascist Party, Terragni's building was the outstanding achievement of Italian Rationalism. Its elegant proportions and subtly layered composition have won many admirers.

Amsterdam, and the Bergpolder apartment block (1933–4) by Van Tijen, Van der Vlugt and Brinkman. The Dutch still played a prominent part internationally, however. Van Eesteren became President of CIAM in 1930, and two years later the progressive groups – 'De 8' in Amsterdam and 'De Opbouw' in Rotterdam – joined forces to publish the bi-monthly magazine *De 8 en Opbouw*. After Van Doesburg's death in 1931 *De Stijl* ceased publication, and the covers of *De 8 en Opbouw* became a showcase for avant-garde layouts.

The ABC group in Switzerland lost much of its radicalism after Hannes Meyer's departure for the Bauhaus and slowly merged with mainstream Modernism. The Neubühl Siedlung in Zurich (1930), a development of 195 dwellings sponsored by the Swiss Werkbund on the lines of the Weissenhof and designed by Haefeli, Hubacher, Steiger, Moser, Artaria and Schmidt, was a quite outstanding example of modern housing, and the provision of outdoor bathing facilities (which became public policy between the wars) yielded some fine complexes. These included the Bad-Allenmoos facility in Zurich (1935) by Alfred Roth and by the engineer Beda Hefti in the highlands above Bern. Roth's 1940 book, *The New Architecture*, confirmed that Swiss architects were skilled but not especially inventive practitioners of Modernism.

In graphic design, however, three world-class figures were at work in Switzerland: Herbert Matter, Jan Tschichold and Max Bill. Matter was an internationally important innovator, his tourism posters and brochures

admired worldwide for heir highly original montages of images which were executed with remarkable economy. The brochures were printed, generally, with only red, blue and black inks and featured cinematic 'dissolves' and a sophisticated layering of images: easy now with an Apple Mac computer and photolithography, but pushing the limits of letterpress printing. The doyen of New Typography, Jan Tschichold, took refuge from Nazi Germany and continued to design books and posters: typical of his minimalist style is a masterpiece of economy and elegance for the 1938 exhibition, *Der Berufsphotograph* (The Professional Photographer). In this poster the negative image subtly announces the theme of the exhibition – a glimpse behind the scenes of photography – and the size and placing of every piece of text is beautifully judged. Max Bill returned in 1929 after two years of study at the Bauhaus, and rapidly established himself as a master of graphic design, as well as a distinguished architect and industrial designer. The extreme formalism and economy of the posters displayed in Bill's Swiss Pavilion at the 1936 Milan Triennale – a masterpiece of austerity in its own right – gave the world a foretaste of the 'Swiss Style' which would dominate graphic design of the 1960s and 1970s.

Nowhere offered a more daunting challenge to Modernism than Great Britain. In the 1920s 'taste' was still thought to have ended in the late eighteenth century, and 'modern' meant a contemporary reproduction of antique furniture. Despite the pre-War energy of the Vorticists, Modernism made only the most tentative of inroads during the 1920s – architecturally, in the Bassett-Lowke house (1925–6) by Peter Behrens and Amyas Connell's 'High and Over' (1929–30), and design-wise in an exhibition of furniture by the Russian emigré Serge Chermayeff at Waring and Gillow in 1928, which the *Design and Industries Association Journal* described as 'by far the best thing yet done in this country'. Intellectually undemanding derivatives of Art Deco such as 'Jazz Modern' and 'New Art' became the favoured style of bright young socialites like the Flappers, and there was a small market for the kind of spare modern style of which, in a *Punch* cartoon, one fashionable Flapper remarked ecstatically to another, 'My dear, how *exquisitely* unfurnished.' The interiors of houses became steadily less cluttered, and the most expensively uncluttered might be furnished by a decorater like Curtis Moffat, an American photographer who opened a gallery in London's newly fashionable Fitzroy Square in 1929. His white rooms with aluminium- or copper-faced doors,

Left: Giuseppe Terragni, Casa del Fascio, Como, 1932–6
Inspired by Mussolini's description of Fascism as 'a house of glass into which all can look', Terragni placed a glass-fronted, top-lit double-height meeting hall at the heart of his masterpiece.

Below: Persico and Nizzoli, Medaglia d'Oro room, Italian Aeronautical show, Milan, 1934
This mesmerizing labyrinth of images suspended on a square grid hovering in space was a major international influence on exhibition design. It probably owed something to Frederick Kiesler's extraordinary De Stijl *City in Space* which was shown at the Paris Exhibition of Decorative Arts in 1925.

steel furniture, African masks and geometrically patterned cushions were greeted in the gossip columns as 'Modernistic', 'Cubist' or 'Futuristic'.

Modernist architecture and design were largely the work of foreigners or ex-colonials – which hardly worked in their favour as anxiety grew about the rise of Nazism in Germany. Connell formed a partnership with the New Zealanders Basil Ward and Colin Lucas; Walter Gropius, Marcel Breuer, Moholy-Nagy and Erich Mendelsohn practised in London during the 1930s; and the British wing of CIAM, known as MARS (Modern Architectural Research Group), was founded by a Canadian, Wells Coates. Moholy-Nagy worked as a graphic designer and as the display director for Simpson's men's store, which moved into a Modernist building by Joseph Emberton in 1936. The much larger Peter Jones store (1936–9), designed by William Crabtree, was London's most prominent example of Modernist architecture, the choice of style reflecting the company's unique organization as a profit-sharing partnership involving the whole workforce.

The Modernist vision of the new life at its most progressive was captured in the Lawn Road Flats in Hampstead (1932–4) developed by Jack Pritchard, an expert on plywood just back from a visit to the Bauhaus – he also founded the Isokon company to manufacture furniture. Designed by Wells Coates, the flats adapted *Existenzminimum* standards to the needs of urban professionals, and were serviced by the collective 'Isobar' and restaurant, central heating and a shoe-polishing service – ideal, thought Pritchard, for 'the new type of man who likes not only to travel light but to live light, unencumbered with possessions and with no roots to pull.' Egon Risse, Breuer and Gropius lived there for a while, and were commissioned to design plywood furniture for Isokon – the production of Breuer's superb Long Chair and Gropius's nest of tables passed to John Alan Designs in the 1960s.

Clients attracted to Modernism were apt to enjoy such suspect pleasures as socialism, sunshine and scholarship. A typical case in point was Earl de la Warr, the Mayor of Bexhill and Chairman of the National Labour Party, who commissioned the seafront Pavilion (1932–4) at Bexhill-on-Sea which bears his name. Designed by Mendelsohn and Chermayeff, it was explicitly intended to introduce modern architecture to the general public – in which it eventually, if belatedly, succeeded beyond de la Warr's wildest dreams by becoming a familiar location in the popular 1980–90s television series *Poirot*.

Left above: A. M. Cassandre, *Nord Express*, Poster, 1927
One of a series of justifiably famous transport posters executed by Cassandre. His stylized forms emphasized the speed and excitement of 'modern' travel.

Left below: Le Corbusier and Pierre Jeanneret, Swiss Pavilion, Cité Universitaire, Paris, 1930–2
The elegant curtain-wall of this student hostel is in striking contrast to the random-rubble facing of the communal facilities behind. Circular pilotis have also given way to muscular concrete shapes, anticipating the sculptural forms of Le Corbusier's post-War buildings.

Opposite: Pierre Chareau and Bernard Bijvoet, Maison de Verre, Paris, 1928–32
This 'house of glass' in a tight Parisian courtyard was imbued with the spirit of the International Style but offered an original vision of a steel and glass architecture. The elevation recalls Bruno Taut's Glass Pavilion, but in place of mysticism and myth Chareau created a poetic interpretation of the house as a machine for living in.

Right top: Piet Zwart, Cover and page from *ook post van u* (Post for you too?), 1929
The offices, telephone kiosks, booklets and stamps of the postal service PTT brought the Dutch into daily contact with Modernist design. This booklet, which was designed to encourage use of a new airmail route, communicates as much visually as verbally.

Right centre: Piet Zwart, Booklet for Dutch Cable Factory in Delft, 1928
Amongst the first to use close-up photographs of industrial products, Zwart here makes powerful use of repetition and a 'monumental' close-up. The asymmetrical composition unites the two pages into a single design.

Right bottom: Piet Zwart, Advertisement, c. 1925
Trio Printers in the Hague, who commissioned this piece, had a stimulating effect on graphic design developments in The Netherlands due to the interest displayed by the director F. Kerdijk.

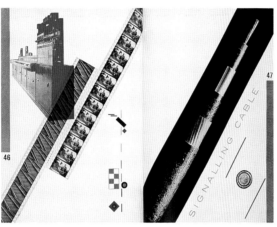

The two Modernist buildings of international importance were the Boots pharmaceutical factory near Nottingham (1930–2), designed by the engineer Owen Williams, and the Highpoint I block of flats (1933–5) by Tecton, a collaborative practice formed around the Russian Berthold Lubetkin. Lubetkin's best work had a clarity and rigour rarely seen in British architecture – the plan of Highpoint I is worthy of Le Corbusier, economical yet wonderfully elegant, and it remains arguably Britain's finest Modernist building. Tecton went on to build a series of popular buildings at London, Whipsnade and Dudley zoos, of which the first, the Penguin Pool (1934) in London, caught the public's imagination like no other Modernist design – having been constructed for animals rather than humans clearly helped. An exuberant, Constructivist tour-de-force in reinforced concrete, its interlocking spiral ramps made a perfect stage for their self-important-looking occupants – a replica was made as a set for Selznick's 1938 film *Young at Heart*. Owen Williams's work for Boots was a superb example of the 'Engineer's Aesthetic', combining a highly inventive reinforced concrete structure with elegant, lightweight steel and glass curtain-walling. Unlike the standardized, repetitive construction of the American factories at the turn of the century, Williams introduced numerous structural and architectural subtleties. One notes, for example, the faceted corners, chamfered mushroom columns, heating pipes doubling as guard rails, the dramatically cantilevered first floor, and the continuous metal track for maintenance and cleaning which forms a distinctive openwork cornice. Amongst industrial buildings, it was rivalled only by the Van Nelle factory in Rotterdam.

In the catalogue of MOMA's 1943 exhibition on 'Modern Architecture in England', Henry-Russell Hitchcock claimed that 'England leads the world in modern architectural activity'. Buildings such as Lawn Road, Highpoint I and the Boots factory justify such a claim, but it was not until after 1945 that Modernism's influence extended beyond a small coterie of practitioners and clients. It was not for want of trying, however, for nowhere was the Modernist cause more energetically promoted – even the ultra-conservative *Country Life* magazine was sympathetic, thanks to the efforts of Christopher Hussey who cast Modernism as the latest manifestation of English Classicism. Several notable books appeared. John Gloag's *Design in Modern Life* was based on popular BBC radio talks by leading advocates of modern design, both of them timed to coincide with an exhibition on 'British Industrial Art' at Dorland Hall in 1933. (The forward-looking BBC was a valuable ally and broadcast various other radio programmes and series backed up by articles in *The Listener*.) The following year saw the British Modernists' bible, Herbert Read's *Art and Industry*, which was written 'to support and propagate the ideals expressed by Dr Gropius', and F.R.S. Yorke's international compilation, *The Modern House*. In 1936 Nikolaus Pevsner's vastly influential *Pioneers of the Modern Movement* (later re-published as *Pioneers of Modern Design*) appeared, presenting Modernism as the culmination of a century of reforming endeavour. By 1937 there were sufficient houses for Yorke to write *The Modern House in England*. Most were routine exercises in the International Style, the conspicuous exception being Chermayeff's own house at Bentley Wood (1937–8) which anticipated his wood-framing experiments in America. Finally, *An Introduction to Modern Architecture* was published by Penguin in 1938; its author J. (later Sir James) M. Richards was one of the leading promoters of modern design (his nickname was Karl Marx) and his book was aimed at the widest possible audience.

Thanks to the efforts of Frank Pick, the best-known client of modern design in Britain was the London Underground. The system's distinctive sans-serif typeface and circle-and-bar symbol by the eminent typographer Edward Johnston date from 1916 – one of Pick's first commissions – and distinguished stations and train interiors followed. The Underground's poster and advertising campaigns, like those of the Dutch oil company Shell (referred to as 'The New Medici' in *The Architectural Review* in 1934), were probably many people's first contact with modern art and design. Pick's most original contribution, however, came from an engineering draughtsman, Henry Beck, who devised a new map of the Underground system in 1933. Based on an octagonal grid, it sacrificed topographical accuracy for clarity in showing routes and interconnections: a graphic masterpiece, it remains essentially unchanged and has influenced similar maps worldwide.

Johnston's student Eric Gill modelled his Gill Sans typeface of 1928 on the Underground lettering. Unlike the rationalized sans-serifs designed in Germany (notably Paul Renner's Futura) Gill Sans retained many of the subtle variations of Roman lettering, and remained the most popular sans-serif in Britain for the next thirty years, especially favoured for timetables and forms where clarity was essential. Gill's influential *Essay on Typography* (1931) advocated the use of evenly spaced

typesetting with ragged right-hand margins, whereas Continental typographers continued to justify both sides to form rectangular blocks. Gill argued, rightly, that regular word-spacing with varied line lengths is easier to read, but despite its (marginal) 'functional' superiority, it was little used until the 1970s. British typography was outstanding, but graphic design lagged well behind the Continent. A conspicuous exception was Penguin Books, founded in 1935 and the spearhead of the paperback revolution, who turned to the New Typography of Jan Tschichold to project a modern image. The leading Modernist commercial artist was Ashley Havinden, who devised advertising campaigns for clients such as Chrysler, the GPO, the Milk Marketing Board and Simpson's of Piccadilly: his style – which drew on Cubism, Futurism and the Bauhaus – was widely imitated. But as in architecture, the best work was by foreign talent – Moholy-Nagy and the German-born, Paris-trained Frederick Henrion who arrived in 1939. He soon found work for the General Post Office and, during the War, for the Ministry of Information, and was set to become a major force in the post-War years.

Anyone brave enough to commission a Modernist house, or seeking to modernize their home, would have been able to furnish and decorate it with examples of good modern design – at a price: few were produced in large quantities, but the quality could be very high. The role of art and design in industry was the subject of a succession of government and industrial enquiries, Councils and Associations were formed and several firms produced Modernist designs. Isokon led the way in wooden – chiefly plywood – furniture, with Gropius as director of design, sales brochures by Moholy-Nagy and Breuer's iconic Long Chair (modelled on Alvar Aalto's bent-ply designs) of 1936 as its flagship. Pel, an offshoot of Tube Investments, commissioned new tubular steel designs, manufactured Bauhaus pieces under licence from Thonet and produced Chermayeff's stacking chair with its canvas seat and back in vast quantities. Designed in 1932, it soon filled village and school halls across the country, not to mention the BBC's prestigious new Broadcasting House in London. Gerald Summers designed a classic for Makers of Simple Furniture – a bent-ply chair made from a single sheet of material, like one of Albers' *Vorkurs* exercises.

The combination of a new material and a new product was grist to the Modernists' mill, and E.K. Cole commissioned designs for bakelite radios from Chermayeff, Coates and Misha Black. For all their modernity, these all looked dated within ten years and if

Johannes Duiker, Handelsblad-Cineac Cinema, Amsterdam, 1934
This elegant and wonderfully light composition of white surfaces, glass and a metal structure with its enormous illuminated sign was influenced by Russian Constructivist projects such as the Vesnins' Pravda Tower.

Below: Max Bill, Swiss
Pavilion at the 1936 Milan
Triennale, 1936

Bill's minimalist interior was in
perfect accord with the
sophisticated graphic design of
the celebrated posters, which
give a foretaste of the spare
'Swiss Style' which dominated
corporate graphics two decades
later.

Opposite: Herbert Matter,
Travel poster, 1936

Herbert Matter's strikingly
innovative posters and booklets
promoting the Swiss travel
industry quickly acquired a
worldwide reputation and led
to his being invited to work in
the USA. The vast face
demands to be seen both
figuratively and abstractly.

one had to single out one widely available British
product of the 1930s which stood the test of time, it
would surely have to be the Anglepoise lamp designed
in 1932 by G. Carwardine for Herbert Terry. It can
hardly be called Modernist in a stylistic sense – the base
retains echoes of Classicism – but as an example of
functional, problem-solving design it is a classic, taking
its model, like so many innovations, from nature – in
this case, the human arm. We saw the same approach
amongst nineteenth-century engineers, and it was
Modernism which made the appreciation of functional
form part of the general culture of the mid-twentieth
century.

There were similar achievements in more traditional
fields. At Edinburgh Weavers, for example, the artistic
director Alistair Morton commissioned one of the most
remarkable collections of textiles produced in the
twentieth century. The 'Constructivist Fabrics' collection,
launched in 1937, included designs by the painters Ben
Nicholson and Duncan Grant, the graphic artist Ashley
Havinden and the sculptor Barbara Hepworth. Marion
Dorn also worked regularly for Morton, and was the
outstanding designer of carpets and rugs which, due to
the emphasis on plain walls and plain or slightly
patterned fabrics, were often the only decorative feature.
Dorn's aim, as in much Modernist painting, was to
achieve flatness (without 'hills or valleys' as she put it)

and her colours (she worked with up to 500, all
specially dyed) recalled Cubism's smoky-café period.

The great success of 1930s ceramics was Clarice
Cliff's modernistic 'Bizarre' ware, and manufacturers
eager to persuade people to buy new services rather
than replace broken items were always on the lookout
for new ideas. These included a succession of geometric
shapes other than round: modernistic 'new concept
tableware' even extended to square cups and saucers
with a matching spoutless teapot with recessed handles
– not at all the sort of thing a rational, Bauhaus-style
analysis was intended to lead to. Surprisingly, it was
that bastion of tradition in pottery, the Wedgwood
factory, which began – following Victor Skellern's
appointment as Art Director in 1934 – to produce
genuinely Modernist pieces. The architect Keith
Murray was entrusted with their design, and produced
elegant, hand-thrown earthenware vases (highly
acclaimed at the time) and austerely rational matt-
glazed tableware, including a beer mug which
Herbert Read declared 'better than anything else in
modern ceramics'.

Modernism posed formidable challenges for the
crafts. It was in pottery that the intellectual dilemmas
were most forcefully confronted, and the tradition most
conspicuously enriched by immigrants. Lucie Rie
arrived from Vienna in 1938, bringing with her a
decorative tradition rooted in the Secession, and the
textile designer Hans Coper came from Germany in
1939. Coper joined Rie's studio after the War and
became, with Bernard Leach, one of the twin pillars of
British pottery – his intellectual approach was an ideal
foil to Leach's Zen-inspired touch. In the depth of the
Depression, Leach went back to Japan for two years,
where, during 1909–20, he had learned his craft and
formulated his philosophy. On his return his pottery in
St Ives, Cornwall, became a mecca for young potters,
and A Potter's Book (1940) their bible. Leach attempted to
refute the influence of Modernism and 'the affirmation
of the mechanical age in art – functionalism' on the
crafts. In doing so he argued for an aesthetic which
demanded that 'a pot in order to be good should be a
genuine expression of life' which implies 'sincerity on
the part of the potter and truth in the conception and
execution of the work.' His ideas may have been
infused by Zen Buddhism and an admiration for
Oriental traditions, but they are difficult to separate
from many a Modernist's philosophy of abstract painting
or sculpture – or the core values, minus the machine,
of the Bauhaus. To save studio pottery from the threat

PONTRESINA

Engadin

Above: Wells Coates, Lawn Road Flats, Hampstead, London, 1932–4
Designed to very tight space standards, the flats were aimed at 'the new type of man who likes not only to travel light but to live light' and became an enclave of Modernist culture in London.

Right: Ben Nicholson, *White Relief*, 1934
With the sculpture of Henry Moore, Ben Nicholson's geometric low reliefs were one of Britain's few original contributions to Modernist art during the 1930s. Their links to Mondrian and Malevich are obvious, but Nicholson found a fresh way of working with minimal means.

Opposite: Erich Mendelsohn and Serge Chermayeff, De La Warr Pavilion, Bexhill-on-Sea, 1932–4
Commissioned by the Socialist Mayor, Earl de la Warr, and designed by two central European exiles, the Pavilion was intended to introduce the British public to Modern architecture.

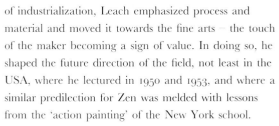

of industrialization, Leach emphasized process and material and moved it towards the fine arts – the touch of the maker becoming a sign of value. In doing so, he shaped the future direction of the field, not least in the USA, where he lectured in 1950 and 1953, and where a similar predilection for Zen was melded with lessons from the 'action painting' of the New York school.

The International Style found more fertile soil in Scandinavia than in much of Europe, 'functional' simplicity and restraint seeming to come naturally in those unforgiving northern climates. The Nordic countries industrialized late, had an abundance of natural materials, above all wood, and strong craft traditions which continued uninterrupted as a living part of the culture – unlike in Britain where the keen interest in arts and crafts was a self-conscious revival. Furniture designers such as Bruno Mathsson in Sweden and Kaare Klint in Denmark were thus able to balance innovation and tradition in a way which made their work widely acceptable – it was undeniably modern, but not quite Modernist. The style known as 'Swedish Grace' in the decorative arts and Nordic Classicism in architecture was much admired at the Paris Exhibition of Decorative Arts in 1925. The emphasis on surface and volume rather than mass proved an ideal aesthetic preparation for Functionalism, as the new architecture became known, and Swedish industry's emphasis on high standards of design was almost unrivalled. The outstanding example was the Orrefors Glass Company, who appointed the designers Simon Gate in 1916 and Edvard Hald in 1917, the first in a succession of outstanding talents.

The breakthrough of Modernism came in 1930 with the Stockholm Exhibition organized by Gregor Paulsson, the influential director of the Swedish Arts and Crafts Association (now known as *Svensk Form*). Paulsson's model was the Weissenhof in Stuttgart, which the architect Sven Markelius had visited in 1927, and the exhibition was designed by Gunnar Asplund, the master of Nordic Classicism, in a Modernist style of great vitality and lightness of touch. The supreme example was the light-filled Paradise Restaurant, whose impossibly slender steel columns, vast areas of glass, circular glass tower and large coloured sunblinds crystallized a vocabulary that would be emulated throughout Europe. The exhibition was a great success and the Finnish architect Alvar Aalto explained that it was 'not a composition in stone, glass and steel, as the Functionalist-hating exhibition visitor might imagine, but rather a composition in houses, flags, searchlights,

flowers, fireworks, happy people and clean tablecloths' which demonstrated 'a whole new kind of joy'. It presented a beguiling vision of the modern lifestyle, with fully furnished model apartments, complete with Frankfurt-style kitchens and modern ceramics, glassware and cutlery – which were, however, markedly less iconoclastic than the architecture. The International Style enjoyed only modest success in Sweden, where architects tempered it with shallow pitched roofs and traditional materials, developing a modern vernacular of low-rise apartment buildings in green settings. They were aesthetically bland, but widely liked – and much admired in Britain. Asplund himself went on to design several distinguished buildings which blended Modernist and traditional ideas, the recent revival of interest in which should not obscure the fact that they exerted little influence at the time.

The Stockholm Exhibition had an enormous impact on young architects and designers throughout Scandinavia. The style was already familiar in Oslo thanks to a celebrated study-trip abroad and Lars Backer's Skansen Restaurant (1925–7), and Frithjof Reppen had already designed a pair of outstanding apartment buildings (1929–32). But in Norway, as elsewhere, the majority of commissions were for private houses: the best were by Ove Bang and Arne Korsmo. Bang also completed some notable public buildings, including the headquarters of the Norwegian Lutheran Home Mission (1934), and the Workers' Association (1939–40) in Oslo, whilst Korsmo exerted considerable influence as a teacher at the Oslo Art and Crafts School. He developed a programme integrating architecture, interior design and crafts, and became internationally known for his industrial designs – with his wife Grete he won a Grand Prix for glass and silverware at the Milan Triennale of 1954.

The restraint and clear, simple order of the International Style fitted well with native Classical and craft traditions in Denmark, and Modernism became a subject of debate in the 1920s thanks to Poul Henningsen's *Kritisk Revy*. Henningsen himself designed the PH lamp in 1928, which became not only a familiar sight in Modernist interiors of the 1930s, but also a stimulus to numerous other designers. Arne Jacobsen quickly emerged as the major Danish talent. In 1930 he began work on the Bellevue beach area outside Copenhagen, which included elegant baths, cabins and kiosks, the Bellavista estate of three-storey apartments, and a theatre with a sliding roof to use the night sky as a ceiling – a favourite theme of Nordic Classicism. Jacobsen benefited from his close friendship with Asplund, acquiring the fastidious attention to detail which became a hallmark of his influential later buildings and furniture.

The giant amongst Nordic architects and the major architect to emerge during the 1930s was Alvar Aalto. In 1928 – at the age of thirty-one – he won the competition for a new sanatorium in Paimio and completed the design of the Turun Sanomat newspaper in Turku for an owner who wished to project a modern image – the paper changed from Gothic to Roman type at the same time as it moved into startlingly modern, and markedly Corbusian, offices and printing works. The Paimio Sanatorium was completed in 1933 and, like his Viipuri Library (1927–35), was sufficiently orthodox to be accepted as a canonical Modernist building, whilst revealing clear hints of radical innovations to come. Aalto designed everything down to the last detail, including door-handles, light-fittings and the Paimio chair which was a bent-wood interpretation of Breuer's metal designs and ostensibly configured to help the patients' breathing. The Modernist ideals of sun, space and greenery and the therapeutic regime for tuberculosis were in perfect accord, and Aalto's machine-for-healing established his international reputation.

For almost half a century, Finland has successfully cultivated an image as a haven of modern design. This began with the Finnish Pavilion at the 1930 Antwerp International Exhibition, designed of plywood by Erik Bryggman in the International Style. The system of architectural competitions for public buildings enabled the new architecture to make inroads into most areas of building, but the cultural climate of the 1930s was intensely nationalistic and favoured traditional design. A few influential clients came from among progressive industrialists, and Modernism was favoured for buildings

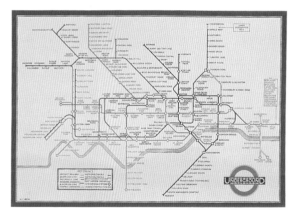

which the government used to project a modern image to the world – chiefly hotels and leisure and sports facilities. In 1935 Aalto's principal clients, Harry and Maire Gullichsen of the Ahlstrom paper and timber company, formed Artek to sell his furniture (light fittings and glassware soon followed) and to promote modern culture. Using the strong and abundant birch, Aalto had already designed several highly innovative bent-wood chairs, tables and stools. First exhibited abroad at Fortnum and Mason's in London in 1933, when *The*

Left above: A. Rogers, 'Speed' poster, 1930
Commissioned for London Underground, the clean lines of this poster demonstrate a new style which was to become universally influential.

Left below: Henry C. Beck, London Underground Map, 1933
By sacrificing geographical accuracy and organizing the map on an octagonal grid, Beck, an engineering draughtsman, produced a classic example of visual communication, the model for similar maps worldwide and, much updated, still in use today.

Opposite left: Tecton, Penguin Pool, London Zoo, 1934
This exuberant essay in reinforced concrete created a perfect setting for its inhabitants and quickly caught the public's imagination. Tecton, a collaborative practice formed around the Russian exile Berthold Lubetkin, designed several other buildings at London, Dudley and Whipsnade zoos.

Opposite right: Owen Williams, Boots Factory, Beeston, 1930–2
Designed by an engineer, the mushroom-columned and continuously glazed Boots Factory remains one of the outstanding industrial buildings of Europe — and of functional, Modernist architecture in Britain.

Above: Advertisement for Pel furniture, 1930s
Pel were the leading British manufacturers of tubular steel furniture and their eclectic range included examples of rigorous Modernist design as well as decorative interpretations of the machine aesthetic.

Below: László Moholy-Nagy, Page layout for *The Architectural Review*, July 1936
The Architectural Review published Modernist work regularly throughout the 1930s, and whilst he was in London Moholy-Nagy contributed photographs, specially prepared collages and layouts such as this. The grid of photographs – now so familiar – was unprecedented in the *Review*'s pages, as of course were the circular 'peepholes' which transform the page into an abstract design.

Architectural Review acclaimed them as 'cheap and seemly furniture, light and easy to move', these chairs made a great impression at the 1936 Milan Triennale and several are still in production. Aalto's light fittings and glassware were also outstanding, and the 1937 Savoy Vase, its undulating profile supposedly inspired by 'a young Eskimo's leather breeches' but looking for all the world like the outline of a Finnish lake, has become almost a national icon. The manufacturers, Karhula-Iittala, also employed Timo Sarpaneva and Tapio Wirkkala, and a similarly distinguished team was established by the ceramics company Arabia under their design director Kurt Ekholm. The work of Aalto and these other designers in the 1930s laid the foundations for Finland's internationally acclaimed design of the 1950s, which played a central role in establishing that Scandinavian Modern style whose continuing, if much corrupted, influence can be seen in the catalogue of Ikea, the Swedish-based company which is now the world's largest furniture retailer.

Aalto's choice of wood for furniture was both pragmatic – it was abundantly available, and Finnish craftsmen and industrial workers were geared to working with it – and ideological: wood was, he thought, more 'human', and as a material could form the basis of a regional/national adaptation of what he saw as a rootless international style. His friend Poul Henningsen considered metal chairs 'so cold they give the modernly dressed woman a cramp in the thigh', and Aalto argued that supposedly 'rational' objects often lacked 'human

qualities'. Writing about lighting – the subject of increasing scientific study – he suggested that 'the candle's yellow flame and the interior decorator lady's inclination to glorify her light composition with yellow silk rags come closer to the mark vis-à-vis human instincts than the electrical technician with his luxmeter and his schematic concept of "white light" – much of rational lighting is inhumane.' Aalto's vision of regional Modernism was given compelling form in his pre-War masterpiece, the Villa Mairea designed for the Gullichsens on their estate near Noormarkku. Aalto combined an astonishing array of materials and forms which can be enjoyed as abstract spatial, visual and textural assemblages, but which also evoke associations with the Finnish vernacular and landscape, Modernist painting, the International Style of modern architecture, the Mediterranean vernacular and so forth. This was no revival of nineteenth-century eclecticism, but a thoroughly Modernist collage of fragments – architecture had seen nothing like it.

Aalto designed the Finnish Pavilions for both the 1937 Paris and 1939 New York World's Fairs, producing for the latter one of his finest designs. Finland could afford only a standard 'box', which he transformed by an undulating screen suspended diagonally across its length above an exhibition of objects on low plinths. The serpentine wall was intended to evoke the Aurora Borealis and clad with closely spaced fins to enhance the optical effect of its surfaces; the metaphor was made even more vivid by washes of coloured light from a

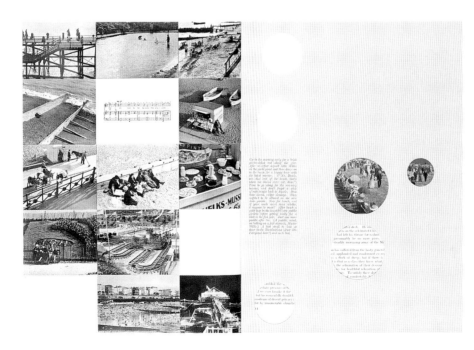

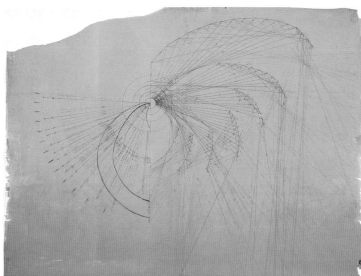

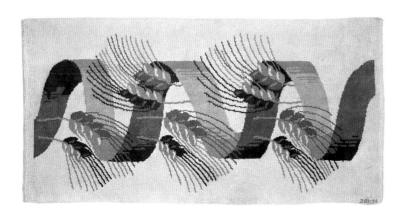

Left top: Poul Henningsen,
PH lamp, 1928
Left centre: **Poul
Henningsen, Design studies
for the PH lamp, 1928**
The PH lamp is a modern
classic, still in production and a
model for many subsequent
designs. Its elegant, organic
forms were ostensibly generated
functionally – to ensure good
light distribution and absence
of glare – and were arrived at
graphically by tracing light
rays.

**Left bottom: Marion Dorn,
Rug, c. 1936**
Designed for the Wilton Royal
Carpet Factory, this rug is an
example of Marion Dorn's bold
use of colour and form.

**Below: Bruno Mathsson,
'Eva' chair, 1934**
Like Aalto in Finland, the
Swede Mathsson experimented
extensively with bent-wood
techniques. This chair, light
and carefully shaped to the
body, has been in continuous
production since the 1930s.

NORTHAMPTON COLLEGE
LIBRARY

**Above: Alvar Aalto,
Tuberculosis Sanatorium,
Paimio, Finland, 1928–33**
The Modernist vision of sun,
space and greenery accorded
perfectly with the treatment for
tuberculosis, and Aalto's great
sanatorium was capped by a
heroic roof deck on which
patients were put out to air, six
storeys above the surrounding
forest.

**Right: Ove Bang, Workers'
Association, Oslo, 1939–40**
Modernism was more readily
accepted in Scandinavia than in
much of Europe, and this essay
in the Corbusian style, little
known outside Norway, can
stand comparison with all but
the most innovative designs of
the period.

battery of spot-lamps mounted on top of the projection booth. In place of the didactic, narrative structure of traditional exhibitions Aalto applied Modernist principles to create an integrated presentation which exploited the latest techniques – vast photographs, cinema, lighting and spatial composition – to project Finland as a modern, creative country with deep roots in the landscape and culture of the forest. Widely acclaimed as the finest interior at the Fair, it established Aalto's reputation in America.

Modernism generally struggled to gain official acceptance in established cultures, but in more volatile circumstances it proved ideal as a means of projecting change. This was the case in the Republic of Czechoslovakia, born from the ruins of the Austro-Hungarian Empire on 28 October 1918, in the future state of Israel and in post-revolutionary Brazil. To young Czechs, eager to help establish an identity for their country, Modernism seemed the obvious inspiration. Several groups consolidated during the 1920s, with the most radical – Devetsil – led by the brilliant theorist and critic Karel Teige. Devetsil's 1922 manifesto *Zivot II* (Life II) featured Teige's Constructivist typography, derived from El Lissitzky and the Bauhaus. His article 'Foto-Kino-Film' – the first on the relationship between the avant-garde and photography – was laid out like a newsreel, with text and illustrations interdependent: pages were then normally laid out individually, with no regard to their sequential effect. Established by 1925 as the dominant tendency in Czech architecture, Modernism was enthusiastically embraced by the young intelligentsia and middle-class as an expression of their progressive, cosmopolitan aspirations. The late 1920s and 1930s saw the construction of commercial and public buildings in Prague and Brno, as well as numerous houses and apartments – more than there were anywhere else except Weimar Germany. The shoe company Bata became a major patron of modern design: its stores in Prague were among the earliest Modernist public buildings, and the centre of the company town, Zlin, was dominated by two buildings by Vladimir Karfik – a community centre and the seventeen-storey Bata headquarters. Karfik, who had worked for Wright and Le Corbusier, designed Tomas Bata's own office as a lift which could visit every floor of the headquarters: the Russian Constructivists would surely have approved of such dynamism!

The Jewish settlement of Palestine began in earnest in the 1920s, and the first seeds of Modernism were

Alvar Aalto, Villa Mairea, Noormarkku, Finland 1937–40
In the Villa Mairea Aalto turned collage to architectural ends, creating a brilliant synthesis of Modernist, vernacular and natural motifs. The interior, with its clustered poles and rattan-wrapped steel columns, offered a vivid abstraction of the Finnish forest, as well as a spatially varied and richly habitable living space.

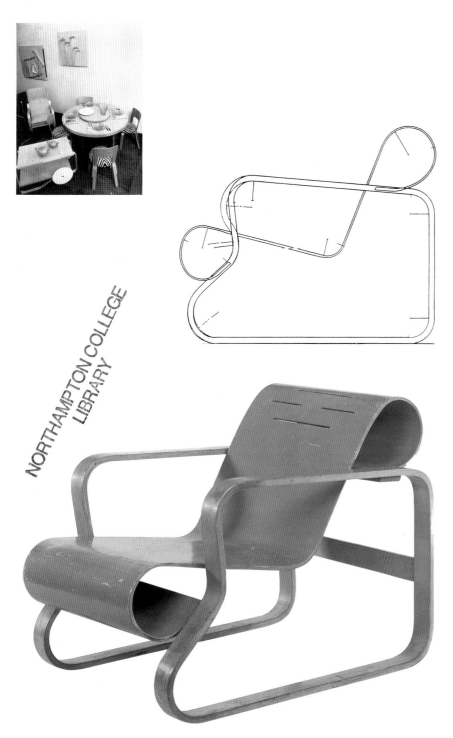

NORTHAMPTON COLLEGE
LIBRARY

Above left: Aino Aalto, Artek room at Milan Triennale, 1936
Artek was formed to manufacture Aalto's furniture and promote modern culture in Finland, and this exhibit was designed by Aalto's architect-wife, Aino. Variants of most of the furniture shown are still in production.

Above: Alvar and Aino Aalto, Paimio Chair, 1930–3
This bent-ply seat hung from a bent-birchwood frame was intended to help the breathing of the patients in the Paimio Sanatorium, and was later produced by Artek for general use. It is still in production.

Opposite: Alvar Aalto, Finnish Pavilion, New York World's Fair, 1939
Widely hailed as the outstanding interior at the Fair, Aalto designed this setting as an evocation of the Finnish landscape. All the objects were of wood, artfully arranged in a multivalent collage which broke new ground in exhibition design.

scattered by the Zionist *Hilfsverein deutscher Juden* (German Jewish-aid Association) which sent architects to Palestine. Erich Mendelsohn visited in the early 1920s and his idea of a regional interpretation of Modernism inspired later European arrivals. The shortage of materials and rudimentary local steel industry commended reinforced concrete construction, and the International Style looked well in the strong sun. The new town of Tel Aviv was planned by Patrick Geddes, and between 1931 and 1948 more than 4,000 buildings were erected in a simple cubic style. With a band of balconies and blinds replacing the *fenêtres en longueur*, they looked much like the timeless Mediterranean architecture Le Corbusier sketched in his early travels. Denounced as Jewish in Germany and as petit-bourgeois in the USSR, and widely feared as socialist elsewhere, Modernism was an ideal way for the Jewish, predominantly middle-class socialists who settled Palestine to declare their new identity and signal the Jewish claim on the land.

Reflecting on the 1920s, the British architects Alison and Peter Smithson observed that 'in Berlin, Mies generated a lot of heat; but in Paris, with Le Corbusier, people caught fire'. Le Corbusier's importance to the development and dissemination of Modernist architecture is difficult to overstate. *Vers une Architecture* became one of the most influential books on architecture ever published, and he continued to produce a stream of brilliant, provocative texts. In 1929 the Swiss publisher Girsberger issued the first volume of Le Corbusier and his partner and cousin Pierre Jeanneret's complete works: the *Oeuvre Complète* eventually ran to eight volumes and enabled Le Corbusier to determine the 'ideal' presentation of the buildings. Published with French, English and German texts, it exerted enormous influence worldwide. The second edition of the first volume was dedicated to a young South African architect called Rex Martienssen (who first visited Le Corbusier in 1925) and his Transvaal Group. The dedication makes interesting reading, and was almost certainly intended as a counter to the International Style: 'Let us have fresh proposals from every quarter of the globe. In a century's time we can begin to talk of "a style". To-day we dare not. All we can do is to think OF STYLE in itself – that is to say the moral probity of every work that is truly and genuinely creative. . . . Architecture must bring to the men of our new mechanical civilization, not just strict utility, but joy itself. Our task to-day is to light this flame . . .'

Right above: Ludvík Kysela, Bata store, Prague, 1928

Modernism flourished in the new Czech republic. Numerous private houses and apartment buildings were constructed in the 1930s, and the Bata shoe company (the most important patron of Modernist design) built several shops in the International Style.

Right below: Lúcio Costa, with Le Corbusier and others, Ministry of Education and Health, Rio de Janeiro, 1936–43

The flagship of Brazilian Modernism, the Ministry building (left) was designed following a visit by Le Corbusier who later included it in his *Oeuvre Complète*. Pilotis and *brises-soleil* were ideally suited to the climate and one of Costa's collaborators, Oscar Niemeyer, became a leading exponent of the Corbusian style.

For many, the flame was lit by working in Le Corbusier's studio at 35 rue de Sèvres, which became a mecca for young architects from around the world. The Spaniard Josep Lluís Sert, for example, worked there at the end of the 1920s and returned home to help form the national organization for contemporary architecture, GATEPAC, which became the Spanish wing of CIAM. Its activities were curtailed by the Spanish Civil War, but not before Sert had designed the Spanish Pavilion for the 1937 Paris World's Fair, which saw the unveiling of Picasso's great anti-war painting *Guernica*. Sert went on to become the Chairman of Architecture at Harvard. Le Corbusier's intense, passionate personality and architecture held a particular appeal in the Latin countries, and the Brazilian Pavilion by Oscar Niemeyer, Lúcio Costa and Paul Lester Wiener at the New York World's Fair in 1939 announced the arrival of a lyrical, hybrid strain of Modernism.

Lúcio Costa was appointed head of the School of Fine Arts in the wake of the Brazilian Revolution of 1930 and the new Ministry of Education and Health Building (1936–43) became the flagship of Brazilian Modernism. Costa led a team of young Modernists, and they invited Le Corbusier to act as a consultant in 1936. During his short visit the basis for the design was established – which he included in the *Oeuvre Complète* – and Corbusian Modernism became, in effect, the new state's 'official' style. Pilotis and *brise-soleil* sunshades were ideal in the tropical climate, and the Brazilians proved superb exponents of the free plan, none more so than Oscar Niemeyer. In buildings such as the New York Pavilion and the Casino, Yacht Club and Restaurant in Pampúlha (1943), Niemeyer brought a brio and fluidity to the Corbusian syntax, which anticipated the master's own late work. Uniquely, the new Brazilian architecture was complemented by vigorous and original landscapes and gardens by Roberto Burle Marx, whose distinctive style exploited the rich variety of tropical plants (on which he became an authority) to create sinuous, interlocking swathes of colour reminiscent of the biomorphic forms of Joan Miró or Hans Arp.

Although christened in New York, the International Style was very much an adopted child. It arrived first on the West Coast in the persons of Rudolf Schindler and his fellow Viennese architect, Richard Neutra. Both left Europe to work for Frank Lloyd Wright, and made their mark with houses for the same client, Dr Philip Lovell. A better embodiment of the 'New Man' than Lovell is difficult to imagine: his Physical Culture Centre

**Oscar Niemeyer, Church of
St Francis of Assisi,
Pampúlha, Brazil, 1943**
One of a group of buildings in
Pampúlha in which Niemeyer
experimented with the formal
freedom made possible by
reinforced concrete
construction.

and 'Care of the Body' column in the *Los Angeles Times*
made him a celebrated advocate of natural remedies,
vegetarianism, exercise and nude sunbathing. Schindler's
Beach House ran slightly over budget and Neutra
managed to impress Lovell as being the more
businesslike. In 1927 he duly secured the commission for
a large house on a steeply sloping site in the Hollywood
Hills near the Pathé Studios – it ran more than 100 per
cent over budget. The rambling, steel-framed structure
with hanging balconies and sleeping porches is a classic
example of a quintessentially Californian, laid-back
version of the International Style. Details such as a
Model T Ford headlight in the staircase, suspended
aluminium light troughs and the predominantly grey,
white and black colour scheme gave it an authentically
'industrial' look, and Lovell hoped his house would
'introduce a modern type of architecture and establish
it firmly in California'. He invited the public to view its
aesthetic and health-giving delights, and the response
staggered him. Some 15,000 Angelenos made the
pilgrimage: in the best traditions of Hollywood, the
'Health House,' as it came to be called, was an
instant star.

In Southern California, Modernism became part of
a developing regional architecture which laid the
foundations for California's pre-eminence in domestic
design after World War II. On the East Coast, by
contrast, Modernism confronted the stale formalism of
the Colonial Revival, which offered nothing to enrich
the import. Again, emigrés were the prime movers. The
Zurich-trained William Lescaze arrived in 1920, and
formed a partnership with George Howe in 1929.
Together they executed the PSFS Building in
Philadelphia (1929–32), the first Modernist tower, and

Lescaze's own house in Manhattan (1934) – the first
International Style building in New York. Although
avowedly opposed to international Modernism, even
Frank Lloyd Wright responded to the invader,
producing in Fallingwater both a great house and one of
the iconic images of modern architecture (1935–9).
Gropius's arrival at Harvard in 1937 was reported in
Time magazine, which described him as 'one of the
founders of the concrete-pipe-and-plate-glass school of
architectural modernism known as the International
Style'. Breuer soon followed, and like Gropius built a
house shortly after arriving – they worked in partnership
until 1941. In 1938–9 Sigfried Giedion gave his
influential Norton Lectures at Harvard, published in
1941 as *Space, Time and Architecture*, an ambitious attempt
to explain Modern Architecture as the embodiment of
the industrial *Zeitgeist* and fulfilment of the Western
tradition. Despite a dearth of actual buildings in the
East, the International Style was established as the
cutting edge of contemporary architecture.

Mainstream American ideas of modernity, however,
had little to do with the European import. New York's
Art Deco skyscrapers and the frenzied 'Zigzag Moderne'
of Chicago's Century of Progress Exposition of 1933
were more familiar, but above all the 1930s were the
Streamlined Decade. Developed to enable objects (such
as aircraft or ships) to penetrate air or water with the
least resistance, streamlining became synonymous with
saving time and energy, and then simply with being, or
looking, modern – one critic was even moved to write
about 'the speedy lines' of Jean Harlow's 'body design'.
The profession of industrial designer appeared first in
America, as a response to desperate sales figures during
the Depression. Designers such as Raymond Loewy,

Norman Bel Geddes, W.D. Teague and Henry Dreyfuss worked closely with engineers, market analysts and sales managers to re-design – or more often simply restyle – products. Loewy made his mark by restyling the Gestetner duplicating machine and thus extending its life cheaply: 'streamlined' was the favourite look, and Loewy was later hailed on the cover of *Time* as the man who 'streamlines the sales curve'. With economic growth depending on a rapid turnover of money, obsolescence became a valuable 'design' feature, rendering products 'out of style' long before they were technically obsolete – so much for the eternal verities of Corbusier and Ozenfant's *objets-types*, or the Bauhaus's commitment to form follows function.

The futuristic designs (for ships, cars, aeroplanes etc.), featured in Norman Bel Geddes's book *Horizons* (1932), did much to popularize streamlining, and Loewy's Coldspot refrigerator of 1932 and Hoover Model 150 vacuum cleaner evoked a feeling of speed and efficiency in housework and were widely emulated. In Britain HMV employed Christian Barman to design streamlined electrical goods, whilst in Italy Olivetti products were clearly influenced – and Corradino d'Ascanio's 1946 streamlined Vespa motor-scooter became almost inseparable from the image of modern Italy. The 'Building the World of Tomorrow' theme pavilions of the 1939 New York World's Fair, which was seen by forty-five million visitors, were designed by the 'big four' American designers. They proved immensely popular, although an architectural critic berated them as 'over-streamlined pseudo-modern (see the soft corners and fungoid bulges on the buildings by some of our most celebrated industrial designers). This may be called *modernoid*.' One hesitates to call anything by Frank Lloyd Wright modernoid, but his masterly Johnson Wax Building had some decidedly streamlined features: it opened to unprecedented national acclaim in 1939, and the company maintained that the publicity generated paid for the building. The bravura main office, with its structure of slender mushroom columns and continuous cornice of daylight, was so popular that some workers were said to be reluctant to leave at the end of the day.

To challenge the American love of styling MOMA organized 'Machine Art' in 1934, an exhibition of rigorously Platonic machines and machine-parts, kitchen- and laboratory-ware, scientific instruments and household fittings. More important still was its major 1938 exhibition on the Bauhaus, organized by Herbert Bayer. Combined with the growing number of exiles, several

Main staircase (opposite) and entrance (left): Richard Neutra, Lovell Health House, Los Angeles, 1927–9
Built in the Hollywood Hills this rambling, steel-framed house, with its balconies and sleeping porches is a laid-back, quintessentially Californian version of the International Style. Dr Lovell was a well-known advocate of healthy living and 15,000 Angelenos took up his invitation to view the wonders of his new house, which became an instant star.

involved in teaching, it helped consolidate European influence in the USA, and the accompanying book, *Bauhaus 1921–28*, was the most comprehensive yet published. It was followed by others which built on the Bauhaus legacy. Moholy-Nagy's *The New Vision* (1942) and *Vision in Motion* (1947), and his fellow Hungarian Gyorgy Kepes's *Language of Vision* (1944) were widely studied.

As in architecture, many of the talents behind the immensely influential American graphic and advertising design were initially imported from Europe. The Russian-born Mehemed Fehmy Agha was discovered in 1928 by Condé Nast, when working for the German edition of his *Vogue* magazine. He arrived in New York the following year and took over as art director of Nast's flagships – *Vogue*, *Vanity Fair* and *House and Garden*. The magazines were quickly transformed by asymmetrical page layouts, bold typography, photographs 'bleeding' off the page and whatever other devices his designers could find in the 'Temple of Constructivism'. Agha largely invented the look of the modern fashion magazine: he was the first to design in double-page spreads, printed his first colour photograph in 1932, and used leading photographers extensively – photographs eventually displaced the work of artists on the covers of most magazines.

Agha's example was followed at *Vogue*'s rival, *Harper's Bazaar*, where another Russian-born designer, Alexey Brodovitch, took over in 1934, four years after emigrating from Paris. He used a stable of outstanding photographers, including Bill Brandt, Brassai, Cartier-Bresson, Man Ray, Richard Avedon and Irving Penn, and commissioned covers and illustrations from the likes of Cassandre, Herbert Bayer and Salvador Dali. Brodovitch was a master of sequencing pages, unorthodox cropping of photographs and the use of white space: under his direction *Harper's* became the

Frank Lloyd Wright, Fallingwater, Bear Run, Pennsylvania, 1935–9
This vacation house was Wright's response to the International Style and quickly became one of the canonical images of modern architecture. Like the Prairie houses, it was organized around a chimney, but the complexity of its spatial composition was unprecedented in Wright's work. At nearly seventy years old, Wright proved he could more than match the interpenetrating spaces of European Modernism.

NORTHAMPTON COLLEGE LIBRARY

first modern 'style' magazine, relying on its own presentations rather than endorsements by the famous or wealthy to establish the clothes' credentials. American designers learnt quickly from Europe: Laurence Beall's superb posters for the Rural Electrification Administration were exhibited at MOMA in 1937, and Alvin Lustig and Paul Rand, in particular, drew creatively on a wide range of Modernist art. Rand was the art director of *Esquire* and *Apparel Arts* magazines during 1935–41 and looked especially to Matisse, Picasso and Miró, as well as to De Stijl and Constructivism; he mixed cut-out paper, photographs, hand-drawing and typography to create exceptionally sophisticated designs.

To many Europeans, modernity and America became almost synonymous. The image was promoted by magazines with sophisticated advertising and photographs of cars and consumer goods, but established above all by the flood of Hollywood movies which swept through the picture palaces of the 1920s and 1930s. Cinema was the dominant mass-medium of the first half of the twentieth century with attendances reaching their all-time peak in the 1930s – there were 85 million at 17,000 cinemas in the USA in 1939. Hollywood's dominance was overwhelming – as many films were made there as in all the other countries combined, apart from Japan. Modernist architecture featured regularly in the movies, most often as a backdrop to an affluent, fashionable lifestyle, but also as a vision of the new and possibly threatening, or

as the object of satire – the technologically advanced kitchen as a means of women's liberation was regularly lampooned.

One of the best and, in terms of the International Style, architecturally most authentic portrayals of the modern lifestyle was in Allan Dwan's 'What a Widow!' (1930), in which Gloria Swanson played a fashionable socialite and archetypal New Woman who held court in an ultramodern town house. The set was designed by the Paris-based American architect Paul Nelson in a style which reflected the influence of both Le Corbusier and Neutra. Swanson was very much the New Woman off set too, commissioning fabrics from Sonia Delaunay before they had become fashionable amongst architects' wives. All the major studios used a 'modern look' during the 1930s, but they were not in the business of stylistic purity or intellectual integrity and freely mixed elements of Art Deco, streamlining, the 'moderne' and International Style, none more so than RKO whose designers introduced Bakelite floors and adored streamlining as a setting for the dance routines of Fred Astaire and Ginger Rogers. The cinema exerted an enormous influence on the way people – especially women – dressed, but its impact on architecture and design was modest. It did nonetheless help shape people's perceptions, and in ways which were inimical to the Modernists' original aspirations: the lasting impressions were probably either of threatening novelty or of a fashionable utopia for wealthy nonconformists – hardly what the predominantly left-

Frank Lloyd Wright, Johnson Wax Building, Wisconsin, 1939

The Johnson and Johnson Building's hypostyle hall with its slender mushroom columns is one of the twentieth century's great interiors. Like the Larkin Building of 1904, Wright designed his new cathedral to work as a totally introverted space, lit from above and by a continuous cornice of perspex tubes – wrapping around its curved corners, they give the exterior a distinctly streamlined look.

Right: A. M. Cassandre, *Harper's Bazaar* **magazine cover, 1939**
Russian by birth and French by adoption, Cassandre was honoured with an exhibition at New York's Museum of Modern Art in 1936. He worked in the USA in the late 1930s and his fellow Russian, Alexey Brodovitch, commissioned this cover which playfully exploits Cubism, Purism and Surrealism to create a memorable image of chic modernity.

Below: The New York World's Fair 1939 poster, 1937
The Fair was designed in a futuristic style by America's leading industrial designers, and its streamlined forms were predictably criticized as being pseudo-modern. Superficial imitation of the International Style's external forms proved easier than mastering its compositional principles.

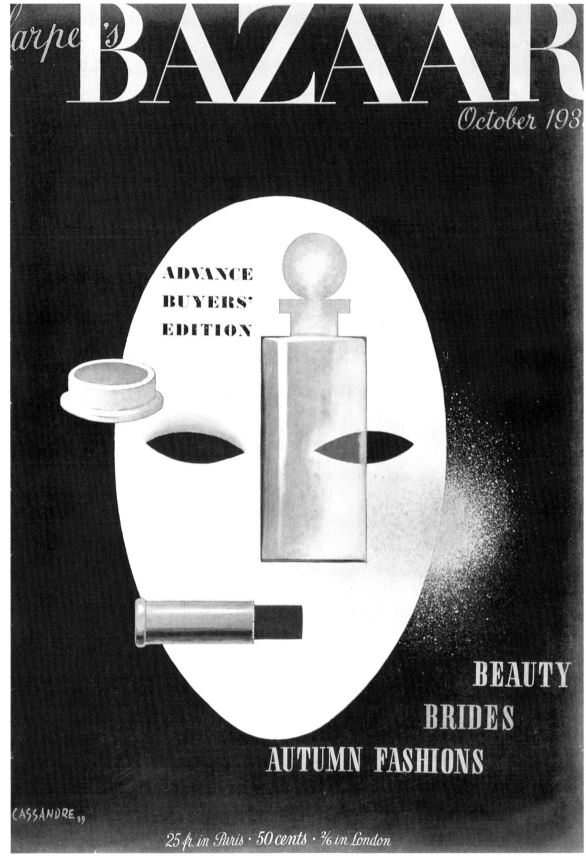

wing, socially committed pioneers set out to achieve.

World War II inevitably put a stop to developments in most fields, but the Modernists' new 'language of vision' was pressed into action to serve the needs of government propaganda. In Britain, Abram Games, F. H. K. Henrion, G.R. Morris and Reginald Mount produced a succession of outstanding posters – Morris and Mount making surprisingly vigorous use of Surrealist-inspired images. Many of the most striking American designs were also Modernist in inspiration, and, typically, the work of Europeans – Herbert Matter, who was tempted to leave Switzerland for New York in 1936, the Amsterdam-born, Italian-educated Leo Lionni, and Jean Carlu, who was in New York when France surrendered. Although propaganda was the War effort's most conspicuous call on design skills, more important in the long run was its insatiable demand for information, clearly presented and easily assimilable to permit rapid decision taking: Information Design came to occupy an important place in post-War graphics, and its foundations lay in the Modernist problem-solving approach and emphasis on legibility and clarity of communication.

By the War, Modernist architecture and design were established as significant elements of the visual culture of developed countries, but most people's day-to-day lives were relatively unaffected – in the average home, only the radio set and occasional advertisements in magazines were likely to look overtly 'modern'. Horizontal and corner windows became a fashion in some new suburban houses, but otherwise they were thoroughly traditional. Apart from a greater restraint in decoration, the only rooms significantly affected by modern design were the kitchen and bathroom. The most conspicuous changes were in women's clothing, whose development falls outside an account of Modernism with a capital 'M'.

After World War II, this all changed. As a vanguard movement in the arts, Modernism was arguably over by 1940, but its public success had hardly begun. Its post-War pre-eminence depended on new clients and new needs: large international corporations, public authorities charged with building houses or schools speedily and in unprecedented quantities, and insatiable consumer markets. America led the way in the fine arts, corporate architecture and consumerism, the European countries, devastated by war, in the construction of the Welfare State. The impact of Modernism on mainstream practice – and hence on everyday life – had scarcely begun: the appearance of the everyday world was set to change out of all recognition.

Below left: Cedric Gibbons, E. B. Williams and William Horning, Dream Office for MGM, 1936
The public was fed dandified visions of the 'moderne' by the cinema long before such furniture was ever widely available.

Below: Raymond Loewy, Coldspot refrigerator, feature in Sears Spring catalogue, 1935
Streamlined forms made obvious sense in the design of locomotives and cars, but in the USA in the 1930s streamlining and modern design became almost synonymous. Loewy's Coldspot refrigerator was hugely popular, and numerous products were given a streamlined face-lift to revive sales and extend their life.

6

We are not at the end but at the beginning of an epoch ... We have science, we have technology, we have industrialization. All are accepted as part of progressive existence, the question is how to guide them in a direction that is beneficial to all of us. Mies van der Rohe

Left: John Follis, *Arts and Architecture* magazine cover, 1949
Under John Entenza's direction *Arts and Architecture* became the vanguard of design culture in California and one of the world's most influential design magazines. The abstract treatment of leaf and pebble neatly summarizes the combination of organic form and Modernist aesthetic promoted by the magazine.

Opposite: Le Corbusier, Unité d'Habitation, roof garden, Marseilles, 1947–52
Le Corbusier's first major post-War building announced a new sculptural freedom in form-making which would characterize his – and much other – work. The roof garden included a running track, and its heroic conception was clearly inspired by the rooftop test-track of the FIAT factory in Turin, on which Le Corbusier was photographed in the 1920s.

Before 1939, Modernism remained predominantly a European affair; in 1945, with the European economies in ruins, America was poised to become the focus of avant-garde art. Entering the War late and remaining unaffected by either fighting or bombing at home, the foundations for post-War supremacy were laid by 1945 – even the Central Intelligence Agency (CIA) was enlisted to promote American culture abroad in the battle to wrest the prestige of cultural leadership from Paris. The War effort was all-consuming in Europe, but in America it was almost business-as-usual for many artists and institutions. The Museum of Modern Art (MOMA) continued to hold major exhibitions, although the show which artists were still assimilating in 1945 was organized by the Director Alfred Barr in 1936-7. Its title was 'Fantastic Art, Dada, Surrealism'. The latest developments in Paris were a revelation, as was the arrival of real live Surrealists in America – Max Ernst, André Masson and André Breton – and other leading artists such as Léger and Mondrian: Modernism was no longer distant, a story told in magazines and museums, but a living, messy reality.

Surrealism was a starting-point for several of the artists – Arshile Gorky, Jackson Pollock, Mark Rothko – who were later known as the Abstract Expressionists. The major painters had found their mature styles by 1950 – Pollock's skeins of dripped paint, Clyfford Still's soaring shards of colour, Barnett Newman's celebrated 'zips' dividing massive colour-fields, Rothko's luminous stacks of soft-edged rectangles – and American critics

and curators soon felt justified in proclaiming 'The Triumph of American Painting'. New York, not Paris, was now the world centre of art: the paintings were fresher, brighter, more original and bigger – a *lot* bigger. Newman's *Vir Heroicus Sublimis* (1950–1) was fully 5.4 metres wide. Critics were quick to provide the new painting with a literature and a lineage, none more influentially than Clement Greenberg who cast Abstract Expressionism as the furthest point on the 'road to flatness' and the heir to what he saw as the key moment in Modernist painting – the development of Analytical Cubism c. 1911-12.

MOMA naturally pressed Modernist exhibition design into service during the War in such shows as *Road to Victory* (1942) and *Airways to Peace* (1943). Both were designed by Herbert Bayer, enabling him to develop ideas about angles of viewing first explored at the Bauhaus – 'Airways' included a ramp to look down on aerial photographs and a globe visitors could enter. Much the most important of MOMA's Wartime design exhibitions was organized by Eliot Noyes in 1940. Entitled *Organic Design*, it included recent work from Scandinavia, notably the bent-wood furniture of Aalto, and helped establish a trend towards voluptuous, biomorphic furniture exploiting the latest industrial materials and techniques such as multiply curved plywood, fibreglass mouldings and synthetic foams. The contrast with embattled Britain could hardly have been greater. There, the craftsman-designer Gordon Russell was welcoming the Utility Furniture scheme as a

Jackson Pollock,
Convergence, 1952
Dubbed 'Jack the Dripper' on the cover of *Time* magazine, Pollock assumed the role of an all-American cultural hero in the early 1950s. The intricate skeins of paint dripped across his huge 'Action Paintings' were the result of calculation, not chance, and constituted a radical expansion of the Modernist aesthetic.

NORTHAMPTON COLLEGE LIBRARY

Mark Rothko, *Orange and Yellow*, 1956
Rothko's luminous – and for many, numinous – fields of colour epitomized the heroic ambitions of Abstract Expressionism. Influential American critics, above all Clement Greenberg, proclaimed the style to be the culmination of the 'road to flatness' of Modernist painting.

British 'Utility Furniture': kitchen cupboard, early 1950s
In Britain, wartime shortages continued into the 1950s, and with them 'Utility Furniture'. Although seen by some leading designers as an opportunity to instil an appreciation of 'honest' design, the furniture soon came to represent dull functionalism to the public.

heaven-sent opportunity to put into practice the Arts and Crafts ideals of usefulness and honest craft, and to raise the national standard of design. Introduced to cope with labour and materials shortages, Utility was the only furniture allowed to be made from 1942 until several years after the War, and it did not cease production until 1952. The strict regulations meant that it was sturdy and hardwearing, but it was visually dull and came to be associated in most people's eyes with drab functionalism.

For architects and designers returning to work after World War II on either side of the Atlantic, Modernism was inescapable, and to those about to embark on their careers it still offered a vision of hope: Modernism could be adopted, adapted or rejected, but it could not be ignored. In Britain, formal education finally replaced apprenticeship as the route into architectural practice, and Modernist principles were increasingly adopted in universities and colleges worldwide. Only in France did the Beaux Arts system maintain its hegemony – although its legacy lived on in America, especially on the East Coast. The 'basic design' exercises of the Bauhaus *Vorkurs* were widely emulated in 'Foundation Courses', and appeals to students' intrinsic creativity displaced the acquisition of craft skills and schooling in the Classical tradition. Education is rarely discussed in general histories of art and design, but the dominance of Modernist principles was vital to its acceptance as orthodoxy. Bauhaus ideas were, as we noted, in part inspired by progressive education for young children, and these in turn, with their emphasis on 'creativity' and 'self-expression', gained added credence from developments in higher education – many an unsuspecting visitor has likened a first-year art or design studio to a kindergarten, without realizing how significant were the similarities!

Modernism bridged the Atlantic, but the situations confronting designers in Europe and America differed radically. The pressing need in Europe was for housing, schools, and industrial and urban reconstruction – precisely the challenges the Modernists aspired to tackle in the 1920s. In the place of 'homes fit for heroes', the people of Britain were promised a new country, with a national health service, jobs and social welfare, schools and dwellings for all. Belief in the utopia that would flow from technology and planning may have been irremediably damaged by the War and the atomic bomb, but faith in science still ran high, and technology had other wonders in prospect – universal television, unlimited power from nuclear energy, the conquest of space, digital computers, antibiotics. The USA's industrial infrastructure was not only intact after the War, but had been honed by its demands – in two years, the time to make a Liberty Ship plunged from some four and a half months to four and a half days: the productive potential in peacetime made the need to promote consumption urgent. Functional problem-solving has a part to play in most designing, but the early Modernists' fixed '*objets types*' and a single 'style of the epoch' had no place in a consumer economy driven by manufactured fantasies and desires rather than by need. However, by an irony of history, the 'universal style' of one of the last believers in the *Zeitgeist*, Mies van der Rohe, proved a perfect match for the global ambitions of American corporations.

To Mies, technology was the true expression of the twentieth century, and by settling in Chicago he found himself in the spiritual home of American building. In Chicago, technology could mean only one thing – the steel frame – and shortly after arriving in 1938 Mies projected his first all steel-and-glass house for a site in Wyoming. In 1945 a commission from Dr Edith Farnsworth enabled him to return to the idea, but it had to wait five years to be built, during which time (in 1947) the Museum of Modern Art gave Mies its stamp of approval with an exhibition and a book by Philip Johnson. The following year he began work on the 860 Lake Shore Drive Apartments (1948–51), for a site overlooking Lake Michigan. Several towers were then in progress, and Pietro Belluschi's elegant twelve-storey slab for Equitable Life in Portland, Oregon, had been completed in 1947: but it was Mies who stamped the type with unique authority. Spatially, he reduced the tower to a column-free 'universal space' around a core of services; formally, to a rectangular prism defined by a lightweight 'curtain wall' hung from the structural frame. By placing two towers at right-angles, rotated through ninety degrees and displaced by one bay, Mies created a subtle visual tension between them, one tower seen obliquely presenting a solid face, the other a play of transparency and reflections. The columns are flush with the glass skin and have I-section mullions planted centrally on them – a 'sign' of the structure within the fireproof concrete. This results in the windows next to the column being narrower than the central pair in each bay, producing a clearly discernible rhythm which enlivens the facades: upon such subtleties rests the success of the Miesian aesthetic.

It was not just aesthetic refinement that commended Mies's skin-and-bones architecture to corporations and developers, however. Curtain-walled towers are so ubiquitous now that it is difficult to imagine how they seemed when new, combining the aura of the most technically advanced country on earth with speed of design, ease of construction, and – thanks to air-conditioning – a could-be-anywhere universality. Here, indeed, was a truly international, replicable style of building which came with the official stamp of cultural approval: it was pioneered by one of the century's recognized masters, exhibited at MOMA and acclaimed in 1951 by America's official historian of modern architecture, Henry-Russell Hitchcock, as 'probably the major achievement of the 20th century'. The slick curtain walls, reflective by day and glowing at night, quickly came to symbolize honest business, efficiency and a future of limitless opportunity: they were soon emulated worldwide. And for developers, economy-class versions could be built *very* cheaply: 'architecture', as opposed to mere building, had never been so affordable.

The demand for new buildings in America was immense and forced major changes in the way architecture was practised. Offices grew larger, more corporate and institutionalized, and buildings were designed by large teams, with different groups specializing in various aspects such as structure, skin and service cores (lifts, stairs, toilets, ducts, etc.). Skidmore Owings and Merrill (SOM) was founded in 1936 and after the War pioneered the application of American business organization to architectural practice, growing rapidly into the largest and most influential commercial firm – by the 1980s they were employing over 2,000

Above: Mies van der Rohe, 860-880 Lake Shore Drive, Chicago, 1948–51
On their completion in 1951 the twin 26-storey towers at 860-880 Lake Shore Drive, seen at the centre of this picture, were the highest buildings along the north shore. The first steel and glass curtain-walled towers, they are now dwarfed by the 100-storey Hancock Tower by Skidmore Owings and Merrill (SOM) and a bustle of other Miesian buildings.

Left: Mies van der Rohe, 860-880 Lake Shore Drive, Chicago, 1948–51
Epitomizing Mies's belief in an architecture of 'almost nothing', these apartments set the pattern for countless later buildings. Developers loved Miesian architecture because it was quick and cheap to build, and clients saw it as embodying the know-how of America's technological supremacy.

Below left: Skidmore Owings and Merrill, Lever House, New York, 1952
The tower and podium form of Lever House set the pattern for countless later buildings. Car-drivers reputedly slowed down to admire its crisply detailed, green-tinted curtain-wall which was in startling contrast to the older stone-clad buildings of Manhattan, with their awkward setbacks to comply with daylighting regulations.

Below right: Mies van der Rohe with Philip Johnson, Seagram Building, New York, 1954–8
The epitome of Modernist corporate architecture, the Seagram Building was clad with a curtain-wall of bronze-tinted glass in bronze mullions. Placed symmetrically on the site and approached centrally, it marked a resurgence of the Classical sensibility which ran through all Mies's work.

Opposite: Skidmore Owings and Merrill, Pepsi Cola building, New York, 1960
Hailed as 'a kind of Pazzi Chapel of corporate design' by the *New York Times*'s architecture critic Ada Louise Huxtable, Gordon Bunshaft's wonderfully elegant design for the Pepsi Cola building showed that it was still possible to say something fresh within the parameters of the Miesian style.

people in six offices in the USA, London and Hong Kong, and had completed projects in over forty countries. Their breakthrough came in 1952 with the twenty-one-storey Lever House – *Life* magazine reported that drivers and pedestrians slowed to marvel at this green-tinted spectacle on New York's Park Avenue. Gordon Bunshaft, the chief designer of SOM's New York office, avoided the daylighting setbacks typical of New York skyscrapers, and the slab-and-podium form proved very influential. In partnership with Philip Johnson, Mies raised the corporate tower to new heights of elegance with the thirty-nine-storey Seagram Building (1954–8), set a short distance from Lever House on the opposite side of Park Avenue. Luxuriously clad with bronze-tinted glass in purpose-made bronze mullions, it was approached axially across a small plaza. Symmetrical and monumental, Seagram radiated corporate power and prestige.

Mies's less-is-more architecture exploited the steel-frame construction which became the commercial vernacular of America, but the beauty of his buildings, arising from perfection of proportion and refinement of detail, is as difficult to achieve as it is unmistakable. Emulated by gifted architects for specific clients wanting a quality building, the results could be superb: as, for example, by Gordon Bunshaft/SOM for Pepsi Cola in New York (1960) – 'a kind of Pazzi Chapel of corporate design' as the *New York Times*'s Ada Louise Huxtable

described it – or by Arne Jacobsen for Jespersen in Copenhagen (1955–6). But these refined essays in idealized technology were worlds apart from the mass-produced banalities of curtain-walled, speculatively built towers and slabs which rose everywhere business flourished in the 1960s. Anonymous buildings for anonymous clients, they gave Mies the dubious honour of becoming the most influential architect since Palladio. The urban towers had their suburban counterpart in the campus of low-rise, curtain-walled pavilions in a park-like setting, usually with reflecting pools and extensive, orderly planting – a benign image of corporate efficiency and largesse pioneered by Eero Saarinen at the General Motors Technical Center in Warren, Michigan (1946–55).

The new corporate architecture was accompanied by a distinctive 'American Look' in furniture, interior design and art. This consisted of an assemblage of new or classic Modern furniture with large potted plants, blocks of bright colour, elegant textiles, and abstract paintings and sculpture – Late Modernist art proved surprisingly decorative. Bright, orderly and comfortable, the 'Look' drew on both geometric abstraction and the biomorphic forms of sculptors such as Constantin Brancusi, Henry Moore and Jean Arp. MOMA's 'Organic Design' exhibition played an important part in its formation, as did the Museum's competition for 'Organic Design in Home Furnishings' which was won

Below left: Alexander Calder, *Janvier* mobile, 1950
Calder's enchanting mobiles, invented in 1932, were an original contribution to Modernist sculpture and came in all sizes – the example shown is 5.4 metres across. Their organic, seemingly weightless forms were much admired by the post-War generation of American designers.

Below: Herbert Matter, Brochure cover for Eero Saarinen's Tulip-Chair, Knoll International, 1956
The page shown was covered by a translucent sheet with a picture of a mysterious brown-paper-wrapped object, which 'unwrapped' to reveal the Tulip Chair. (A two-page advertisement played the same trick.) Designed of moulded polyester with a coated metal base, the chair was the latest product of the American designers' post-War exploration of organic form.

Bottom: Charles Eames, Lounge Chair and Ottoman, Knoll International, 1956
This classic chair, exploiting the potential of the two-way bending of plywood developed in the 1940s, became an epitome of sitting comfort.

by Charles Eames and Eeero Saarinen with two influential ideas: a sculptured seat on a spindly substructure – which Saarinen developed into his Womb Chair (1946–8); and modular storage units – pioneered in the mid 1920s and ubiquitous in the 1950s. The classic Modernist chairs of the 1920s were *constructed*, whereas these were *sculpted* – indeed some were designed by sculptors, such as Harry Bertoia, whose 'chickenwire' chairs were made from bent grids of slender chrome-plated steel bars (1952–), and Isamu Noguchi who designed a free-form low table in 1945. The new furniture was manufactured primarily by two companies: Knoll International and Herman Miller. By the mid-1950s the Knoll catalogue featured European classics (including Mies's Barcelona chair, never intended for mass-production but soon to grace many a corporate foyer) and designs by Charles and Ray Eames, Harry Bertoia, Eero Saarinen and others. Herman Miller supported Charles Eames's early research and went on to lead the field in office systems – such as the celebrated 'Action Office' range. Eames's furniture often recalls the stabiles and mobiles of the sculptor Alexander Calder, but the forms were based on careful ergonomic analysis and were highly innovative technically. The chairs eventually sold by the million, the 1956 Lounge Chair and Ottoman becoming an epitome of modern comfort.

The graphic skills which began to establish the image of a consumer society through advertising and magazine layout in the 1930s soon found their way into American business and industry. Paul Rand's influential *Thoughts on Design* appeared in 1947, and advocated a wide repertoire of Modernist techniques – asymmetry, photograms, collage, adaptations of painters' motifs (from Arp, Miró and Klee amongst others) and so on. Rand pioneered the New Advertising, which demanded the viewer's involvement in 'completing' the message, and was also the leading figure in corporate identity work: his masterly logotype for IBM was designed in 1956, and he worked for many other corporations including ABC Television, Westinghouse Electric and United Parcel Service (UPS). Rand was appointed to work for IBM by Eliot Noyes, their corporate design consultant (a role modelled on Olivetti's design management policies); it was also through Noyes that Marcel Breuer was commissioned to design IBM's buildings. Noyes himself had a worldwide impact in the 1960s as the consultant to Mobil Oil, his standard petrol stations spreading inexorably around the globe. American advertising, style magazines such as *Harper's*

Bazaar, *Vogue* and *Esquire*, and corporate image-making were a major influence worldwide during the 1950s, but what became the International Style of corporate design – the counterpart of the reductive architecture of Miesian towers – developed in Switzerland.

Max Bill and a talented younger generation of Swiss designers were leading advocates of rational Modernism. American advertisements were the work of art directors, whereas those of the Swiss were patently design solutions to a problem, using orderly arrangements of type and relevant images to convey information – not to intrigue or puzzle, like the New Advertising. Two of the most widely used sans-serif typefaces – Univers and Helvetica – were designed by Swiss typographers in the 1950s, and the Swiss style combined sans-serif text with photographs – often dramatically shot or cropped – using a systematic underlying order, generally based on a grid. Developed by designers such as Emil Ruder, Armin Hofmann and Josef Müller-Brockmann, the Swiss style – or International Typographic Style as it became known – established an overwhelming dominance in the 1960s and 1970s, which was identified particularly with the corporate style of major graphic design firms like Landor Associates of San Francisco (who designed the identities of Coca Cola, Levi Strauss, 3M, Heinz, General Electric and many US and foreign airlines), Chermayeff and Geismar in New York (who were responsible for hundreds of schemes including Mobil Oil and Xerox), and Pentagram in London (whose clients included Olivetti, IBM, Reuters and Penguin Books).

The cool sophistication of international corporate design found its counterpart in the industrial design emanating from Germany. The strong design base established between the wars played a significant part in the German 'economic miracle' and found a key post-War focus in the Bauhaus's avowed successor, the Hochschule für Gestaltung at Ulm. Founded in 1955, it was designed and directed for a year by Max Bill, and then by the Argentinian Tomás Maldonado, who favoured rigorous analysis, teamwork and system – ideas which became fashionable in the 'Design Methods' movement of the 1960s. Maldonado established close links with the Braun company of Frankfurt, and Otl Aicher, Hans Gugelot and Dieter Rams all taught in Ulm and designed for Braun. Their minimalist style, like Mies's architecture, depended on perfection of detail and won prizes for Braun at the Milan Triennale of 1960; the following year they were awarded the prestigious Rinascente Compasso d'Oro. Fêted in the international magazines, the Braun style epitomized 'Good Design'. To Maldonado it was not a 'style' – he redefined industrial design as 'scientific operationalism' – but it was quickly imitated, both by other German companies such as Siemens, AEG-Telefunken and Bosch, and abroad. In Denmark, Jakob Jensen designed the ultimate elegant boxes for Bang and Olufsen (1969–73): unsightly knobs were replaced by push-buttons and sliding controls, and the famous tangential pick-up arm. Governmental and corporate promotion of design was probably stronger in Japan than anywhere

Below left: Arne Jacobsen, 'The Ant' stacking chair, 1952
In this wonderfully elegant design Jacobsen exploited the elasticity of laminated wood and lightness of slender metal legs to create an exceptionally comfortable stacking chair. Originally designed to furnish the canteen of the manufacturers Novo in Copenhagen, it became a classic of 1950s design and is still in production.

Below right: Room in 'New Furniture Designed by Charles Eames' exhibition, Museum of Modern Art, New York, 1946
As well as three variants of the sculptural bent-wood chair, behind the table can be glimpsed a prototype metal-based three-legged chair which, like most of the early three-legged designs, tended to tip over – and never went into production.

NORTHAMPTON COLLEGE LIBRARY

Hans Gugelot, Braun Razor, model no. 26, 1962
The Braun name became almost synonymous with coolly minimal Modernist design during the 1960s, and both Rams and Gugelot taught at the Hochschule für Gestaltung at Ulm, founded to continue the Bauhaus tradition.

else in the world, and the products of Sony, Sharp, Canon and other corporations soon came to rival the sophistication and elegance of Braun and other European trendsetters.

By the 1960s Miesian architecture, a modified American Look in interiors (with a strong bias towards 'classic' modern rather than biomorphic furniture), the International Typographic Style and the slick minimalism epitomized by Braun combined to create a style more consistent and pervasive than the first International Style. It was referred to by many, not surprisingly, as 'Bauhaus' – a usage which MOMA described as 'popular' but 'incorrect' in its 1959 *Introduction to Twentieth Century Design*, but which it had done much to encourage through its focus on the Bauhaus as the single fount of modern design. The relationship to the Bauhaus was more problematic than might appear, because our image of it has been greatly influenced by the 1960s revival. By assimilating the significantly different work of Le Corbusier and Mies van der Rohe to the new Bauhaus look, and by eliminating colour almost entirely, a homogeneous image of Modernist design was presented which overlooked the variations between its sources. The new cool, austere, monochromatic design had more to do with the corporate values of the 1960s than with the revolutionary zeal of the 1920s, and by being imputed to the original buildings and furniture helped promote the misleading view of 1920s Modernism which became the object of such ill-informed assaults as Tom Wolfe's *From Bauhaus to Our House* (1981).

The domestic counterpart of the new corporate architecture also began in America with Mies's Farnsworth House, finally built in 1950. This epitomized his architecture of *beinahe nichts* ('almost nothing') since it consisted simply of a 'universal space' defined by two horizontal planes slung between steel I-beams, infilled with glass and made habitable by a narrow service core and Shantung-silk curtains. Hovering above a bucolic flood-plain, it remains the archetypal Modern house-as-temple, although its image was sullied by an acrimonious lawsuit with Dr Farnsworth who declared it too expensive to live in. Almost as radical were the 'Case Study Houses' in California. They were the idea of John Entenza, who transformed *California Arts and Architecture* (1911–38) from a provincial homes-and-gardens magazine into *Arts and Architecture* (1943–67), a vehicle for the Los Angeles avant-garde, with a worldwide readership and cutting-edge layouts by Alvin Lustig: the historian Reyner Banham described it as 'the

most ruthlessly pinned-up and cribbed-out-of magazine of the hour'. The Case Study Programme began in 1945, and twenty-seven houses were built and published by 1963, the best – and best known – by Charles and Ray Eames in 1945–9. A poetic assemblage of industrial steel framing filled with small, Japanese-style rectangles of translucent and transparent glass, the Eames House had a flexible plan, used standard components and materials 'honestly' – everything exposed – and formed a perfect foil to their chairs, paintings, fabrics, folk art and other collectibles. The laid-back, Californian answer to the Farnsworth house, it pointed the way to a more relaxed Modernism. Just as important as the Case Study Houses in epitomizing the California lifestyle were the post-War houses of Richard Neutra, beginning with the spectacular Desert House for Edgar Kaufmann Jr. (1946) – the complete integration of house and landscape is typical of Neutra's late style and clearly reflected his longstanding interest in Frank Lloyd Wright's Prairie Houses.

Arts and Architecture's Case Study Programme was but one of many efforts to introduce good design to the American public. MOMA ran a competition for 'Low Cost Furniture' in 1948, won by the English designers Robin Day and Clive Latimer with storage units of a type later to be found in many homes, and the following year it exhibited a house by Marcel Breuer in its sculpture garden. Although architecturally feeble – the diagrammatic plan had only a tenuous relationship to the 'butterfly' form – the house was much imitated and the vertical boarding, zoned plan and butterfly roof found their way on to many suburban lots. In 1949 the Detroit Institute of Arts held a major exhibition entitled 'For Modern Living' which was designed by Charles and Ray Eames, and in 1950 MOMA began a public education programme promoted around a series of twice-yearly 'Good Design' exhibitions, which were directed by Edgar Kaufmann Jr. 'Good Design' awards and labels were introduced and proved popular with retailers, but they were seen as a 'tyranny of the Modern' by those who did not share MOMA's taste: *House Beautiful* decided 'to speak out and appeal to your common sense' about 'something rotten in the state of design' in April 1953. But it spoke in vain: the new Modernism became the dominant style of the 1960s, as one can see from a book like Werner Weidert's *Private Houses – An International Survey*, published in London in 1967 and full of American-style houses with 'flowing', open interiors on several levels – several with that Californian favourite, the 'conversation pit' – and

Mies van der Rohe, Farnsworth House, Fox River, Illinois, 1946–50
Although completed after Philip Johnson's Glass House, Mies's masterpiece was immediately recognized as a fulfilment of the Modernist dream of floating, weightless planes made habitable by glass. Its simplicity belies great refinement – and expense – in detail and composition: the house has the timeless presence of a Greek temple.

Above: Charles and Ray Eames, Eames House, Pacific Palisades, California, 1945–9
One of the century's classic houses, the Eames House was reputedly made from components available at the local builder's merchant. Built as part of *Arts and Architecture* magazine's Case Study programme, its relaxed, seemingly casual style was the antithesis of the inviolable perfection of Mies's Farnsworth House.

Opposite: Richard Neutra, Moore House, Ojai, California, 1952
Conceived as an oasis in the arid Ojai desert, the house is surrounded by lily-ponds which also serve as reservoirs for irrigation and help humidify the dry air. Its beautifully proportioned rooms, dissolved at their corners by glass-to-glass joints, frame spectacular views of the surrounding mountains.

furnished with Knoll or similar modern furniture. Few could afford the luxury of a one-off house, but the style was regularly featured in *House and Garden* and similar magazines – and could be emulated in furnishing and decoration, and by knocking out a wall or two to achieve the requisite spaciousness.

The 1951 Festival of Britain introduced a decorative and rather effete version of Modernism to a nation laid low by twelve years of rationing, make-do-and-mend clothes and Utility furniture. Designed as 'A Tonic to the Nation' and coinciding with the return of a Conservative government elected to 'Set the People Free' from socialist planning, it also signalled the arrival of the consumer society. The architectural set-pieces on the south bank of the Thames – including the Royal Festival Hall, the Dome of Discovery and the Skylon – were complemented by a landscape which influenced countless civic centres. Responding to the post-War excitement in science, the Festival Pattern Group co-ordinated fourteen manufacturers who used designs derived from molecular crystal structures on furnishings and tableware, murals and carpets. The Festival style lacked the vigour and confidence of the American Look or Californian Modern and reflected the similarly anaemic 'humanized' Modernism of post-War Swedish architecture which the *Architectural Review* christened 'The New Empiricism'. Surprisingly, the big guns of Nikolaus Pevsner, Herbert Read and J.M. Richards all threw their weight behind what Pevsner

called a 'less puritanical, less exclusive' Modernism, and it would not be long before the *Review* was singing the praises of Victoriana.

The New Empiricism's counterpart in furniture and furnishings also emanated from Scandinavia, but was happily more sophisticated than the architecture. Alvar Aalto's 'humane' Modernism was already well known internationally, but Finland was also home to several minimalists, who won six Grand Prix at the 1951 Milan Triennale – three going to Tapio Wirkkala's wonderfully elegant glass and ceramics. The Finnish design renaissance revealed in Milan received detailed coverage in the influential Italian magazine *Domus*, and also loomed large in a major exhibition called 'Design in Scandinavia', which toured the USA and Canada between 1954 and 1957. In Kaj Franck, Finland found a brilliant advocate of functionalist design – his glass pitchers of 1954, for example, were modelled on the kind of laboratory-ware featured in MOMA's 'Machine Art' exhibition. Aalto added several pieces to Artek's catalogue, including stools and tables using the exquisite fan-shaped leg invented in 1954, and throughout Scandinavia furniture was being produced which gained ready international acceptance. Bruno Mathsson's curvilinear armchair designed in 1934 typified the sort of furniture displayed at the Berlin *Interbau* exhibition in 1957, and designs such as Hans Wegner's teak dining-chair and smoke-oak folding chair of 1949 were widely imitated. By the early 1960s few, if any, major Western cities were without a distributor of Scandinavian furniture and domestic wares, and a pseudo-Scandinavian style, based largely on the use of oiled teak wood rather than on a real understanding of the originals, rapidly became a cliché. Scandinavian fabrics were also highly influential: Sweden's Astrid Stampe won a Grand Prix at the 1954 Milan Triennale for her abstract print *Windy Way*, and Finland's Marimekko company became famous for its bold, abstract patterns.

Scandinavian designers also did much to promote the trend towards more organic forms in tableware. In Denmark, Henning Koppel exploited biomorphic analogies with great sophistication – his dishes derived from fishes are sufficiently abstract not to look cute, and sufficiently figurative to hint amusingly at their source – whilst Soren Georg Jensen designed a condiment set in 1951 which suggested by turns miniature machine parts or Brancusi sculptures. Sigurd Persson's sculptural stainless steel Jet Line cutlery (1959) designed for Scandinavian Airlines (now SAS) was easy to mass-produce and radical in form – it is difficult to imagine

HEAL'S for that
can't-wait-to-get-it-home feeling

Serendipity is the word. Horace Walpole invented it to describe the art of making pleasant discoveries. Serendipity is what you acquire the moment you step into Heal's and start exploring all six floors. Some of the many things you'll discover with pleasure include the plastic foam and rubber upholstered chair (shown above)... pure white Swedish sheepskins for only £5/15s... matching sets of American sheets, towels and bedspreads lavishly decorated with large carnations now arriving . . . prints by the famous Bernard Buffet from as little as 6 -...and scores of other fascinating things for people with an eye for good design. Come along soon and serendipize to your heart's content.

Heal & Son Ltd. 196 Tottenham Court Road London W1   Telephone: Museum 1666   Buses 1, 14, 24, 29, 39, 73, 134, 176 or Goodge Street Underground

Advertisement for Heal's, 1960
The happy couple are driving home with a Swan chair (1958) by the Danish architect Arne Jacobsen. Heal's, as the advertisement states, was intended for 'people with an eye for good design' and became a leader amongst shops catering to the newly design-conscious young professionals.

any other airline adopting them then, or even now. Arne Jacobsen's 1957 cutlery range was far more reductive, but curves still dominated over straight lines, as they had in his plywood and metal three-legged 'Ant' chair of 1950 and sinuously curved 'Egg' and 'Swan' chairs of 1958 which emulated the organic furniture pioneered in America. In the 1960s, in line with trends in architecture and industrial design, organic curves gave way to Platonic geometries: Jacobsen's Cylinda Line tableware (1967) epitomized the trend, which found its way into many a home in the form of squat, cylindrical stainless steel tea-services. Its use having been pioneered by sophisticated designers, stainless steel acquired a certain cachet, but many of the cheap mass-produced versions were let down by poor detailing.

'Good Design' – meaning Modernist design – became a significant marketing strategy during the 1950s and 1960s. The Council of Industrial Design opened its Design Centre in London in 1956, and the following year introduced tags for selected products along the lines pioneered in New York – similar schemes, following MOMA's initiative, had started in France in 1955 and in Belgium in 1956. In Britain, modern design became almost synonymous with Terence Conran's chain of Habitat shops, the first of which opened in London in 1964. Conran had worked as a designer on the Festival of Britain and, as a lifelong Labour Party supporter, he made bringing modern design to a mass audience a personal mission. Habitat's eclectic blend of modern classics – from Thonet to Eames – and stripped pine folksiness made him a fortune, appealing initially to the 'switched-on' younger generation of London, and entering the mainstream in the 1970s.

Miesian architecture, the 'American Look' and 'Good Design' were the products of corporations and commerce. The other major strand of Modernist design was promoted by national and local governments and came to epitomize the aspirations, and ultimate failure, of the Welfare State. In Britain, the Labour Party swept to power in 1945 on promises of providing comprehensive health, education and social services. The Luftwaffe having made a start on slum clearance, new houses and flats were needed in huge numbers; the 1944 Education Act had raised the school-leaving age to fifteen, and new buildings were also urgently required. Although thoroughly unfashionable by the 1970s, British achievements in public-sector building were internationally admired and exercised some of the country's finest talents. The opportunity to help build a new Britain drew gifted young architects to leading

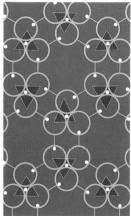

local government offices such as the London County Council (LCC), where Robert Matthew, Leslie Martin, Alan Colquhoun, William Howell and Colin St John Wilson amongst others worked in the early 1950s. Idealistic and soaked in the ideology of the Modern Movement, the younger generation set the pace. They had a body of wartime research, as well as Modernist principles, to guide them – most influential, perhaps, was Gropius's advocacy of *Zeilenbau* in *The New Architecture and the Bauhaus* (1935). This meant parallel rows of eight twelve-storey blocks, aligned north-south, spaced to provide adequate sun- and daylight, and surrounded by green space – a potent symbol of escape from the Dickensian gloom of urban slums.

Several *Zeilenbau* schemes were designed by outside consultants, such as Tecton in Finsbury (1946–50) and Powell and Moya in Westminster (the acclaimed Churchilll Gardens estate in 1962), as well as by the LCC architects, but their uniformity was soon considered irksome and the more picturesque possibilities of Swedish-style tower blocks found many advocates. The most celebrated of the LCC designs, the Roehampton estate (1952–5), was designed in two phases: the first by the point-block loving empiricists, the second by the *Zeilenbau* rationalists. Pevsner acclaimed the resulting picturesque juxtaposition of buildings and landscape to be a specifically English version of International Modern, and whilst schemes such as Churchill Gardens and Roehampton were of undeniable quality, the architects were soon victims of their own rhetoric. Many Local Authority Directors of Housing became firm believers in towers as a means of achieving high densities and 'liberating' surrounding land as parks, and from the late 1950s they were built throughout Britain. Their staunchest advocates during the 1960s were the political leaders of large cities who vied with

each other in exceeding production targets. To meet demand and keep costs down, industrialized systems were introduced – initially from France and Denmark – which used visually crude structural concrete panels. The architectural input into such systems was minimal, and quantity came at the expense of quality.

Faced with more extensive rebuilding than Britain, the French government promoted vast projects using Modernist housing types and layouts and realized by what rapidly became the world's most industrialized construction industry. Auguste Perret was entrusted with the reconstruction of Le Havre, André Lurçat with Maubeuge and Marcel Lods with Sotteville-les-Rouen.

Above left: Henning Koppel, Fish platter and cover, 1954
The Danish designer Koppel gave a new twist to the 1950s love of organic shapes by designing overtly biomorphic forms. Fortunately, they remained sufficiently abstract not to look cute.

Above right: Wodell, Wallpaper, Festival of Britain, 1951
Despite the terrors wrought by military technology, faith in science was undimmed in the 1950s and in Britain the Festival Pattern Group was formed to co-ordinate fourteen manufacturers to produce designs for furnishings, tableware, murals and carpets based on molecular crystal structures.

Left: Tapio Wirkkala, Vases 55, 1955
A star of the 1951 Milan Triennale, which established 'Scandinavian Modern' as an internationally recognized style, Wirkkala worked as a designer for the leading Finnish glassmakers Iittala from 1946 to 1985. The sculptural forms and thick walls of these vases exploit the refractive qualities of glass.

NORTHAMPTON COLLEGE LIBRARY

**Giacomo Matté-Trucco, FIAT
factory, Lingotto, Turin,
1915–20**
FIAT's founder, V. G. Agnelli,
brought Ford-style production
lines to Italy, and his
pioneering reinforced concrete
factory culminated – heroically,
if not entirely logically – with a
test-track on the roof. It
became an icon of modernity –
emulated by Le Corbusier, for
example, on the roof garden of
the Unité d'Habitation at
Marseilles – and its spirit lived
on in the 'streets in the sky' of
the 1950s and 1960s (opposite).

Le Corbusier advised on several town plans, most
famously for Saint-Dié, but his utopianism was out of
tune with the prevailing attitude to reconstruction. At
Marseilles, however, he had the chance to build the
apartment block of his dreams – the first of several
Unités d'Habitations. The huge building (1947–52) was
165 metres long and contained 337 apartments, a
shopping 'street', hotel, community services, and a
rooftop nursery and sports facilities: a 'social condenser'
along almost Soviet lines with the 'cross-over' apartment
section owing something to the OSA collective housing
projects of c.1930. The mix had its problems – the
shops were not economically viable – but socially it was
far from the disaster claimed by Le Corbusier's
detractors, and a world apart from the monuments to
overweening bureaucracies created under his influence
by French planners, such as the ghastly *grands ensembles*
of Sarcelles, Cergy-Pontoise and their ilk. Le Corbusier
had not only created the first post-War masterpiece in
Europe – the FIAT-factory inspired rooftop landscape
truly deserving the epithet 'heroic' – but he had also
announced a radical new aesthetic. The vigorous board-
marked concrete (*béton brut* as he called it) was clearly in
tune with developments in painting, most obviously the
graffiti-inspired *art brut* of Jean Dubuffet and the *tachisme*
of Antoni Tàpies and others or, at some remove, the
dripped canvases of Jackson Pollock or the paint-
spattered walls photographed by Aaron Siskind.

School building in Britain proved less controversial
than housing. The main focus for innovation was

Hertfordshire, where the County Architect Herbert
Aslin and his charismatic deputy Stirrat Johnson-
Marshall pioneered system-building, using prefabricated
components rather than units of structure – the 'kit of
parts' approach advocated by Gropius. Like the LCC,
the Hertfordshire office was a magnet for talented
young architects. The most theoretically inclined of
them, Bruce Martin, observed that 'bricks and stones,
tiles and concrete are materials for defence against a
hostile world. . . . We must build lightly for a life of
free and changing activity, for families with the space in
which to grow as needs and ideas change.' Charles and
Ray Eames might have said much the same about their
house. The Hertfordshire schools were steel-framed and
filled with light; inside, there were bold splashes of
colour (inspired by Ozenfant's pre-War lectures in
London) and, at the Chief Education Officer John
Newsom's insistence, commissioned artworks such as
large murals, sculptures or specially designed curtains.
The system-building approach was taken up by many
other authorities faced with massive school-building
programmes; several formed consortia to benefit from
bulk orders, and a school built using one such system
(CLASP) was exhibited to great acclaim at the 1960
Milan Triennale, winning several awards. When he died
in 1981, *The Architects' Journal* described Stirrat Johnson-
Marshall as 'the most influential architect in the United
Kingdom'. Compared with the arresting images in the
architectural magazines of the 1990s, the Hertfordshire
schools seem scarcely 'Architecture' at all. Johnson-

Marshall challenged his colleagues to 'approach the whole problem of building afresh' and their work represents an architecture almost extinct now. It is the product of rational thought untroubled by questions of 'style', and made for everyman, not a social or intellectual elite, through a process of collaborative design involving educationalists and building scientists as well as architects – a fulfilment, in all essentials, of Gropius's vision for the Bauhaus. Open-plan, flat-roofed buildings and progressive teaching became inextricably linked in people's minds – not always to either's benefit – and a combination of technical failures, fashion and reduced demand saw the disappearance of system-building in the 1980s.

In America, Gropius put his belief in teamwork into practice by forming TAC (The Architects' Collaborative) with six younger architects in 1945. They designed a Graduate Center for Harvard (1948–9), bringing the International Style into confrontation with the neo-Georgian favoured by the university between the wars, but the design lacked conviction, and by the mid-1950s TAC's work had become unmistakably formalist, using elements of the Modern language in a decorative rather than functional way. Mies's increasingly reductive architecture also became problematic. Crown Hall at IIT (1952–6) was immaculately proportioned and detailed – visually, if not in places technically – and the 'universal space' worked adequately as studios. But the single-storey pavilion-form was won at the expense of banishing a lot of habitable accommodation to a semi-

basement: Mies, as Paul Rudolph observed, made good buildings by ignoring most of the things a building has to do. Amidst proliferating circular and polygonal geometries, Frank Lloyd Wright's organic architecture was also descending into a version of form-for-form's-sake. As a gallery, the Guggenheim Museum (1943–59) is less than ideal, but as an urban spectacle it is unrivalled – people, if not always art, look wonderful there. But elsewhere, and nowhere more than in Marin County Civic Center in California (1959–64), circles swarm meaninglessly – the 'arches', for example, are in tension, not compression.

The masters' flights into formalism ran counter to the ground rules of Modernist (indeed of good) architecture, but were widely acclaimed in the architectural press: not surprisingly, younger and lesser talents followed suit. With their Beaux Arts foundations, the American schools had a strongly academic tradition and under the guise of teaching Modern architecture Gropius's Harvard became a finishing school for some of America's leading formalists – Philip Johnson, Paul Rudolph, I.M. Pei and John Johansen, amongst others. Johnson's fall from grace was especially notable, and the 12-metre high decorative arched colonnade of his Amon Carter Museum of Western Art in Fort Worth (1961) became almost the leitmotiv of the American formalists. The grandest formalist extravaganza of all came in Brazil, where the new capital – Brasilia – was planned by Lúcio Costa and Oscar Niemeyer as a homage to the Corbusian 'Radiant City'. Costa's 1957 plan was

Above left: London County Council, Housing estate at Roehampton, London, 1952–5
The small towers were designed by 'empiricists' who stressed human needs and looked to Sweden as an exemplar, and the slabs by 'rationalists' who followed Gropius's advocacy of parallel rows of linear blocks generated by daylighting requirements. Both believed in the Corbusian vision of housing as communal blocks set in parkland.

Above right: Jack Lynn and Ivor Smith, Park Hill, Sheffield, 1961
One of the preeminent examples of English Brutalism, Park Hill was organized around continuous pedestrian walkways referred to as 'streets in the sky'. Although frequently vilified as an example of all that went wrong with modern architecture, the estate has attracted fierce loyalty from a surprising number of residents who value the social ideals behind its design.

shaped like a giant bird, with 'wings' of apartments in enormous super-blocks, a 'body' of repetitive slabs for the ministries and, at the 'head', the executive, legislative and judicial powers. These were accommodated in monumental buildings arranged around the Plaza of the Three Powers and complemented by reflecting pools the size of small lakes. Although they were hailed by patriotic critics as 'the highest peak of Brazilian architecture' the homage turned out to be a parody and the city a practical and artistic disaster thrown up on the cheap by corrupt contractors and bureaucrats. Niemeyer's ceremonial buildings (1958–63) are built diagrams – conceptually thin, formally lifeless and indifferent to climate. The president's palace has a notably cloying version of the grand colonnade – this time of inverted 'arches' – and the main chambers of the congress were accommodated in flying saucers, one landed the right way up, the other inverted. Max Bill had seen it all coming when he described Niemeyer's Palace of Industry in São Paulo (1954) as 'a riot of anti-social waste . . . thick *pilotis*, thin *pilotis*, *pilotis* of whimsical shapes lacking any structural rhyme or reason' and recoiled in horror at 'the spirit of decorativeness, something diametrically opposed to the spirit which animates architecture, which is the art of building, the social art above all others.'

NORTHAMPTON COLLEGE LIBRARY

Le Corbusier, Unité d'Habitation, Marseilles, 1947–52
This enormous 165-metre long building contained 337 apartments, a shopping 'street', hotel, community services, and a rooftop nursery and sports facilities. Its heroic scale and rough, board-marked concrete (*béton brut*) marked the beginning of a new phase in Le Corbusier's work.

The most potent alternative to the slick, technically sophisticated Modernism which stemmed from Mies became known by the confusing term 'Brutalism'. It was first used publicly – as 'The New Brutalism' – by Alison and Peter Smithson, and intended as the antithesis of the *Architectural Review*'s 'New Empiricism'. Setting out to recover the moral probity of that strand of theory stemming from Pugin through Viollet-le-Duc and Berlage, the Smithsons attributed ethical value to hard materials and exposed pipes. The first New Brutalist building was their Hunstanton Secondary School (1949–54), which combined Palladian formality with the steel, glass and brick aesthetic of Mies's early IIT buildings. Brutalism was characterized by tough, roughly textured materials used inside as well as outside, and by boldly articulated forms. Its exponents drew heavily on Le Corbusier's post-War work – the name resonated with the *béton brut* of the Marseilles Unité. The Mediterranean vernacular-inspired concrete vaults and rough brickwork of his Maisons Jaoul (1952–6) on the outskirts of Paris were also widely emulated, and the incomparable pilgrimage chapel at Ronchamp (1950–4) opened the door to sculptural form-making – which in lesser hands produced some unspeakable horrors. Alvar Aalto also turned to brick after the War, in buildings such as the Baker House dormitory at the Massachusetts Institute of Technology (1947-8) and the masterly Säynätsalo Town Hall (1949–52) – one of the most admired jewels of post-War architecture. The entrance elevation of Baker House was dominated by boldly expressed staircases – articulation of such secondary elements as lift towers, services and rainwater gargoyles became a favourite Brutalist ploy.

The retreat from the commitment to machine-age materials was also apparent in Louis Kahn's extension to the Yale Art Gallery in New Haven (1951–3), which featured a structural concrete ceiling and exposed services. Kahn's mature style, with its division into 'served' and 'servant' spaces, emerged in the Richards Medical Research Building at the University of Pennsylvania in Philadelphia (1957–60). The square stacks of laboratories are 'served' by 'servant' brick towers containing lifts, escape stairs and ventilation ducts – which Kahn referred to as 'hollow stones'. The planning is rigorously cross-axial – Kahn's Beaux Arts education was evident in everything he designed – but the resulting composition is beguilingly picturesque, suggesting by turns an Italian hill-town or futuristic apartments. Aged fifty-nine and almost unknown when the Richards Building was finished, Kahn was catapulted

to international fame by what quickly became one of the most influential post-War buildings.

'Brutalist' was not a label many architects cared for, but buildings reflecting the style's chief traits – hard, unfinished materials inside and out; bold, sculptural forms; strongly articulated parts – appeared worldwide during the 1960s. In Britain, the universities offered outstanding opportunities, and few buildings anywhere made a greater impact than the crystalline glass roofs, patent-glazed tower and faceted brickwork of Stirling and Gowan's Engineering Building at Leicester University (1959–63). The dramatically cantilevered lecture theatres surely derived from Melnikov's Rusakov Club and the detailing recalled the machine aesthetic of the 1920s; the composition owed something to Wright's Johnson Wax building – and possibly Kahn's laboratories – and the 'heroic' character had the confidence and vigour of the great Victorian engineers. Each form could be explained 'functionally', but this was an unmistakably eclectic composition of remarkable power. No other British building rivalled its originality, and only the Smithsons' Economist Building (1964) was of comparable importance. This gracious, mixed-use ensemble of three buildings around an intimate piazzetta was one of very few urban projects built anywhere to

suggest an alternative to the mono-culture of American-style office tower or slab-and-podium stereotypes spreading across the cities of the world. Japanese architects made particularly inventive use of the Brutalist syntax, transposing traditional timber structural forms into concrete. The results – as for example in Kunio Mayekawa's Municipal Festival Hall in Tokyo (1958–61) and Kenzo Tange's City Hall in Kurashiki (1958–60) – could be highly expressive, modern yet unmistakably Japanese: they laid the foundations for Japan's continuing engagement with Modernism which was to produce some of the most innovative and provocative architecture of the 1980s and 1990s.

CIAM continued to meet after the War, and at the ninth session, held in Aix-en-Provence in 1953, the Smithsons led an attack on the Athens Charter: it marked the beginning of the end for the uneasy consensus which bound progressive architects to a common cause. 'The narrow street of the slum succeeds,' the Smithsons asserted, 'where spacious redevelopment frequently fails.' This was heresy, but their aim was reform, not rejection, of Modernist principles, and with other dissenters (notably the Dutchman Aldo van Eyck) the Smithsons were invited to formulate the agenda for the tenth meeting. Their

Above left: Mies van der Rohe, Crown Hall, Illinois Institute of Technology, Chicago, 1952–6
Crown Hall was the pavilion counterpart of the Seagram tower: symmetrical, perfectly proportioned and immaculately detailed. Inside, its open-plan 'universal space' worked surprisingly well, but at the expense of banishing a lot of accommodation to a semi-basement.

Above right: Hertfordshire County Council, Monkfrith School, East Barnet, 1949–50
Hertfordshire pioneered prefabricated systems of construction for schools and classrooms such as this. Its lightweight steel columns and lattice beams, generous glazing and children seated in groups around trapezoidal tables became potent emblems of progressive, child-centred education in Britain.

critique focused on the failure to address the human experience of cities and buildings, and proved to be so vigorous that in Dubrovnik in 1956 CIAM fell apart and was formally wound up. The Smithsons' alternative to Modernist orthodoxy in housing, as demonstrated in their Golden Lane project of 1953, featured two-storey maisonettes organized along 'streets in the sky'. The Smithsons were still sufficiently wedded to Modernist ideals not to see that these buildings could hardly sustain real community life, and the concept was eventually realized on a grand scale in Jack Lynn and Ivor Smith's designs for Park Hill in Sheffield (1961), one of the major monuments of British public housing and the Brutalist aesthetic. Aldo van Eyck's work was similarly motivated by the desire to re-create a human scale in oversized buildings and cities administered by ever-growing bureaucracies. His idiosyncratic but persuasive advocacy of concrete 'place' rather than abstract space was widely influential and found expression in the Amsterdam Orphanage (1957–60). The plan, generated by an L-shaped repeating unit and circles at several scales – sandpits, thresholds, steps, lights, tiny mirrors embedded in unexpected places like the floor – was evocative of an African casbah: van Eyck called it 'labyrinthian clarity'.

The Industrial Design equivalent of CIAM, the International Congress of the Societies of Industrial Design (ICSID) was not founded until 1962, although events such as the Milan Triennale and the Aspen Conference in Colorado (which began in 1951) provided opportunities for the world design community to gather and debate. Superficially, there was general agreement about the neo-Bauhaus style – sometimes referred to as 'the transatlantic mainstream modern look' – but the design world was experiencing a crisis of values similar to that which led to the dissolution of CIAM. Design theory had progressed little beyond the Modern Movement's advocacy of standardization for mass-production, but industry was developing batch-production methods using sophisticated, electronically controlled machine-tools which enable products to be tailored to different groups or cultures. Uniform, mass-produced goods for international mass markets would become the exception rather than the rule and Japan, eager for world markets, was leading the way in adaptations designed to suit different national 'tastes'.

One of the first historians and critics to address the changes in design was Reyner Banham, who wrote regularly for the *Architectural Review* and the left-wing weekly *New Statesman* (later *New Statesman and Society*). A recurring theme of his writings was the need for the elitist worlds of architecture and design to come to terms with popular culture, transience and expendability. In a throwaway consumer society, he argued, architectural theory was an inappropriate model for design, which should avoid becoming part of 'the great progressive do-gooder complex of ideas' promulgated by the older generation. In 1955 he wrote about *The Machine Aesthetic*, emphasizing that it was an *aesthetic* – a theme developed in his seminal book *Theory and Design in the First Machine Age* (1960). Modernism, Banham argued, could only be understood as a style: the early Modernists had deceived themselves in thinking they could transcend style, a fact ignored by apologists such as Pevsner who should have known better. Widely accused of being 'inhuman' and 'mechanical', modern architecture and design would become human again, Banham believed, by embracing the values of popular culture – music, cinema, television, advertising etc. He was withering in his criticism of the Council of Industrial Design – which he dubbed 'H M Fashion House' – arguing that 'Good Design' products were often anything but functional, whereas the 'vulgarly' styled American alternatives were both popular and worked well.

Public awareness of design increased with the rapid growth of the advertising industry, the increasing sophistication and variety of lifestyle magazines, and the arrival of colour supplements with weekend newspapers. The British *Sunday Times* introduced the first such magazine in 1962, and many others quickly followed its example: regular 'lifestyle' features and the blurring of distinctions between advertising and editorial pages were highly effective in promoting style-conscious consumption. In consumer products, stylistic pluralism was good for business, and whilst Modernism enjoyed a prolonged reincarnation, it was by no means the only style available for the design-conscious. Beginning with the young of late 1950s America, highly profitable youth markets were established through successive waves of Pop culture, and although most of the results – like 1960s psychedelia – were ephemeral, some had lasting impact, most obviously in graphic design but also in architecture (the British Archigram group's plug-in, drop-out fantasies were later taken up by exponents of High Tech).

Italy became the dominant trendsetter in consumer products in the 1960s, and Italian designers excelled in creating stylish products which retained intellectual credibility. In 1972 MOMA created 'Italy: The New

Opposite above: Oscar Niemeyer, Congress Building and Ministries, Brasilia, 1958
Intended as a model of Modernist planning in the style of Le Corbusier's Radiant City, Costa's Brasilia plan was functionally zoned, with showpiece buildings and large pools in sweeping green spaces. The result, sadly, was a lifeless, artificial showpiece designed with little reference to the climate. The 'flying saucers' in Niemeyer's Congress Building house the two meeting chambers.

Opposite below left: Stirling and Gowan, Engineering Building, Leicester University, 1959–63
This expressive celebration of function looked back to the Heroic Period of modern architecture (with its 'nautical' detailing, Melnikov-inspired lecture theatres, etc.) but the boldly articulated forms, complex geometries, and vocabulary of engineering bricks and patent-glazing were new and won worldwide acclaim.

Opposite below right: Aldo van Eyck, Municipal Orphanage, Amsterdam, 1957–60
Conceived as a miniature city and generated by a repeating, vaulted module, this orphanage exemplified van Eyck's belief that architects had to rediscover ways of recreating human scale amidst the inhuman vastness of modern industries and bureaucracies. It proved to be one of the seminal buildings designed during the 1950s.

Domestic Landscape', a showcase for such sophisticated but undogmatic Modernists as Tobia Scarpa, Vico Magistretti, Joe Colombo and Richard Sapper whose work for Cassina, Tecno, Kartell, Flos, Artemide, Olivetti and Alessi, amongst others, had established Italy's reputation. The exhibition was also a forum for the pioneer of Anti- or Radical Design, Ettore Sottsass Jr, and two studios founded in Florence in 1966, Archizoom and Superstudio. Both designed visionary utopias – or anti-utopias – steeped in Modernist archetypes: the Continuous Monument (1969) consisted of an endless framework covering the whole earth. Both were also influenced by American Pop Art, seen at first hand in the 1964 Venice Biennale, and Archizoom's Andrea Branzi delighted in designing aggressively vulgar objects.

No Italian design of any pretension came without theoretical baggage, and semiology – the newly fashionable 'science of signs' of which the Italian Umberto Eco was a leading exponent – was pressed into service, leading to endless debates about design as a 'language'. Enzo Mari wrote in the MOMA catalogue that 'the only correct undertaking for "artists" is that of language research – that is the critical examination of the communications systems now in use.' At times it seemed that talking could replace doing, and similar debates raged in art schools around the world. For a decade or so from 1965 until 1975, practitioners of Conceptual Art and related tendencies such as Performance, Narrative and Body Art abandoned both the permanence of the traditional art object and its hallowed ground, the museum. This final blossoming of ideas latent in Dada, above all in the work of Marcel Duchamp, spread like wildfire through the art colleges. Caught up by the seeming radicalism of this last-ditch attempt to challenge the hegemony of the market (or, as conservatives saw it, evade criticism of inept drawing and bad brushwork), some designers even opted to work conceptually, offering statements in place of drawings, criticisms in place of objects.

The Italian debate about competing directions in design came to public notice in 1968, when the Milan Triennale was closed following protests against its exclusivity and its failure to address wider social and cultural problems. Architecture loomed surprisingly large in the political and cultural manifestoes issued in Paris, Berlin and Rome as students across Continental Europe took to the streets in the spring of 1968. The impoverished environments produced by state and corporate bureaucracies were cited as proof of the

bankruptcy of the establishment, and radical, often frankly utopian, alternatives were proclaimed with all the optimism of the German Activists fifty years earlier. Amidst growing concern about pollution and urban dereliction, architecture and the environment were causes worth fighting for, and the overthrow of the Beaux-Arts system in French architectural education was a tangible result of the protests. Having been born on the boulevards of Paris in the 1860s it is perhaps fitting that any lingering hopes of salvaging the Modernist belief in a planned utopia were extinguished there a hundred years later amidst the barricades of the Paris Spring. Socialism, the welfare state, economic and social planning – all were soon to be in full retreat before the ideologies of the New Right and the 'free play' of 'market forces'.

To the generation of 1968, versed in the Neo-Marxist writings of the Frankfurt School, Herbert Marcuse and Henri Lefebvre, buildings necessarily represented a 'dominant class ideology'. In response they advocated either a neutral architecture, a 'responsive' open framework or the active participation of users in design. These ideals were more talked about than implemented but they did find partial expression in three outstanding – and very different – buildings completed during the 1970s. The residential and communal facilities designed for the Medical Faculty of the University of Louvain near Brussels by Lucien Kroll were known as 'La Mémé' (1968–72) – they consisted of a fixed skeleton of structure and services infilled by a 'kit of parts' from which the students could select. The Centraal Beheer insurance company's offices in Apeldoorn, The Netherlands, by Herman Hertzberger (1968–72) were an attempt to combine the advantages of individual offices with open *Bürolandschaft* planning, the concrete-block walls deliberately left bare to encourage staff to personalize their workspaces. And at the Pompidou Centre by Piano and Rogers (1971–7) ideas explored in Cedric Price's 'Fun Palace' (1962–7) and Peter Cook's Plug-in City (1964) were combined with a Modernist exposure of structure and services and Miesian 'universal space'. Intended as a 'dynamic communications machine' and 'a people's centre, a university of the street', it proved a dark and difficult place in which to show art but has nevertheless become Paris's most popular attraction, drawing around seven million people a year – all counting as proof of the thriving culture industry even if they only come, as many do, to take the glass-tube escalators to enjoy the view from the roof.

NORTHAMPTON COLLEGE
LIBRARY

MOMA played host to five Modernists of a very different sort in 1969, known as the 'New York Five' after the book *Five Architects* was published in 1972. Their early work was largely houses and extensions in a revival of early Modern styles: the influence of Le Corbusier, the Bauhaus, De Stijl and Terragni were all apparent. Of the five, three have achieved major reputations. Michael Graves lapsed and became a leader of Postmodernism. Richard Meier developed his elegant early houses into an easy-going brand of post-Corbusian white architecture which has found favour with government and corporate clients in Europe as well as America – he has built several museums, including 'the commission of the century' for the Getty Center in Los Angeles, but the Atheneum in New

Harmony (1974) remains his best building. And finally there was Peter Eisenman, master of Modernism at its most abstract and self-reflexive. His houses were generated by transformations of grids – a procedure modelled on Noam Chomsky's 'generative grammars' – and display a famous disregard of function. House VI (1972) features an unclimbable 'staircase' and a gap in the master bedroom floor – the owners spent many years in separate beds before modifying their work of art in an orgy of pragmatism.

By treating Modernism as a style to be revived, the New York Five implicitly consigned Modernism to the history books and cast themselves as Postmodernists who revived it, rather than Modernists who continued. The book which is widely seen as announcing the

Louis Kahn, Richards Medical Research Building, University of Pennsylvania, Philadelphia, 1957–60
The laboratories' service ducts, stairs and lifts were accommodated in independent towers, creating one of the most memorable images in post-War architecture. This distinction between 'served' and 'servant' spaces formed the basis of Kahn's work, and was emulated worldwide.

Above: *Sunday Times*
magazine cover, 1962
This is the first cover of the
first national newspaper colour
magazine, published on 4
February and entitled 'A sharp
glance at the mood of Britain'.
With their fusion of editorial
and advertising copy,
newspapers' Saturday and
Sunday magazines were highly
influential in promoting more
'stylish' consumption and living.

**Below: Joe Columbo,
'Central Living Block' of
Wohnmodell 1969, Visiona
exhibition, shown at
International Furniture
Exhibition, Cologne**
Columbo's vision of the space-
age home was essentially
Modernist: sophisticated
'machines' service a generalized
living space. The sphere
contains the bath/shower and
to its left is a sitting/reclining
area below a rotating bookcase
and television. Kartell had
begun producing the plastic
dining chairs in 1968.

beginning of the end of the Modernist hegemony in architecture – Robert Venturi's *Complexity and Contradiction in Architecture* – was published in 1966 by (who else?) MOMA. Venturi pleaded for evolution rather than revolution and the acceptance of 'honky-tonk elements' in a hybrid architecture. Less was not more but a bore and he preferred messy vitality to obvious unity, ambiguity to clarity, and thought that 'Main Street is almost all right'. From Main Street it was a short trip to the ultimate strip – Las Vegas – and in *Learning from Las Vegas* (1972, with Denise Scott-Brown and Steven Izenour) the relentless kitsch of the hotels and casinos (far less Baroque then than now) became the object of High Camp reverie: rarely have form and content been so cynically separated. Venturi and his colleagues admired Las Vegas as an architecture of communication and in *The Language of Post-Modern Architecture* (1977) the American historian and critic Charles Jencks, who wrote his doctorate under Banham, made communication the basis of his theory. Jencks dated the 'death of modern architecture' to 'July 15, 1972 at 3.32 pm', when several slab-blocks in Minoru Yamasaki's Pruitt Igoe housing development (1952–5) were dynamited, and argued that Modernist buildings failed to communicate outside the coterie who understood their abstract 'language'. Postmodern buildings, by contrast, are 'double-coded' – like the front of a Greek temple which is 'a geometric architecture of elegantly fluted columns below, and a riotous billboard of struggling giants above' – Platonic delights for the

patricians, gawdy entertainment for the plebs: a perniciously divisive definition whose social implications did not appear to trouble Jencks or his followers.

Architecture, for once, found itself in the vanguard of broader cultural developments: Jencks was amongst the first to discuss Postmodernism, but his version (which I will refer to as PoMo) is misleading as a representative of the wider debate. PoMo was associated primarily with stylistic eclecticism, not the issues which preoccupied theorists and practitioners in literature and the fine arts – representation as reality, the politics of identity, rejection of 'grand narratives', suspicion of discourse and the re-evaluation of images, etc. In design, Italy again led the way. The Alchymia studio, founded in Milan in 1976 by Ettore Sottsass Jr with Andrea Branzi, Alessandro Mendini and others, articulated a new language for furniture and objects based on bright colours, pattern-printed laminates and playful, dysfunctional forms such as wildly asymmetrical furniture and sloping shelves. Alchymia was displaced by Memphis – with Sottsass again the leading figure – in 1980–1, and they turned the subversive Alchymia ideas into a marketable style, creating limited-edition pieces whose influence can be seen in many late 1980s products. In architecture, PoMo turned out to be surprisingly leaden. The old warhorse of the International Style, Philip Johnson, created one of its flagships by designing the AT&T building in New York (1978–82) as a Chippendale tallboy, whilst the ornamental, collage-like facade of the Public Services

Richard Meier, The Atheneum, New Harmony, Indiana, 1975–9
Meier first came to notice in MOMA's 'New York Five' exhibition in 1969 as the designer of sophisticated white houses in a post-Corbusian style. The Atheneum, a visitors' building for the 'ideal community' of New Harmony, was amongst his first public commissions and remains arguably his finest composition.

**Michael Graves, Public
Services Building, Portland,
Oregon, 1980–2**
Hailed as a flagship of Post
Modernism or reviled as an Art
Deco pastiche, Michael
Graves's Portland building
attracted worldwide attention.
It helped open the floodgates
to a decade of paste-on
'architecture', and its eye-
catching facades conceal
surprisingly ordinary spaces.

Building in Oregon (1980–2) by Michael Graves became
a *cause célèbre* – and looked very much better as a drawing.

In graphic design, the rejection of Modernist
orthodoxy began in its heartland, Switzerland, with the
work of Odermatt and Tissi in Zurich and Wolfgang
Weingart in Basle. Weingart was particularly influential
through his teaching, and promoted an eclectic,
anarchic style of typography which sacrificed legibility
for expressive vitality. In Britain, the so-called New
Wave was at its most creative in Neville Brody's
transformation of the anarchic graphics of Punk into a
major consumer idiom of the 1980s, exemplified by his
work for *The Face* magazine. The Dutch Studio Dumbar
produced a trend-setting postmodern corporate identity
for the privatized post and telephone service – PTT – in
1989. Javier Mariscal turned into a design phenomenon
in Spain, his work becoming familiar worldwide through
the 1992 Barcelona Olympics; and in the USA, the New
Wave surged vigorously in California, where a former
student of Weingart, April Greiman, emerged as
arguably the outstanding new talent on the world scene.
The rise of Postmodernism coincided with the arrival of
new technologies – computer typesetting, colour copying
and the Apple Mac computer with its sophisticated
graphics software – which gave designers complete
control of the design process and opened up new formal
possibilities. No one exploited these more imaginatively
than Greiman, her complex, layered images being

designed to admit of many 'readings' – artful
embodiments of the postmodern condition.

Postmodernism catered to a rapidly growing market
for design, and the 1980s also witnessed a considerable
vogue for Modernism, with familiar pieces of Bauhaus
furniture entering high street shops at eminently
affordable prices, and designs by less well-known first
generation Modernists such as Eileen Gray, René
Herbst and Rob Mallet-Stevens coming back into
production to serve the needs of a wealthier clientele in
search of something more exclusive. In London, Paris
and New York the Joseph shops became havens of chic
modernity, and many of the outstanding talents
continued to work in the Modernist tradition: Dieter
Rams in Germany refining Braun minimalism, David
Mellor and Kenneth Grange in Britain, Richard Sapper
in Italy – amongst many others. PoMo buildings dated
with unseemly haste, and the carnival of competing
looks threatened to reduce architecture to the status of
another consumer durable, prompting many to resist by
reaffirming Modernist ideals in buildings of marked
austerity. 'Truth to materials' and abstraction made a
comeback, and 'critical' forms of regionalism developed
to counter global homogenization. Amongst the latter,
the concrete 'bastions of resistance' of the Japanese
architect Tadao Ando stood out, their combination of a
Modernist aesthetic and native traditions of spatial
composition and habitation producing an architecture

unmistakably Japanese, yet free of the sentimentality which debases much so-called regionalism.

In Britain, High Tech architects took many of the characteristic tropes of the Modernist aesthetic to their limits. Mies's architecture of 'almost nothing' materialized as slick skins of frameless glass; the free plan, with its endless grid of columns, or column-free 'universal space', assumed exciting new forms in projects like Norman Foster's Willis Faber Dumas offices in Ipswich (1972–6) or the Sainsbury Centre for the Visual Arts at the University of East Anglia (1978); tension-structures, structural glass and new materials like teflon-coated fibreglass were exploited; and industrial pre-fabrication achieved accurate, rapid, dry construction: truly a Machine Aesthetic. High Tech is at its most persuasive in the kinds of buildings at which the Victorian engineers excelled – Norman Foster's Stansted Airport (1991) and Nicholas Grimshaw's Waterloo Euro-Terminal (1993) are distinguished recent examples – but it was also the preferred style for two of the major commercial buildings of the 1980s – Foster's Hong Kong and Shanghai Bank (1978–86) and Richard Rogers' Lloyds Building in London (1979–84). But for all their bravura – for which a coterie of outstanding London engineering consultancies deserve considerable credit – there is something unsatisfying about many High Tech buildings: cold, shiny and unforgiving, they are as much about image as the PoMo buildings which appear to be their antithesis.

Perhaps the most talked-about of the Modernist flowerings of the 1980s was Barcelona Minimalism – part of a general creative outpouring in Spain following Franco's death in 1975. Tolerated but given little breathing-space during the previous forty years, Modernism flourished as regional governments, enjoying the new decentralization of power, became major patrons. Like large corporations, they used architecture and design to establish their identity: complete transport systems were redesigned, parks created, benches scattered along streets, logos adopted. The *new* Madrid or Barcelona or Valencia had to look the part, and after years of suppression Modernism was ideal – it distanced governments from the old regime and connected the commercial world to international culture. In Barcelona, regional aspirations were overlaid with the promotion of Catalonian culture, creating a highly charged atmosphere in which architects such as Enric Miralles, Piñon and Viaplana, and Martorell Bohigas and Mackay, amongst many others, continue to flourish. Barcelonans go out to see and be seen – the Ramblas has long catered to the

need – and the city's new bars, fashion shops, and parks (over 150 of all shapes and sizes) are amongst the most imaginatively designed in Europe. The dominant style is minimalist – spindly steel supports, thin slabs of stone, sheets of clear, translucent and sand-blasted glass, straight lines and taut, shallow curves – and sufficiently distinctive to have become, despite the variations between designers, a regional style.

For all its particularities, what happened in Barcelona was clearly part of the style-obsessed 1980s, of the narcissistic obsession with body culture, proliferation of designer-brands marketed as keys to distinctive lifestyles and the promotion of cities as centres of cultural consumption. For architects lucky enough to secure the plum commissions in this global festival – and there were cultural projects aplenty – the 1980s seemed like very heaven, but all the excitement about 'architectural communication' and 'style' whipped up by advocates of stylistic Postmodernism could not conceal the fact that in most commercial projects the architect's role had shrunk to the provider of external packaging or short-lived interior 'fit-outs'. The professionals whose decisions and expertise really mattered in structuring the public realm were developers, bankers, planners and letting agents. Architects might be called on to add a cultural veneer, but it hardly mattered if this was a mute Late Modern slick-glass skin or a talkative PoMo coat of many colours.

The most radical reaction to this reduction of architecture to more or less stylishly packaged slabs of lettable space announced itself to the world in 1988 in yet another attempt by MOMA to make instant history. The exhibition – 'Deconstructivist Architecture' – featured the work of seven designers, amongst whom Frank Gehry and Peter Eisenman had built the most, and Zaha Hadid was closest stylistically to the implied Russian roots. The rediscovery of Constructivism and Suprematism allied to an interest in literary/philosophical deconstruction as practised by Jacques Derrida, Paul de Man and others were advanced as keys to the Deconstructivists' pedigree, but the new *rappel à désordre* was based more on superficial similarities arising from fragmented and colliding geometries than on any shared body of ideas. In a Decon design, to paraphrase MOMA's catalogue, every element contorts as the 'suppressed alien' of the 'unconscious of pure form' is released.

What the Deconstructivists clearly shared was a commitment to Modernist principles of composition, including techniques associated more with painting than

Top: April Greiman, US postage stamp, 1992
The Apple Macintosh computer transformed graphic design in the 1980s and few made more inventive use of its capabilities than Greiman. The multiple layers and 'floating signifiers' of this image are generally referred to as 'postmodern' but are rooted in early Modernism – the Futurists' 'words in freedom', Cubism, etc.

Bottom: Neville Brody, *The Face* magazine cover, 1985
Whilst art director of the British style magazine *The Face* during 1981–6, Brody developed an explosive, Postmodern style of graphics which challenged most conventions of editorial design. It proved highly influential, but Brody soon tired of it and in 1987 produced a much calmer design for the magazine *Arena*.

**Above: Tadao Ando,
Koshino house extension,
1983–4
Right: John Pawson,
Pawson house (conversion),
London, 1992**

The dream of a universal style died well before the 1980s, when the Modernist aesthetic was variously reinterpreted in economically booming Japan. Tadao Ando's fusion of abstraction and a traditional Japanese sensibility was a reaction against consumerism.

He described his houses as 'bastions of resistance' against consumerism, within which the play of light on finely made concrete evokes the presence of nature. A similar sensibility is at work in John Pawson's house, where Western Modernism is infused by Japanese-inspired austerity – a style which also found favour in up-market shops and art galleries calculated to appeal to the design-conscious.

design: the steel and glass structures of the Austrians' Coop Himmelblau, for example, are materializations of an expressive sketch made, at the moment of revelation, with closed eyes – the nearest architecture has come to Surrealist automatism. Peter Eisenman's disdain for function which is evident in his early houses is now sustained by the fashionable (especially, it seems, amongst some of New York's Jewish intellectuals) belief that after the Holocaust man must be 'de-centred', or eliminated altogether, as the subject of architecture. The 'violated perfection' (a favourite postmodern theme) of his Nunotani Headquarters project in Tokyo (1994), with its suggestion of built-in earthquake damage, seems designed to deter rather than invite occupation. 'Dis-' and 'de-' are the linguistic keys to Deconstructivist architecture – distortion, decentring, disruption, deflection, deviation etc. – and whilst the catalogue of the MOMA exhibition was at pains to stress that it was not a new '-ism', it was already spreading like wildfire. 'Decon' projects could be seen worldwide in schools of architecture by 1990, and in America the style enjoyed a transitory appearance of orthodoxy not seen, perhaps, since the Beaux Arts reigned supreme. With few completed buildings to inspire this devotion, it was a remarkable phenomenon, driven by magazines, dazzlingly presented competition projects, trend-setting institutions and impressively impenetrable texts. It remains to be seen where Decon will lead, but as Eisenman's burgeoning practice

confirms, there is a market for an architecture designed to 'dis-comfort' in every sense – physically, perceptually and intellectually.

Although Modernism has repeatedly been consigned to history, in the mid-1990s reports of its death seem greatly exaggerated. In the early 1980s the situation appeared very different, due in part to the hype surrounding Postmodernism, in part to the rejection of the reductive commercial buildings and public housing which flooded the world during the 1960s. A cursory glance through current architecture and design magazines confirms that Modernism, at least as a repertoire of formal systems and techniques, has by no means been rejected, and that much avowedly Postmodernist art and design draws heavily on ideas developed three quarters of a century ago. But the optimism which fired the first generation of Modernist architects and designers, the belief in reason and progress, in the possibility of building a better world, have gone. The 'incredulity towards [such] metanarratives' – Jean-François Lyotard's characterization of postmodernism – and the levelling of values by critical deconstruction has discredited Modernist beliefs, only to replace them with feelings of bewilderment and powerlessness: much art and design in the 1990s seems to be merely rummaging over history, or living off the astonishing creative ouburst of early Modernism, rather than extending or transforming the tradition of the new.

Above left: Herzog and de Meuron, Private gallery, Zurich, 1992
The Swiss architects Herzog and de Meuron emerged in the 1980s as outstanding exponents of a restrained Modernist style which found favour amongst the new generation in Europe. The emphasis on clear geometric forms, immaculate detailing and quality of materials was a reaction to the Postmodernists' preoccupation with imagery.

Above right: Coop Himmelblau, Falkestrasse 6, Vienna, 1988–9
Formed in 1968, the year of would-be revolution, Coop Himmelblau see architecture as confrontational, an expression of the tensions in a place. This 'explosion' on the roof of a traditional Viennese apartment building was proclaimed one of the first built manifestations of deconstruction – or 'deconstructivism' – in architecture, but its revolutionary charge is purely aesthetic.

The Modernist dream of transcending the separation of art and life in a rationally planned world lingered on in Europe into the 1960s, but with the ascendancy of America the avant-garde lost its radical charge: it became a commodity, and the 'style of the epoch' was appropriated as the corporate identity of big business. The corporate embrace rendered resistance futile. No activity was too outrageous to enter the museum, no work too slight, minimal or conceptual to sell. The museum was the natural habitat of Late Modernist art and architecturally innovative museums became the focus of civic pride in many cities. Universities and colleges made an industry out of the history and criticism of Modernism; government agencies supported Modernist art and artists; and galleries packaged the avant-garde – movement succeeded movement, style followed style, as the 'tradition of the new' boosted sales.

With the 1980s boom came a vigorous challenge to American dominance by resurgent Japan, where Modernist ideas had been thoroughly absorbed and hybridized with native traditions. Tokyo, vilified in the 1960s as the epitome of the chaotic, ugly, unplanned cities the Modernists wanted to replace, was hailed as a model for postmodern settlements of the twenty-first century. Chaos was the new 'hidden order' (the title of a seminal 1986 book by Ashihara Yoshinobu) and Tokyo's amorphous, amoeba-like structure became an organizational metaphor for politics, business and culture in the Digital Age, and the inspiration for designs such as Fumihiko Maki's beautiful 'Spiral' building. Housing a mix of cultural and commercial spaces, it is like a city in miniature – the antithesis of Modernist zoning – and the facade both mirrors the complexity within and projects a frozen, highly abstracted image of the teeming vitality of Tokyo. Superficially it is everything that the calm elevations of Le Corbusier's Cook House, were not. Yet Maki's work is deeply rooted in Modernism (he studied at Cranbrook and Harvard, and worked for SOM), drawing on both the 'rational' mainstream and the techniques – collage, fragmentation, simultaneity – which the Cubists, Futurists, Dadaists and others developed to represent the chaos and complexity of urban experience now claimed as their own by Postmodernists.

Seen against the achievements of the first three decades of the century, most avowedly Postmodern art and design looks thin and mean-spirited, and if the example of Japan is any guide, the aesthetic and technical resources of Modernism will prove a continuing source of inspiration in other rapidly developing Asian countries. The history we have traced *is* an extraordinary story: from a cluster of loosely related movements scattered across a few enclaves in Europe, with only the barest foothold in a couple of dozen countries by 1939, Modernism emerged all-conquering after the War. In terms of the pioneers' ambitions it was, perhaps, a Pyrrhic victory, but whatever glosses and qualifications one might wish to add, future historians will surely measure our century by the works discussed in this book. Modernism, the greatest transformation in Western culture since the Renaissance, is the style of individual freedom and of the twentieth century – and may well prove to have been the first, exhilarating step towards a manifold World culture.

Fumihiko Maki, Spiral Building, Tokyo, 1985
No image captured the teeming, apparently chaotic, 'Postmodern' reality of 1980s Tokyo better than the marvellous street elevation of Maki's Spiral Building. However, like the International Style buildings to either side, its composition is firmly rooted in Le Corbusier's 'Five Principles of a New Architecture', enriched by such Modernist compositional techniques as collage, fragmentation and simultaneity.

NORTHAMPTON COLLEGE LIBRARY

Modernism is the expression by individual human beings of how they will live their own present, and consequently there are a thousand modernisms for every thousand persons. Octavio Paz (Nobel Prize reception speech)

Select bibliography

The literature on Modernism is vast, and new books are appearing in ever-increasing numbers. This bibiliography is therefore highly selective, containing a mixture of recognized classics, general histories and accounts of particular topics or periods. Monographs on individual architects and designers are given with the short biographies.

For the social and cultural contexts in which Modernism developed:
Forty, Adrian. *Objects of Desire: Design and Society Since 1750*. London: Thames and Hudson, 1986.
Hobsbawm, Eric. *Age of Extremes: The Short Twentieth Century, 1914-1991*. London: Abacus, 1995.
Kern, Stephen. *The Culture of Time and Space 1880-1918*. London: Weidenfeld and Nicolson, 1983.
Johnson, Douglas and Madeleine. *The Age of Illusion: Art and Politics in France 1918-1940*. London: Thames and Hudson, 1987.
Willett, John. *The Weimar Years: A Culture Cut Short*. London: Thames and Hudson, 1984.

For the history of modern art:
Green, Christopher. *Cubism and its Enemies*. New Haven: Yale University Press, 1987.
Hughes, Robert. *The Shock of the New: Art and the Century of Change*. London: Thames and Hudson, rev. ed. 1991.
Lynton, Norbert. *The Story of Modern Art*. London: Phaidon Press, rev. ed. 1992.
Varnedoe, Kirk. *A Fine Disregard: What Makes Modern Art Modern*. London: Thames and Hudson, 1990.

General histories of modern architecture and design:
Curtis, William. *Modern Architecture since 1900*. London: Phaidon Press, rev. ed. 1996.
Frampton, Kenneth. *Modern Architecture: A Critical History*. London: Thames and Hudson, 1980.
Frampton, Kenneth and Yukio Futagawa. *Modern Architecture 1851-1945*. New York: Rizzoli, 1983.
Heskett, John. *Industrial Design*. London: Thames and Hudson, 1980.
Hollis, Richard. *Graphic Design: A Concise History*. London: Thames and Hudson, 1994.
Sembach, Klaus-Jürgen, Gabriele Leuthäuser and Peter Gössel. *Twentieth-Century Furniture Design*. Cologne: Taschen, n.d.

Early propagandist books on Modernist architecture and design are essential – and often exciting – reading. They include:
Hitchcock, Henry-Russell and Philip Johnson. *The International Style*. New York: WW Norton, 1966.
Giedion, Sigfried. *Space, Time and Architecture*. Cambridge: Harvard University Press, 3rd ed. 1959.
Le Corbusier, trans. by Frederick Etchells. *Towards a New Architecture*. London: The Architectural Press, 1970.
Mendelsohn, Erich. *Russland Europa Amerika: An Architectural Cross Section*. Basel: Birkhäuser (with English text), 1989.

Pevsner, Nikolaus. *Pioneers of Modern Design*. Harmondsworth: Penguin Books, 1975.
Yorke, F. R. S. *The Modern House*. London: The Architectural Press, 8th ed. 1957.

All the major Modernist movements have been exhaustively documented and analyzed, and many are covered in popular series such as Thames and Hudson's 'World of Art Library'. The following cover architecture and design:
Etlin, Richard A. *Modernism in Italian Architecture, 1890-1940*. Cambridge, Mass: MIT Press, 1991.
Friedman, Mildred ed. *De Stijl: 1917-1931 – Visions of Utopia*. Oxford: Phaidon Press, 1982.
Hulten, Pontus ed. *Futurism and Futurisms*. London: Thames and Hudson, 1986.
Naylor, Gillian. *The Bauhaus Reassessed*. London: The Herbert Press, 1985.
Wingler, Hans M. *The Bauhaus: Weimar, Dessau, Berlin, Chicago*. Cambridge, Mass: MIT Press, 1969.
Whitfield, Frank ed. *The Bauhaus Masters and Students by Themselves*. London: Conran Octopus, 1992

The opening-up of the former Soviet Union led to an explosive growth in literature on the post-Revolutionary period, including:
Art into Life: Russian Constructivism 1914-32 (exhibition catalogue). Seattle: Henry Art Gallery, 1990.
Bobko, Jane ed. *The Great Utopia*. New York: The Guggenheim Museum, 1992.
Cooke, Catherine. *Russian Avant-Garde*. London: Academy Editions, 1995.
Khan-Magomedov, Selim O. *Pioneers of Soviet Architecture*. London: Thames and Hudson, 1987.
Lodder, Christina. *Russian Constructivism*. New Haven: Yale University Press, 1983.

The following deal primarily with developments since the Second World War:
Blueprints for Modern Living (exhibition catalogue). Cambridge, Mass: MIT Press, 1989. (On John Entenza's 'Case Study Houses')
Dormer, Peter. *Design Since 1945*. London: Thames and Hudson, 1993.
Goldstein, Barbara ed. *Arts and Architecture - The Entenza Years*. Cambridge, Mass: MIT Press, 1990.
Jackson, Lesley. *'Contemporary': Architecture and Interiors of the 1950s*. London: Phaidon Press, 1994.
Jencks, Charles. *Modern Movements in Architecture*. Harmondsworth: Penguin Books, 2nd ed. 1985.

For Postmodern critiques of Modernism:
Betsky, Aaron. *Violated Perfection: Architecture and the Fragmentation of the Modern*. New York: Rizzoli, 1990.
Jencks, Charles. *The Language of Post-Modern Architecture*. London: Academy Editions, 3rd ed. 1981.
Venturi, Robert. *Complexity and Contradiction in Architecture*. New York: Museum of Modern Art, 1966.

Biographies

Since Modernism is such a vast field, and the main thrust of the book concerns architects and designers, I have limited myself to those who were active in these fields. This list of biographies is also necessarily limited, within that category, to those that I feel made a significant contribution to the Modernist aesthetic and is thus by necessity an arbitrary and subjective choice.

Alvar Aalto (1898-1976) was the leading Finnish Modernist. After working in the Nordic Classical style he turned to Modernism, producing in the Paimio Sanatorium (1928-33) one of the major buildings of the period. Like many Scandinavian architects, Aalto frequently designed purpose-made furniture and fittings for his buildings: the Paimio Chair was the product of experiments with bent-wood which also led to the famous Stacking Stool designed for the Viipuri Library (1927-35) and numerous later designs, many still produced by Artek, the gallery and company formed in 1935 by his patrons Harry and Maire Gullichsen. The free-form Savoy Vase (1937) later assumed the status of a national icon. In the Finnish Pavilions at the Paris (1937) and New York (1939) World's Fairs and in the Villa Mairea (1937-41) designed for the Gullichsens, Aalto crystallized ideas for a regional Modernist style rooted in Finnish materials, landscape and culture and characterized by collage-like compositions and free-form geometries. After the Second World War his 'humanized' Modernism, exemplified in buildings such as Baker House at MIT (1946-7) and Säynätsalo Town Hall (1949-52), proved widely influential. His numerous later commissions ranged from university campuses (Jyväskylä, 1950-6; Otaniemi, 1955-64) and town centres (the most complete at Seinäjoki, 1952-89), to museums, opera houses and concert halls (Finlandia Hall and congress centre, Helsinki 1970-5). Amongst this vast output, the Church of the Three Crosses in Imatra (1956-9) stands out for the Baroque virtuosity of its spatial composition, and the tiny summer house at Muuratsalo (1953) as a masterly statement of his lifelong meditation on the interaction between culture and nature, architecture and landscape.

Weston, Richard. *Alvar Aalto*. London: Phaidon Press, 1995.

Herbert Bayer (1900-85) was born in Austria and studied architecture before attending the Bauhaus in 1921-3, where he took up wall-painting under Wassily Kandinsky. Returning to the Bauhaus in 1925 to be master of the print workshop and teach visual communication, he established lower-case sans-serif type for use in all its printing. Amongst the first to introduce photography into graphic design, he made advertising part of Bauhaus teaching. He left for commercial practice in Berlin in 1928, where he developed a style based on retouched photographs, montage and Surrealist imagery which exerted a considerable influence on advertising in the 1930s. After organizing and designing the major Bauhaus exhibition at New York's Museum of Modern Art in 1938, Bayer stayed in the USA. Nostalgic for the mountains of Austria, he was drawn to the old mining town of Aspen in the Colorado Rockies which Walter Paepcke, head of the Container Corporation of America, was determined to turn into an educational and cultural retreat for busy executives. Bayer designed several buildings there, and acted as design consultant to Paepcke's and many other corporations before turning increasingly to painting.

Chanzit, Gwen F. *Herbert Bayer: Collection and Archive at the Denver Art Museum*. Seattle and London: University of Washington Press, 1988.

Max Bill (1908-) studied silversmithing in Switzerland and art at the Bauhaus and worked as an architect, painter and sculptor, as well as being involved in exhibition, stage, graphic and industrial design. A leading figure in the emergence of the widely influential Swiss School in graphic design of the 1930s, he embraced the ideal of 'concrete art' advocated by Theo van Doesburg as the basis of a universal art of absolute clarity, subsequently employing grids and mathematical progressions to impose a strict visual discipline on the disparate elements of a design. Bill designed the Swiss Pavilion at the 1936 Milan Triennale which, combined with the extreme formalism and economy of the posters displayed in it, gave the world a foretaste of the austere style which would dominate much corporate design of the 1960s and 1970s. Bill has remained committed to Bauhaus ideals throughout his long career, and in the 1950s he designed the 'new Bauhaus' – the Hochschule für Gestaltung at Ulm – and also served as its first rector (1951-7).

Max Bill: Retrospektive: Skulpturen Gemälde Graphik 1928-1987 (exhibition catalogue). Frankfurt: Schirn Kunsthalle, 1987.

Marcel Breuer (1902-81) was born in Hungary. As a student at the Bauhaus from 1920-4 he concentrated on furniture design, working under the strong influence of Constructivism and De Stijl. After graduating in 1925 he was appointed head of the carpentry workshop following the Bauhaus's move to Dessau where, fascinated by the strength and lightness of his new bicycle, he produced the Wassily Chair (1925), the first of several original and immensely influential bent-metal designs. The following year the Cantilever Chair, also known as the B32, appeared. Made from a single length of tube, supporting panels of wood and caning, the cantilever principle was probably influenced by a slightly earlier design by Mart Stam, and in turn became the model for numerous similar designs worldwide. In 1928 Breuer turned to architecture and left the Bauhaus for Berlin. In 1935 he moved to England, where he designed a plywood reclining chair for Isokon. But commissions were hard to come by and in 1937 he followed other emigrés from Nazi Germany to the USA, where he taught under Gropius at Harvard until 1946, designed more experimental furniture, and built his own house at New Canaan in 1947 which became a place of pilgrimage for students. In 1952 (with Pier Luigi Nervi and Bernard Zehrfuss) he was selected to design the UNESCO Building in Paris (1953-8), and in 1956 he set up Marcel Breuer and Associates in New York. Their work included buildings for major corporations – including several, thanks to the patronage of Eliot Noyes, for IBM – and the Whitney Museum of American Art in New York (1963-6). Almost all his later designs were characterized by strongly articulated volumes, reflecting the decisive influence of Constructivism.

Blake, Peter. *Marcel Breuer: Architect and Designer*. New York: 1949.

Charles Eames (1907-78) studied architecture and after several years in practice became head of the department of experimental design at the Cranbrook Academy of Art (1937-40). During the Second World War he experimented with new materials, notably plastics, with the architect Eero Saarinen and together they won a prize in the Museum of Modern Art's (MOMA) 'Organic Design in Home Furnishing' competition in 1941 with three multiply-curved plywood chairs. With his sculptor-colleague Harry Bertoia, Eames was one of the first to design furniture to be seen in the round – as it would so often be viewed in modern, open-plan interiors. In 1941 Eames married the abstract painter Ray Kaiser – all subsequent work was jointly credited – and they moved to Los Angeles. MOMA staged an exhibition of Eames's plywood chairs in 1946, and the rights to produce them were bought by Herman Miller, the beginning of a long and profitable association. Herman Miller began production of moulded fibreglass seats with slender rod bases in 1950 and they became ubiquitous in both domestic and commercial settings into the 1980s. Although rightly celebrated for its furniture, the Eames studio also produced outstanding work in exhibition and film design, and the house (1945-9) which Charles and Ray created for themselves as part of John Entenza's Case Study Programme epitomized the Californian lifestyle and remains one of the most admired post-War designs.

Kirkham, Pat. *Charles and Ray Eames: Designers of the 20th Century*. Cambridge, Mass: MIT Press, 1996.

Walter Gropius (1883-1969) was born into a family of architects and after studying in Munich and Berlin worked for Peter Behrens for two years before setting up his own practice in 1910, completing the first curtain-walled building, the Fagus Factory, the following year. He joined the Deutsche Werkbund in 1910, siding with Henry van de Velde in defence of individual creativity against Herman Muthesius's advocacy of standardization. After service in the War, he became director of the applied and fine arts schools in Weimar, merging them to form the Bauhaus in 1919. Intended as an expression of the unity of the arts – an ideal strongly advocated in German Expressionist circles – the Bauhaus quickly became a focus of avant-garde art and design. Gropius had a genius for picking staff, and managed to keep together what amounted to a roll-call of leading and individualistic Modernists. In 1922 Gropius re-directed the Bauhaus onto functionalist lines, and in 1925 transferred the school to Dessau, where in 1926 it moved into the new building he designed. Weary of the constant struggle with the authorities in an increasingly hostile Germany, Gropius resigned as director in 1928. In 1929 he became Vice-President of CIAM, and in 1934 moved to London, where he formed a partnership with Maxwell Fry from 1936-7 before leaving for the USA to become Professor of Architecture at Harvard. In 1945 he formed The Architects Collaborative, and although his later work rarely rose above the ordinary, he remained an influential educator and spokesman: his lifelong contribution to the dissemination of Modernism is hard to overstate.

Fitch, J. and I. Gropius. *Walter Gropius: Buildings, Plans, Projects 1906-1969* (exhibition catalogue). Cambridge, Mass: MIT Press, 1973.

Arne Jacobsen (1902-71) was born in Copenhagen and educated in the strong Danish neo-classical tradition. In 1925, whilst still a student, he travelled to Paris, where he encountered Le Corbusier's work, and in 1927-8 to Berlin where he saw an exhibition on Mies van der Rohe. He rapidly assimilated the lessons of Modernism and in 1929, with Flemming Lassen, created a sensation with an exhibition 'house of the future' replete with rooftop helipad. Over a period of five years at Copenhagen's Bellevue beach area (1930-5) he created bathing cabins and kiosks, the Bellavista housing estate and a theatre with a sliding roof which epitomized the International Style. Jacobsen's work was characterized by his restrained, fastidious taste and after the War he worked undogmatically in a variety of manners and materials, producing in the Jespesen office building in Copenhagen (1955) an exceptionally light and refined version of the Miesian glass slab, and for St Catherine's College, Oxford (1960-4) a design which also drew creatively on Mies's work of the 1920s – and which, in keeping with Scandinavian tradition, was designed down to the teaspoon. Excited by Charles Eames's plywood experiments, Jacobsen designed a highly refined chair for Fritz Hansen in 1953, following it with the famous Egg and Swan chairs in 1958. He also designed cutlery and tableware, and – in the Vola range – the ultimate in minimalist kitchen and bathroom fittings.

Shriver, P. *Arne Jacobsen: A Danish Architect*. 1972.

Le Corbusier (pseudonym of Charles-Edouard Jeanneret, 1887-1965) was born in Switzerland, where he received an Arts and Crafts training before embarking in 1907 on travels around the Mediterranean. In 1908-9 he worked for August Perret in Paris and in 1910-11 for Peter Behrens in Berlin, where he came into contact with the Deutsche Werkbund. The Dom-ino house (1914) announced a new architecture based on reinforced concrete construction but its aesthetic potential was not realized until the 1920s. With the painter Amédée Ozenfant he founded Purism and edited the journal *L'Esprit Nouveau* (1920-5), expounding theories – soon published in such seminal books as *Vers une Architecture* (1923) – which became central to the Modernist vision. Formally, this was articulated in 'The Five Points of a New Architecture' in 1926, and embodied in a series of houses culminating in the Villa Savoye in Poissy (1929-31). The houses were complemented by radical visions of a new urbanism based on tower and slab-blocks in open spaces criss-crossed by highways, and by chairs (designed with Charlotte Perriand) which have become modern classics. In the 1930s Le Corbusier worked on large-scale plans in North Africa and South America, applying the principles of CIAM's 1933 Athens Charter, and turned to the vernacular for inspiration. The rough *béton brut* surfaces of his first major post-War building, the Unité d'Habitation at Marseilles (1947-52), anticipated the brutalism which came into vogue later in the 1950s. His sculpturally expressive mature style – exemplified in the chapel at Ronchamp (1950-4), the monastery of La Tourette (1957-60), and the capitol at Chandigarh (1952-64) – was widely, and all too often ineptly, emulated. Le Corbusier published prolifically throughout his life and through his polemical texts, eight volumes of work (the *Oeuvre Complète*) and buildings in three continents, left an indelible mark on the twentieth century.

Le Corbusier, trans. by Edith Schreiber Aujame. *Precisions On the Present State of Architecture and City Planning*. Cambridge, Mass: MIT Press, 1991 (first published in French in 1930)

Curtis, William. *Le Corbusier*. London: Phaidon Press, 1992.

El Lissitzky (Eleazar Markevich, 1890-1941) was born near Smolensk in Russia and studied architecture under Josef Maria Olbrich in Darmstadt for five years from 1909. On returning to Russia in 1914 he worked in architectural practice, but also took up fine art and illustration. The painter Marc Chagall invited him to teach in Vitebsk, where he came under the influence of Kazimir Malevich and adopted Suprematism, producing his famous revolutionary poster *Beat the Whites with the Red Wedge* and collaborating on the design of the first 'Prouns', which he described as 'half-way stations between architecture and painting'. He taught in Moscow in 1921 and then embarked on extensive travels around Europe in 1922-5 as a free-roving cultural ambassador for the Soviet Union. He taught in Germany and Switzerland and consolidated links with the European avant-garde, notably the Dadaists, De Stijl and Bauhaus. Van Doesburg published his picture book *Of 2 Squares* in 1922 and it had an immediate impact on graphic design, as did the *Proun Room* he exhibited in Berlin in 1923 on architecture. In 1924-5 with the Dutch architect Mart Stam he designed the visionary 'Cloud Props' project. During the politically difficult years of the 1930s in the USSR, El Lissitzky concentrated on photography and photomontage. But by then his decisive impact on the West had been made: a prolific writer and publicist and the most important direct link to the revolution in Russia, he was also a major innovator in graphic design.

Lissitzky, El, trans. by Eric Dluhosch. *Russia: An Architecture for World Revolution*. Cambridge, Mass: MIT, 1984 (originally published in German in 1930).

Lissitzky-Kuppers, Sophie. *El Litssitzky: Life, Letters, Texts*. London: Thames and Hudson, 1968.

Ludwig Mies van der Rohe (1886-1969) was born in Aachen and worked as a draughtsman there before moving to Berlin in 1905. Three years later he joined Peter Behrens's office and met Walter Gropius. He began independent practice in 1912, but did not identify himself with the progressive Deutsche Werkbund until after the War. The Expressionist project for a glass tower on Friedrichstrasse (1919) was the first of his celebrated 'Five Projects' (the others were a second glass tower, a concrete office building, a brick villa and a concrete house) in which, by 1924, he had anticipated many of the key technical and formal innovations of the next thirty years. In 1927 he directed the Werkbund's Weissenhofsiedlung in Stuttgart, the most extensive early manifestation of Modernist architecture, and in 1929 he designed the German – the so-called Barcelona – Pavilion for that city's International Exhibition. The ceremonial Barcelona Chair – designed for the king of Spain – was manufactured by Knoll from 1947, becoming almost ubiquitous in corporate interiors of the 1950s. Mies directed the Bauhaus from 1930 until its closure by the Nazis in 1933, and finally left for America in 1938 where he taught at the Armour Institute (later Illinois Institute of Architecture) in Chicago, beginning work in 1940 on the master-plan for its new campus. Mies believed that architecutre, as an expression of the epoch, must reflect the dominant technology and his post-War buildings were all essays in pared-down steel (or reinforced concrete) and glass construction. The apartments at 860-80 Lake Shore Drive (1948-51) in Chicago set the standard for tall buildings; the 39-storey Seagram Building (1954-58) was unrivalled as an emblem of corporate power; and in the single-storey pavilion of the Farnsworth House (1946-50) he gave definitive expression to the Modernist dream of the glass house. Imitated worldwide, Mies became arguably the most influential architect since Palladio.

Johnson, Philip. *Mies van der Rohe*. New York: Museum of Modern Art, 1947, republished 1978.

László Moholy-Nagy (1895-1946) was born in Hungary, where he began studying law. Injured in the War, during his convalescence his interest in drawing revived and he made contact with the Russian-inspired group of artist-activists *Ma* (Today). After the War he moved via Vienna to Berlin where he took up painting and photography, soon adopting a Constructivist approach. He greatly impressed Walter Gropius on their first meeting in 1921 and two years later was invited to teach at the Bauhaus. His influence was central in the school's shift to a functionalist, materials-based approach to design, and the foundation course he developed was described in 1929 in the influential book *Von Material zu Architektur* (published in English as 'The New Vision' in 1932); he also designed and (with Gropius) co-edited the entire series of Bauhaus books. In 1928, shortly after the appointment of Hannes Mayer to succeed Gropius, Moholy-Nagy left the Bauhaus, finding work as a graphic and exhibition designer, photographer and film-maker in Berlin, Amsterdam and London, before moving to the USA in 1937. In Chicago he became director of the school of design at the Association of Arts and Industries – which he optimistically renamed 'The New Bauhaus: American School of Design'. With Sigfried Giedion as director, he founded the Chicago Institute of Design Research: in 1949, three years after his early death, it was absorbed into the Illinois Institute of Technology.

Passuth, Krisztina. *Moholy-Nagy*. London: Thames and Hudson, 1985.

Richard Neutra (1892-1970) was born and educated in Vienna. He met Adolf Loos in 1910 and discovered Wasmuth's publications of Frank Lloyd Wright's work the following year. After the War he worked in Switzerland, where he met Erich Mendelsohn, who invited him to his office in Berlin in 1921; two years later he left for the USA, alternating between Holabird and Roche's office in Chicago and

Wright's Taliesin. In 1925 he moved to Los Angeles to work for the Viennese-born Rudolf Schindler, taking over Schindler's client Dr Lovell to build the so-called 'Health House' (1927-9) in the Hollywood Hills. This launched his own practice and was soon hailed as the first major example of the International Style in the USA. Neutra's career reached its peak immediately after the Second World War in designs such as the Kaufmann Desert House at Palm Springs (1946-7) and the Tremaine House at Santa Barbara (1947-8) in which the International Style aesthetic of lightness, openness and spatial continuity with the landscape was brought to a peak of refinement. Neutra built numerous major buildings during the 1950s and 1960s, but none matched the quality of his houses.

Hines, Thomas S. *Richard Neutra and the Search for Modern Architecture*. New York and Oxford: Oxford University Press, 1982.

Gerrit Thomas Rietveld (1888-1964) was born in Utrecht in the Netherlands and trained, like his father, as a carpenter. He took classes in architecture and in 1918 made the chair which Theo van Doesburg seized upon as a model of De Stijl design: the Red and Blue Chair, as it became with Van Doesburg's help, quickly assumed the status of one of the first icons of Modernist design. Rietveld became a full member of the De Stijl group in 1919, designing a series of outstanding successors to the Red and Blue Chair and, in 1924, the Schröder House in Utrecht. This was a collaboration with the client Truus Schröder-Schräder, who lived there all her life. By far the most important built example of De Stijl architecture, it was also stylistically the most advanced building of its date in Europe, the first floor being designed as a transformable interior with sliding partitions, fold-down furniture and a host of other innovations. Although neither academically nor professionally trained, Rietveld participated fully as a member of CIAM from its foundation in 1928 and practised as an architect until his death in 1964. The sculpture pavilion in the Sonsbeek Park in Arnhem (1954, re-erected at Otterlo, 1965) recaptured the De Stijl spirit, but none of his later buildings – most famously the Rijksmuseum Vincent van Gogh in Amsterdam (1963-72) – matched the quality, let alone innovative brilliance, of the De Stijl years.

Brown, Theodore M. *The Work of Gerrit Rietveld, Architect*. Cambridge and Utrecht: 1958.

Alexander Rodchenko (1891-1956) was a pioneer and leading exponent of Russian Constructivism in the 1920s. Trained in painting in Kazan and, briefly, in graphic design in Moscow, he came under the influence of

Futurism before becoming acquainted with the work of Malevich and Tatlin. By 1915 he was producing abstract paintings, and in 1918 his first three-dimensional constructions appeared. He taught composition at the Vkhutemas and with his wife Varvara Stepanova and Alexei Gan formed the First Working Group of Constructivists in 1921. In keeping with the Constructivists' opposition to 'fine' art, Rodchenko worked primarily as a graphic designer during the 1920s, producing posters for government trade organizations, the cinema, the journal *LEF* and its successor from 1925 *Novyi LEF* in a striking style based on limited, strong colours counterchanged around a central axis of symmetry. He designed a model Workers' Club for the Soviet Pavilion at the 1925 Paris Exhibition of Decorative and Industrial Arts, and explored the possibilities of transformable, multi-functional furniture (generally far from flexible in practice). In 1928 he acquired a Leica camera and turned to photography as his main medium, developing a theory of the snapshot which, like most avant-garde developments in the Soviet Union, soon fell foul of Stalin's ideal of socialist realism.

Noever, Peter ed. *Aleksandr M Rodchenko • Varvara F Stepanova: The Future Is Our Only Goal* (exhibition catalogue). Munich: Prestel, 1991.

Eero Saarinen (1910-61) was born in Finland, the son of the celebrated architect Eliel, and with his parents emigrated to America in 1923. He studied sculpture in Paris and architecture at Yale University where, in 1934, he won a two-year travelling scholarship to Europe. On his return he joined his father in his office and as a teacher at Cranbrook Academy of Art. He first came to public attention in 1940 as a furniture designer and the following year, with Charles Eames, won a prize in the Museum of Modern Art's Organic Furniture competition. His Womb chair (1946) epitomized the emerging aesthetic, its spindly metal legs supporting a sensuous, sculptural seat, and ten years later in the Tulip chair (1956) he united the base and seat into a visually homogeneous form. At the General Motor's Technical Centre in Michigan (1948-56) Saarinen produced a low-rise counterpart of the Miesian steel and glass tower, but his interest in the rational mainstream of Modernism was short-lived and the freer forms pioneered in sculpture and furniture became the basis of his mature style, most famously in the soaring concrete 'wings' of the TWA Terminal Building at New York's John F Kennedy Airport (1956-62).

Kuhner, Robert A. *Eero Saarinen: His Life and Work*. Monticello, Illinois, 1975.

Skidmore, Owings and Merrill (SOM) was founded by Louis Skidmore and Nathaniel Owings in Chicago in

1936 and opened a New York office the following year; John Merrilll joined the partnership in 1939. From the outset, it was unlike previous architects' offices, being modelled on American business practice and emphasizing individual anonymity within an ethos of teamwork. SOM's breakthrough came in 1952 with the 21-storey Lever House in New York. Designed by Gordon Bunshaft, its tower and podium form and sophisticated steel and glass curtain-wall set the standard for commercial buildings; later, building on Eero Saarinen's pioneering work for General Motors, they also perfected the low-rise rural or suburban company headquarters as a campus of buildings in a park-like setting. SOM rapidly secured commissions across the USA and consistently outdid most of their many imitators in visual refinement, responsiveness to clients' needs, and business efficiency. Engineers played a major role in SOM's design teams and structural expression was central to much of their work: skeleton construction achieved archetypal expression in the Business Men's Assurance Co. of America building in Kansas City (1963). Increasingly since the 1970s SOM has worked abroad, notably in Islamic countries, and in 1980 were employing over 2000 people and building worldwide.

Danz, Ernst. *Architecture of Skidmore, Owings & Merrill 1950-62*. New York, 1962.

Jan Tschichold (1902-74) studied calligraphy in Leipzig and after visiting the Bauhaus exhibition in 1923 embraced Modernist principles. In October 1925 he published a manifesto entitled '*Elementare Typographie*' (Elementary Typography), and the same year Paul Renner appointed him to teach at the prestigious Munich School of Master Book Printers, where he began to write the seminal *Die Neue Typographie* (1928), the first attempt to define typographic principles. Tschichold's advocacy of typographic Functionalism – economy of expression, sans-serif typefaces and asymmetrical design – was hugely influential, reaching working printers as well as avant-garde artists and designers. In 1933 he emigrated to Switzerland where in 1935, much to the dismay of dogmatic Modernists such as Max Bill and Kurt Schwitters, he published an article stating that symmetrical layouts were acceptable. He spent 1947-9 in England, at the invitation of Sir Allen Lane, revising the design of the entire output of Penguin books: his strict standards and keen eye subtly but unmistakably transformed the appearance of these ubiquitous paperbacks. Tschichold devoted much of his later life to researching and writing about a medium to which he had made the most far-reaching contributions of the century.

McLean, Ruari. *Jan Tschichold:*

typographer. Boston: David R Godine, 1975.

Theo van Doesburg (1883-1931) was the leader of the Dutch De Stijl group. Born in Utrecht, he formulated the ideas of Neo-Plasticism which underpinned De Stijl's development and in 1915 began a correspondence with Mondrian who became its most prestigious member. He also recruited Gerrit Rietveld, painting a chair he had made red and blue, thereby transforming it into one of the movement's most famous icons. A tireless writer and propagandist, Van Doesburg produced the De Stijl magazine and travelled and lectured widely around Europe to disseminate the group's revolutionary ideas. A gifted painter, typographer and graphic designer, he also made a major contribution to the development of the Modernist aesthetic in architecture through his collaboration with the architect Van Eesteren on the Maison d'Artiste (1922) and Maison Particulière (1923). In 1923 he visited the exhibition of El Lissitzky's *Proun Room* in Berlin and saw in the use of the diagonal a way of refreshing the De Stijl aesthetic, which in 1926 he announced as the new concept 'Elementarism' – soon exemplified in the conversion of the Café Aubette (1927-8) in Strasbourg, where he set up diagonal counter-compositions to the existing rooms to destroy the cubic enclosure visually. A perpetual innovator, in 1930 Van Doesburg articulated his ideal of a 'concrete art' of universal clarity which was taken up most notably by the Swiss designer Max Bill.

Van Straaten, Evert. *Theo van Doesburg: Painter and Architect*. The Hague: SDU Publishers, 1988.

Frank Lloyd Wright (1867-1956) was born in Wisconsin and joined Adler and Sullivan in Chicago in 1888. He made Sullivan's ideas on 'organic architecture' his own and five years later went into partnership with Cecil Corwen. In 1896 he set up his own office in suburban Oak Park, where he executed numerous houses and developed the Prairie Style. This was given definitive expression in two projects published in 1901 in the *Ladies' Home Journal*, and reached a climax in the Robie House in Chicago (1907-9). Wright also completed two other major buildings, the Larkin Building (1904-5, demolished 1949) in Buffalo and Unity Temple (1905-7) in Oak Park. Professionally and personally disillusioned, he left his wife and family in 1909 and travelled to Europe with his mistress. In Berlin Ernst Wasmuth published two portfolios (1910-11) of Wright's work which decisively influenced developments in Europe. Returning to Wisconsin in 1911 Wright built his home and studio – 'Taliesin' – at Spring Green. During the 1920s he designed houses in California using concrete 'textile blocks' (eg Millard

House – 'La Miniatura' – in Pasadema, 1921-3), and after several years with little work, the 1930s saw three masterpieces: Fallingwater in Pennsylvania (1935-9), the administration building of S C Johnson & Sons in Racine, Wisconsin (1936-9), and Taliesin West in Arizona (1937ff). Of his later buildings, much the best known remains the Guggenheim Building in New York, idealistically conceived as a 'Temple of Non-Objectivity' but much compromised in execution. Wright remained on the periphery of Modernism, hostile to its machine-aesthetic, yet equally committed to abstraction and spatial continuity. A prolific author and shameless self-publicist, Wright epitomized the American myth of the pioneer. As our concern with the environment grows, his work increasingly claims attention as one of the great artistic achievements of the twentieth century.

Wright, Frank Lloyd. *An Autobiography*. First published in 1932; new, rev. edition New York: Horizon Press, 1977.

Levine, Neil. *The Architecture of Frank Lloyd Wright*. Princeton: Princeton University Press, 1996.